Wild Music

A pianist plays in front of the riot police during the Maidan Revolution.
Copyright Eliash Strongowski after a photograph by Oleg Matsekh, 2013.

Maria Sonevytsky

WILD MUSIC

Sound and Sovereignty in Ukraine

Wesleyan University Press   Middletown, Connecticut

Wesleyan University Press
Middletown, CT 06459
www.wesleyan.edu/wespress
© 2019 Maria Sonevytsky
All rights reserved
Manufactured in the United States of America
Designed by Mindy Basinger Hill
Typeset in Minion Pro

Library of Congress Cataloging-in-Publication Data available upon
request

Hardcover ISBN: 978-0-8195-7915-7
Paperback ISBN: 978-0-8195-7916-4
Ebook ISBN: 978-0-8195-7917-1

5   4   3   2   1

What a view from the West-North of these regions,
when one day the spirit of civilization (*Kultur*) will visit them!
The Ukraine will become a new Greece: the beautiful heaven of this
people, their merry existence, their musical nature, their fruitful land, and
so on, will one day awaken: out of so many little wild peoples (*kleinen wilden
Völkern*), as the Greeks were also once, a mannered (*gesittete*) nation will
come to be: their borders will stretch out to the Black Sea and from there
through the world. Hungary, these nations, and an area of Poland and Russia
will be participants in this new civilization (*Kultur*); from the northwest
this spirit will go over Europe, which lies in sleep, and make it subservient
(*dienstbar*) to this spirit. This all lies ahead, and must one day happen;
but how? When? Through whom?

Johann Gottfried Herder, Journal meiner Reise im Jahr 1769

«Будь ласка, давайте не будемо варварами!»
(Please, let's not be barbarians!)

Sign hanging in the entryway of an apartment building in Kyiv, 2011

CONTENTS

KEY SITES REFERENCED IN THIS BOOK

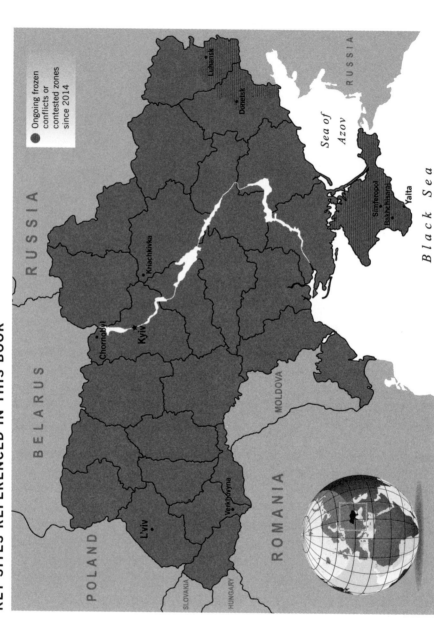

PREFACE

Sovereignty, a key term of this musical ethnographic study, emerges from the exigencies of Ukrainian political instability. The revolutionary upheavals of the Maidan in 2013–2014 called Ukrainian political sovereignty into question for the second time in a decade, disrupting the lives of many of my interlocutors and demanding that I acknowledge how much the conceptual terrain had shifted since I began my research in Ukraine in 2004. As the previously unthinkable challenges to Ukraine's territorial integrity increased in 2014 with Russia's opportunistic seizing of Crimea and provocations on the eastern borders, I had the opportunity, as an ethnographer, to see my own investments in the project of Ukrainian statehood come into relief. Until then, Wildness—the other key term of this study—had been my focus; in the first iteration of this project, I studied two borderland populations (Crimean Tatars and Hutsuls), observing how modern-day discourses of civilization and barbarism were made audible through musical practices. After the borders of contemporary Ukraine became contested in the aftermath of the Maidan, I was forced to confront the ways in which I had been taking the political sovereignty of Ukraine as an overly convenient way to bound my comparative project.

Apart from the fact that I had largely studied the musical practices of Ukrainian citizens for whom the state's political sovereignty was meaningful and important, I had to reexamine the assumptions of my own politicized subject position as a child of the postwar Ukrainian-American diaspora, which carried with it a baseline belief that Ukrainian statehood was a legitimate project. (In Abu-Lughod's [1991] memorable term, this split identity marks me as a "halfie.") As Crimean Tatars were ordered to trade in their Ukrainian passports for Russian ones, as Hutsuls became newly caricatured by Russian media as part of a rabid neofascist takeover of Ukraine, as the Russian state vowed to defend its

Russian-speaking compatriots abroad, I could no longer take the legitimacy of the state for granted. Pragmatic questions about how to continue research in certain regions led to conceptual ones, such as whether to refer to the people who were fleeing from Crimea or the conflict zones in the eastern Donbas and Luhansk regions as internally displaced persons (IDPs) or refugees—a difference in terminology that belied a larger political reality as to whether these territories of Ukraine had been, in fact, absorbed by another sovereign power.

Inspired by Madina Tlostanova and Walter Mignolo's (2012) call that scholars situated in the West must strive to "learn to unlearn in order to relearn," I offer this prefatory note to situate myself within this musical ethnographic study of Wildness and sovereignty, in the hope that it lays bare the continuing process of my own (re)education.[1] In Ukraine, people who get to know me well have sometimes referred to me as *nasha Amerykanka* (our American).[2] I have long recognized that this term of intimacy, while endearing, risks obscuring just how different my lived experience and horizons of opportunity—as a middle-class American citizen who was working toward and eventually earned a PhD at a prestigious university in New York City—were from the limited conditions I often encountered throughout Ukraine. At the same time, my inability to pass fully as Ukrainian in many contexts made me a target of suspicion (I was accused of being a spy on a number of occasions), derision (especially for those Ukrainians who had soured on the diaspora and its interventions in Ukraine's internal affairs), or hostility (when my inability to speak Russian fluently—I was raised speaking only Ukrainian, which remains rare—was interpreted as evidence that I was a nationalist zealot who must be refusing to switch to Russian). Marked through my upbringing and affiliation with the North American Ukrainian diaspora, sanctioned by the knowledge-production frameworks of the Western academy, this book represents a reckoning with my own assumptions about what I thought Ukraine was before beginning this research.

My parents left Western Ukraine to flee westward across the "bloodlands" of World War II (Snyder 2010a). With their families, they spent years in displaced persons (DP) camps after 1945, before they won visas that allowed them to emigrate to North America (my mother's family to Coaldale, Alberta; my father's to New York City).[3] Born in the 1980s, I was instilled with an intense and politicized nostalgia for what I understood to be my ancestral homeland of Ukraine. My childhood idea of Ukraine was articulated in a prewar Western Ukrainian dialect that I took to be unmarked. It was informed by the sensibilities of a cohort of refugees who had largely been among the urban intellectuals and religious leaders of pre-Soviet Western Ukraine, many of whom believed they were keeping the "real Ukraine" alive during a period of intense Russification and Sovietization.[4] My imagination of Ukraine centered on the literary culture of L'viv and the Carpathians and Eastern-rite Catholicism; images of yellow wheat and blue sky; the bright red boots and billowing *sharovary* pants of the folk dance costume; *pysanky* (batiked Easter eggs); stories of lionhearted *Kozaky* (Cossacks) battling marauding Tatar hordes and Russian imperialists; the unquestioned evil of the Soviet Empire; the lachrymose nationalism of the romantic poet-hero Taras Shevchenko; meals of *varenyky* (pierogies) and borsch. The Ukrainians I knew lived in the East Village of New York and summered in the Catskill Mountains, or in the Ukrainian diaspora communities of Munich, Innsbruck, and Vienna (where parts of my widely dispersed family who did not win the DP camp immigration lottery settled). My Ukraine was a Ukrainian scouting summer camp held in the wooded outskirts of an Ohio Amish town, where we sang "Blowin' in the Wind" with Ukrainian lyrics around the nightly campfire and patriotic Ukrainian anthems every morning ("When we grow up big / brave soldiers / we will defend Ukraine / from enemy hands").[5]

In the summer of 1991, my family secured Soviet visas and prepared to travel to Ukraine. Leaving from Vienna on a massive, fume-filled train, we rumbled eastward on August 24, 1991, the very day that Ukraine declared its independence from the Soviet Union. At the age of ten, I could not comprehend the scale of historical events that we had stumbled into, but I remember bottles of champagne when we arrived at the train station in the Western Ukrainian city of Truskavets; my father's tears upon reuniting with family that he had not seen since the 1940s; the grey shops with prosaic names ("Milk," "Bread") and bare shelves; the black market machinations my mother undertook to acquire a toothbrush; the visit to a family village where there was no running water; and the rock-bottom prices of hand-whittled souvenirs that my brother and I bought for our friends back in the United States. When we left Ukraine after that first trip, I was inconsolable as the train lurched out of the L'viv train station and all of my new uncles, aunts, and cousins waved goodbye to their American relatives. I discovered on that trip that my childhood Ukraine had been a mirage: the real place was alien, full of real people with complex and disadvantaged lives. In it, I was a strange misfit speaking an archaic dialect imprinted with privilege and distance. And yet, I wept at leaving.

As an American teenager, I staged my rebellion against a Ukrainian-American diaspora culture that I found stifling, and deepened instead my interest in

Ukraine proper. Determined to question the Cold War logics that underpinned my upbringing in the diaspora, I traveled back after graduating from high school in 1999. I spent three months exploring the country, a trip that broadened my eyes to its regional diversity. It was on this journey that I first encountered Western Ukrainian mountain music, performed by Hutsul highlanders in the village of Rakhiv, and that I first learned about the Crimean Tatar repatriate community fighting to reestablish itself in Crimea. I listened to the cool new bands that were emerging seemingly everywhere. I got acquainted with a team of young ethnomusicologists based at the L'viv Conservatory, and joined them for a field expedition in the Bukovina region. The trip was cut short by rains that flooded out our fieldsite, but it gave me my first sense of what motivated much of post-Soviet Ukrainian ethnomusicology at that time.

When I entered graduate school at Columbia University, I was trained in the style of North American ethnomusicologists, who are expected to conduct lone immersive fieldwork over extended periods. During my doctoral fieldwork in 2008–2009, I spent eighteen months traveling between several sites in Crimea and Western Ukraine, timing my arrivals and departures to coincide with key social events in both communities. At the same time, I started to develop contacts at the Tchaikovsky National Music Academy of Ukraine in Kyiv and began to learn about the Central and Northern Ukrainian vocal styles that were part of a broader urban revival of village styles often glossed as *avtentyka*. My presence in host communities was, often, more disruptive than I intended, in part due to the symbolic capital I embodied as an American citizen whose presence and interest offered validation for many locals. Since many people knew me as a musician as well as an ethnographer, I was (often spontaneously) called to perform at community celebrations: I once sang a traditional Crimean Tatar song for a bride and groom as revelers danced around me at a wedding palace outside of Bakhchisarai, was featured playing the banjo on Crimean Tatar television and in Hutsul newspapers, and was asked to sing Gloria Gaynor's hit "I Will Survive" for a young Hutsul couple at their wedding dinner.

After 2009, I have returned to Ukraine whenever professional and personal circumstances have allowed. In 2010 and 2012, I had the occasion to visit as a performer in a variety of musical and theatrical projects. Since 2014, I have conducted interviews with Crimean Tatars who had relocated to Kyiv and L'viv. I returned to post-annexation Simferopol for a brief visit in the summer of 2015. Additionally, in recent years I deepened my study of *avtentyka* singing practices and pedagogy. My research in this area has been guided primarily by Yevhen

Yefremov, a senior professor of ethnomusicology at the National Music Academy of Ukraine, whose ethnographic research in the region of Kyivan Polissia that is now better known as the "Chornobyl Zone" formed the raw material for the Chornobyl Songs Project, a performance-based project that we developed collaboratively in 2011.[6]

Through Professor Yefremov and other *avtentyka* teachers, I have learned a bit about distinct regional and local village styles of Northern and Central Ukraine and how they have been studied and differently valorized by Soviet versus post-Soviet ethnomusicologists. As part of this research, I made a pilgrimage to the village of Kriachkivka, a famous Soviet-era "singing village" in the Poltava region that has also been symbolically important for the urban *avtentyka* revival. Opening up this third area of inquiry warmed me to communities with perhaps less overt investments in Ukrainian statehood than many of the Hutsuls or Crimean Tatars I had spent time with in 2008–2009. Though I cannot profess to represent the views of the Ukrainians who enthusiastically side with Russia in the ongoing war (I have done no research in the Donbas or Luhansk regions, but had some exposure to pro-Russian Crimeans before the annexation), the world of *avtentyka* singing has offered me a third perspective on contemporary Ukrainian modes of localized affiliation, and contributes to my understanding of how contemporary Ukrainian music reflects many varied internal discourses of Wildness.

ACKNOWLEDGMENTS

My intellectual, social, material, and spiritual debts should be voiced in many languages, so дякую, сагъолыныз, спасибо, thank you. Flattened on the page, these words fail to capture the deep reserves of gratitude I carry for the many individuals who contributed to this book during its long gestation. Intellectual labor is anything but a solo project, and without the network of interlocutors, friends, mentors, colleagues, students, and accomplices listed here, this book would simply not exist. I hope that I have captured in it at least some partial truths. I take full responsibility for its deficiencies.

First, and profound as the Black Sea, is my appreciation for the individuals who nourished, welcomed, educated, and guided me during many research trips to Ukraine. I wish I could offer more satisfying modes of reciprocity than this book. In 2008–2009, Oksana Susiak and her late mother, Sophia Petriivna Susiak, provided me with a cozy, lively, and safe home base in Verkhovyna. In Simferopol, I benefited immensely from the boundless generosity of the Settarov/a family. Ukrainian colleagues in ethnomusicology in Kyiv and L'viv shared their knowledge and taught me about how our ethnomusicologies compare. I thank especially Iryna Dovhaliuk, Iryna Fedun, Iryna Klymenko, Olia Kolomyiets', and Yevhen Yefremov. Local scholars—such as Vasyl Zelenchuk in Kryvorivnia; Fevzi Aliev and Dzhemil Karikov in Simferopol—shared their life's research with me and gave me an intellectual grounding as I pursued the research questions of this project, which often seemed at odd angles to their work.

So many musicians, artists, friends, activists, and community leaders in L'viv, Kyiv, Simferopol, Bakhchisaray, and other villages throughout Ukraine opened doors for me, agreed to allow me to hang out for a while, and answered my pestering questions (sometimes years later). I thank especially Gulnara Abbasova, Alim Aliev, Abduraman Egiz, Marko Halanevych, Pavlo Hrytsak, Khalil

Khalilov, Ruslana Khazipova, Ostap Kostiuk, the late Mykhailo Nechai, Roman Pechizhak, Marta Shvets', Rolan Salimov, Tamila Tasheva, the Tafiychuk family, Zeyneb Temnenko, and others whose names I have withheld for reasons of confidentiality. The artful ways that Ukrainians have negotiated the hardships of everyday life in a volatile, precarious state has been one of the deepest lessons of my life. To all of the individuals who entrusted me with their words and experiences: дякую, сагъолыныз, спасибо, thank you.

Wide as the steppe is my gratitude to my network of colleagues and friends who offered feedback on various parts of this book. Tyler Bickford, Katherine Boivin, Farzaneh Hemmasi, and Olga Touloumi read most or all of the manuscript at various stages. All four of these brilliant scholars and friends allowed me to test out ideas without judgment, while pushing me to sharpen my claims and clarify my arguments. I continue to learn so much from our writerly exchanges. Larissa Babij, my friend on the ground in Kyiv, raised provocative questions and challenged me to elucidate crucial connections among my key terms. Marié Abe, Alexandre Benson, Andrea Bohlman, Delia Casadei, Adriana Helbig, Laura Kunreuther, Lauren Ninoshvili, and Emily Zazulia helped me think through the problems of specific chapters. Two anonymous reviewers provided instructive critique and helpful suggestions for the revision of this book. David Novak stepped in to offer immensely generous and generative feedback on the introduction during the end of my revisions.

This work began its life as a doctoral dissertation at Columbia University, where I was fortunate to work with Aaron A. Fox, who continues to invigorate my thinking whenever we talk. Tyler Bickford, with whom I entered graduate school, has taught me so much about collegiality, reciprocity, and ethical ways of being in the academy. He has restored my confidence when my own confidence was failing. A deep bow to my professors—especially Lila Ellen Gray, Ana Maria Ochoa, Vitaly Chernetsky, Timothy D. Taylor, Mark von Hagen, Frank Sysyn, Christopher Washburne, and the late Catherine Nepomnyashchy—who impacted me in lasting ways, many of which continue to reveal themselves to me. At Columbia, I was so lucky to be among an inspiring community of graduate students who shaped my thinking then and continue to do so now. Thanks especially to Tyler Bickford, Ryan Dohoney, Andrew Eisenberg, Shannon Garland, Adriana Helbig, Niko Higgins, Farzaneh Hemmasi, Brian Karl, Elizabeth Keenan, Toby King, Morgan Luker, Lauren Ninoshvili, Marti Newland, David Novak, Jason Lee Oakes, Matt Sakakeeny, Ryan Skinner, Anna Stirr, and Whitney Slaten.

I received support from various granting agencies at different stages of this work. The American Councils Foreign Language Training Grant supported my study of the Crimean Tatar language; the Social Science Research Council and the IREX Individual Advanced Research Opportunities Grant funded the bulk of my fieldwork; and the Canadian Institute of Ukrainian Studies and various small grants from the Harriman Institute of Columbia helped support the writing of this book.

Much of this book was written in between semesters during my four years at Bard College. The impact of the faculty who took part in the interdisciplinary Experimental Humanities "sound cluster" at Bard—Laura Kunreuther, Matthew Deady, Olga Touloumi, Alexandre Benson, Danielle Riou, Julianne Swartz, and Drew Thompson—cannot be underestimated. Thank you for modeling how to mix scholarship with innovative teaching, and for pushing me to think more critically about how sound and music relate. At Bard and beyond, I clarified my thoughts, vented my anxieties, and learned a lot about writing and music through conversations with Austin Charron, Nick Emlen, Rory Finnin, Kyle Gann, Sage Gray, Brent Green, Joe Hagan, Samantha Hunt, Adrian Ivakhiv, Alex Kahn, Thomas Keenan, Arseny Khakhalin, Peter Klein, Susan Merriam, Maia McAleavey, Sophia Micahelles, Greg Moynahan, Thomas Porcello, Tanya Richardson, Kate Ryan, Stephanie Savell, Alina Simone, Corinna Snyder, Elsa Stamatopolou, Yuka Suzuki, and Olga Voronina.

I am grateful to the Harvard Ukrainian Research Institute, where I spent a stimulating fall semester after completing my dissertation, and where I first started to conceive the shape of this book. Kay Kaufman Shelemay stepped in as a mentor during my time at Harvard, for which I remain so grateful. During a postdoctoral fellowship at the University of Toronto, I benefited from the meetings and moral support of the Ukrainian Research Group as we witnessed the Maidan Revolution from our screens. In Toronto, I was also lucky to have Joshua Pilzer and Farzaneh Hemmasi for ethnomusicological discussions.

Too many students to name have challenged, inspired, and educated me. Students in my "Musical Exoticisms" seminars at the University of Toronto and at Columbia University helped me think through a broad literature on Eastern European otherness. The advanced Bard College students in my "Contemporary Ethnographies of Music and Sound" offered productive feedback on an early version of my introduction.

Many versions of this work were presented at conferences, including the Society for Ethnomusicology; the International Association of Popular Music Studies; the International Council for Traditional Music; the Association for Slavic, East

European, and Eurasian Studies; the Soyuz Symposium; the Danyliw Seminar; the Imperial Reverb: Exploring the Postcolonies of Communism conference at Princeton University; the Sonic Contestations of Nuclear Power conference also at Princeton University; the Experience Music Project Pop Conference. I am grateful to the colleagues who invited me to present portions of this work at Amherst College, Arizona State University, Boston University, Harvard University, McMaster University, University of Toronto, University of Cambridge, Wilfred Laurier University, and York University. An earlier version of Chapter 2 appeared in the *Journal of Popular Music Studies*; it is reprinted here by permission of the copyright holder, John Wiley & Sons, Inc. A version of Chapter 4 was previously published in *Public Culture*; it is republished by permission of Duke University Press.

I revised this book after beginning a new position at the University of California, Berkeley, where I have been welcomed into an extraordinary community of scholars. I am grateful to my colleagues in ethnomusicology, Jocelyne Guilbault, Ben Brinner, T. Carlis Roberts, and Bonnie Wade, for their encouragement. Mary Ann Smart has been a wonderful supporter in navigating my new institutional terrain. Delia Casadei and Emily Zazulia quickly became friends who patiently endured me as I brought this book to completion. On walks along the shoreline, I benefited greatly from dialogues with Richard Taruskin. Over meals, I have gained from conversations with Daniel Fisher, Marika Kuzma, and Alexei Yurchak. Charles Briggs offered a crucial suggestion and then allowed me to run with it. My wonderful seminar of graduate students at Berkeley read the close-to-final version of the introduction and encouraged me to finally send it off.

Marla Zubel acquired this book for Wesleyan University Press; Suzanna Tamminen and Mary Garrett kindly shepherded it through to publication. I thank the editorial board of the Music/Culture series—Sherri Tucker, Jeremy Wallach, and Deborah Wong—for supporting this project from the outset. Sashko Danylenko generously agreed to conceive the art that decorates the cover of this book.

In ways big and small, many others have supported this project over the years. In particular, I acknowledge Alison Cartwright Ketz; Julian Kytasty; Ethel Raim and the Center for Traditional Music and Dance; Mariana Sadovska; Yuri Shevchuk; Marta Soniewicka; Genevieve Smith; Virlana Tkacz of the Yara Arts Group; Morgan Williams; Ihor Poshyvailo and the Honchar Musum in Kyiv; Hanya Krill and Maria Shust of the Ukrainian Museum in New York; and Alla Rachkov. Margo Brown and David Romtvedt offered me a blissful quasi-residency in Buffalo, Wyoming. And I wish to acknowledge the vast infrastructure of childcare that undergirds this work: I thank Sara Foglia, Annemieke de Wildt, Carol Murray and the wonderful teachers of the Abigail Lundquist Botstein Nursery School at Bard College, in addition to a number of incredible Bard students—especially Bernardo Caceres, Maddie Hopfield, Eleanor Robb, Izzy Spain, and Sienna Thompson—for allowing me the space and peace of mind to know that my children were in good hands whenever I retreated to my office to write.

Finally, high as the Chornohora mountains is my appreciation for my family. A network of guardian aunts supported me through various stages of fieldwork: Ira Lasowska in L'viv, my safe harbor in Ukraine; Marta Bilas in Austria, who, among other things, helped me buy the beat-up Mazda that became key to my fieldwork; and Natalia Sonevytsky, my inspiring *strianka*. My late father, Rostyslav Sonevytsky, diligently practiced the piano every morning before going to work. This model of creativity and discipline has informed my life as a musician and a scholar. Words fail to express my debt and gratitude to my mother, Chrystia Sonevytsky, whose kindness appears to be infinite. She set an example of how to balance career with family; I thank her for her sustaining love for me and my family. My children, Lesia and Artem, teach me every day about the wild possibilities of human connection. And Franz Nicolay—my first reader, my worthy adversary, my companion, and my love—thank you for accompanying me on this adventure.

NOTE ON NAMES AND
TRANSLITERATION

This book contains translations and Romanizations from three different languages with complex and politicized relationships to orthography and transliteration. Where possible, I have included the original Cyrillic for readers familiar with that alphabet.

For Ukrainian, I generally follow the transliteration standards adopted in 1996 as the Ukrainian national system. I prefer to use the Ukrainian transliteration of places located in Ukraine, even when norms of transliteration into English favor the Russian transliteration. For example, I write Kyiv (from the Ukrainian Київ, rather than Kiev), Chornobyl (Чорнобиль, rather than Chernobyl), and L'viv (Львів, rather than Lvov). When Romanizing Russian, I use the ICAO system that was adopted in 2013, in part to minimize the use of diacritics in the text. I hold to these standards unless an individual or group represents their names or terms using different systems of transliteration. In such cases, I follow their lead.

The Crimean Tatar language presents some especially complex issues. Typically, in this book, I transliterate from the Cyrillic system that was adopted in the mid-twentieth century because the majority of texts I depended on were either produced during the Soviet period, or in post-Soviet publications that favored Cyrillic over Turkic (or Arabic) rendering of the language. However, I do occasionally transliterate terms to connote the specific sounds of Crimean Tatar that are difficult to convey with strict transliteration from Cyrillic, so instead of the term "Khaytarma," (rendered in Cyrillic frequently as "Хайтарма"), I opt for the transliteration as "Qaytarma," which indicates that the initial phoneme is a voiceless uvular stop. (In Cyrillic, this phoneme is better approximated with the combination of "К" followed by the hard sign from Russian, "ъ.")

A final note: some activists have moved to refer to themselves as "Crimeans" (in Ukrainian: Кримці or Krymtsi; in Turkic: Qirimli or sometimes Kirimli) rather than "Crimean Tatars." I have not observed these practices due to the fact that "Crimean Tatar" remains the dominant internationally recognized ethnonym for the group. For this reason, I also write "Crimea" instead of Krym or Qirim. That said, I acknowledge the importance of the campaign to jettison the vague and colonial term "Tatar," which was applied as the generic term for all Muslim subjects living on the territory of the former Russian Empire.

The vast majority of the formal and informal interviews for this project were conducted in either Ukrainian or Russian and have been transcribed and translated on the basis of field recordings. When I have reconstructed dialogue from field notes, I do not represent speech in quotation marks, unless I jotted it into my fieldnotes with quotation marks. Unless otherwise noted, translations are my own.

I present the identities of my interlocutors in various ways. In some cases, with their permission, I include full names. In others, in cases of more sensitive information, I do my best to fully anonymize sources. When I write about well-known musicians and bands, I typically use the full names of individuals if there is other information presented that would make them identifiable. In the case of celebrities, since my access to such individuals was for the most part restricted to their publicly available speech, I use full names.

Wild Music

INTRODUCTION

On Wildness

Wildness cannot tell because it frames telling as another tool of colonial rule. Wildness cannot speak without producing both the colonial order that gives it meaning and the disruption of that order through temporal and spatial and bodily excess and eccentricity.

J. Jack Halberstam, Wildness, Loss, Death

An audience of thousands wave national flags in a riot of color. Onstage, four dancers stand in a circle of red, pulsating light. The arena resounds with the sampled blare of the *trembita*, the massive slender horn associated with the Western Ukrainian mountain highlanders known as Hutsuls. Each dancer slowly raises a *trembita* so that the horns radiate outward from the circle. As the blurting opening sounds of the horns become more recognizable as melodies, they are interrupted by an orchestral hit, and a pop star—Ruslana, wearing a long fur draped Tarzan-like over one shoulder—enters from the back of the stage. She and five dancers wearing identical fur cloaks storm toward the audience. With each thunderous orchestral hit, they roar "Hey!" Bursts of flame erupt on the projection screens encircling the stage, as the dancers flank Ruslana in pyramid formation. They rip off their furs to reveal skin: tan midriffs, leather microskirts, and tall heeled boots with metal-studded seams. Their muscular tattooed arms bear Ruslana's "Wild Dances" insignia. As they turn, the tinny sound of *tsymbaly*—the hammered dulcimer also prevalent in rustic Hutsul music—momentarily cuts through the thumping electronic tune, and the dancers jump into synchronized choreography that recalls mid-1990s Janet Jackson more than Western Ukrainian village dance. The observer confronts a rapid stream of ambiguous yet redolent gestures: flashes of Xena the Warrior Princess or Britney Spears, Scythian gold or Celtic crests, the amped-up *oom-tzah* of a discotheque, an echoing Carpathian yodel, global sex, local folk, Amazons, Genghis Khan.

The performance of this song—called "Wild Dances"—took place in 2004 and signaled post-Soviet Ukraine's emergence into the arena of international pop music. It was Ukraine's second year participating in the Eurovision Song Contest (ESC), the televised song competition that has for decades staged European harmony and discord through the extravagant battle of folk-pop singers representing their countries (Tragaki 2013; Raykoff 2007). While *trembita* and *tsymbaly* samples in "Wild Dances" sonically marked the song as having something to do with the Western Ukrainian borderlands, other features skewed toward the generic dance-pop conventions of the early twenty-first century. The song's lyrics juxtaposed Hutsul vocables (*shydy-rydy-da-na*) with vague desires ("I want you to want me") sung in both English and Ukrainian. When "Wild Dances" was televoted to Eurovision victory, fans and media interpreted the song and its performance as an allegory of Ukraine's tortured post-Soviet geopolitical position. In interviews, and in her own (brief) political career following her Eurovision stardom, Ruslana herself supported such an interpretation, framing her victory as evidence that Ukraine was a European state that had finally left the orbit of Russian influence.[1] But if "Wild Dances" was a message about Europe-facing aspiration, why voice that message using a lexicon of exoticism?

There is more to this Eurovision story—about how the pop singer's triumph was variously received within Ukraine with pride, with ambivalence, or with embarrassment—especially as Hutsuls were forced to have a "rueful" reckoning with entrenched stereotypes of their "wildness" that had suddenly become internationally visible (Herzfeld 2005). I will take up these themes later on in this book. But here I wish to emphasize this watershed moment in post-Soviet Ukrainian pop music as a prominent instantiation of what I call "wild music," when tropes of exoticism are strategically integrated in musical performance in order to make political claims. Such wild music, I will argue, draws upon a discursive (uppercased) Wildness that has long defined Ukraine's liminal position in the world.[2] "Wild Dances" is perhaps the neatest example of such a phenomenon—especially as the song migrated, later in 2004, from the Eurovision stage to that of the Orange Revolution. There, as Ruslana repeatedly performed her ballad of auto-exoticism, it became an emblem of revolutionary hope for a less precarious future. Almost a decade later, the Maidan Revolution set in motion

FIGURE INTRO.1 Following the finals of the 2004 Eurovision Song Contest, Ruslana waves the Ukrainian flag at the Abdi Ipekci Arena in Istanbul, Turkey. Ukraine won the 49th Eurovision Song Contest with 280 points. AP Photo/Osman Orsal.

another cycle of revolutionary hope, eventual disappointment, then fatigue. Ruslana and scores of other musicians again deployed their own forms of musical Wildness on the revolutionary stage, suggesting new ways forward for Ukraine, trying to push past the binary choice of alliance with Europe or Russia, liberal democracy or authoritarianism, capitalism or socialism. In each new context of revolution, musicians performed hope for the future of Ukraine through wild music.

We can begin to understand the political utility of Wildness as a representational tool by observing its historical resonance in modern Ukraine. In a global context, Ukraine is not likely to leap to mind as an extreme space of otherness. The historian Larry Wolff, for example, documents how Ukraine (along with the rest of Eastern Europe) was "invented" during the Enlightenment as "an intellectual project of demi-Orientalization" (1994, 7). Indeed, for centuries, travelers, diplomats, and writers framed Ukraine as a space of liminality, tantalizingly close to the spaces of civilization. To Johann Gottfried Herder, the original theorist of musical nationalism, its inhabitants were the nearby "little

INTERESTING

wild peoples" (2011, 57) who—from their practices of sounding, and Herder's practices of listening—inspired his rhapsodies about the essence of the national spirit expressed through folk music.[3] For many nineteenth-century Polish and Austro-Hungarian ethnographers gazing eastward, Ukraine became a site of pilgrimage in pursuit of such *völkisch* authenticity. For such observers, Ukraine was a zone of un-civilization, one that they aspired to make intelligible through ethnographic inscription.[4]

Meanwhile, from the north, Catherinian narratives of imperial domination turned on the taming of the "wild field" (дикое поле) that flowed into the Crimean peninsula.[5] From the Russian imperial perspective, Ukraine was frequently depicted as an eternal "little" (мала) province of Russia, its unruly younger sibling. Such metaphors of kinship that subordinated Ukraine to Russia flourished in the Soviet twentieth century and have been revived again in the twenty-first.

Ukraine has been, in other words, a quintessential borderland, a buffer, a threshold, the closest "elsewhere" to a European or Russian "here." Its "wild" peoples and territories, observed by so many outsiders, have been tempered by its proximity to those "civilized" observers. Historically, then, Ukrainian Wildness has not been construed as the inscrutable Other of Orientalism, but instead as the proximate unruliness, the quaint immaturity, of the border. Like Orientalism, however, this discursive formation of Wildness is formed in "the ensemble of relationships between works, audiences and some particular aspects of the Orient [or the Wild that] . . . constitut[e] an analyzable formation" (Said 1979, 28).

Today, this discursive Wildness thrums through daily life not only as a current of history, but also as a pulse of the present. In a precarious Ukrainian state, Wildness manifests in everyday instabilities, in economic insecurity, in the untrustworthiness of authority, in the churning violence on the country's

borders, in the rise of restive militias, and—key to my project—in the creative expressive practices of citizens who survive and innovate under conditions of precarity. Wildness manifests in the political and aesthetic concepts, techniques, and shared assumptions through which Ukrainians contest their liminal position in contemporary global politics. Contemporary Ukrainian Wildness, then, can be understood as a "border epistemology" in Tlostanova and Mignolo's terms: a response "to the violence of the imperial territorial epistemology and the rhetoric of modernity with its familiar defects, from forced universal salvation to taking difference to sameness, from subject-object split to naturalization of Western epistemic privilege" (2012, 7). Ukrainian Wildness, therefore, also anticipates new modes of governance; scholars such as Jack Halberstam have also turned to "thinking about 'wildness' as a space/name/critical term for what lies beyond current logics of rule" (2014, 138).[6]

In the twenty-first century, the discursive force of Wildness has been harnessed by many Ukrainian musicians who remediate burdensome histories of exoticism in order to foster unexpected citizenly solidarities across the fault lines of ethnic, linguistic, and religious identity. From their borderland vantage, Ukrainians use Wildness as a source of knowledge, which rankles binaries of nature and culture, undermines geopolitical taxonomies of "West" and "East," and—instead—motivates strategies of self-representation that defiantly recenter local ways of knowing and sounding (cf. Ochoa Gautier 2016). Let me clarify here that I am aware of the dangers of reproducing damaging stereotypes of exoticism in my examination of Wildness. In my approach, I reject the notion of any a priori wildness (which might suggest an equivalence between the wild and an absolute or primordial state of nature), despite the fact that some Ukrainians hear such "real" wildness contained in specific acts of sounding. I am not interested in arbitrating the relative truth of such claims here, but rather in investigating how discursive Wildness has been circulated through aestheticized sonic expressive practices that enable contemporary actors to make a diversity of claims to political status. ⭐ M𝐴IN IDEA ↓

This book asserts that Wildness structures much of how Ukrainians today envision their horizons of possibility, and that wild music is a key vector through which citizens debate what Ukraine has been, what it is today, and, even more urgently, what it ought to be. It considers the ways that wild music—and the potential of Wildness expressed in sound and performance—fosters affective alliances among the diverse citizens of an imperiled state. While Wildness suggests riotousness, the refusal to be rationalized, tamed, or domesticated, *wild music* should be understood as a container that traps Wildness, because the music I analyze is always recognizable as a rationalized form of sounding.[7] In other words, musical form, along with its contexts of performance, circulation, and commercial exchange, naturalizes and domesticates those sounds that are construed to be "wild"—those ungovernable, uncategorizable, unexpected sounds of Ukraine's internal others that become intelligible—and thus commodifiable—as "music" when framed by specific acts of performance, audition, or circulation.

As a sonic representational resource, Wildness is expressed musically in many different ways: as outward-facing strategic auto-exoticism (as in the Eurovision example given); as nested and internal otherness (witnessed in the urban fetish of "village authenticity"); as ecological activism, totemic "folklore," anarchic hedonism; or as a reflection of Ukrainian experience that refracts the gazes of external viewers. It functions, at times, as a "weapon of the weak" (Scott 1985), though it can be coopted by the powerful. The Wildness of wild music seeks to surprise, to call attention to itself—and, at times, to refuse. Wild music can present as campy ironic distance (wildness as "wildness"), as utter sincerity (wildness as "nature" or "pristine wilderness"), or as an ambiguous blur of these two extremes. In any of its guises, the Wildness of wild music is disruptive in the present. Wildness rattles the cage of musical culture; it seeks to unsettle conventional sense, even as it is framed within colonial and postcolonial logics of sense-making (cf. Taussig 1987). Still, Wildness affords new modes of expression that musicians artfully link to the ways of life that they seek to bring into being.

Wildness is also a matter of perception. Many listeners—especially those alienated by, excluded from, or not conversant in internal Ukrainian discourse—will not hear the same Wildness that I identify in this music. Musical sound is, perhaps, an inherently unstable index of cultural territory.[8] But this book traverses the edges of this interpretive site, seeking a "border thinking"—and listening—grounded in culturally situated "interpretive moves" that center local ways of knowing through sound (Feld 1984).

SOVEREIGN IMAGINARIES

The period investigated in *Wild Music* is loosely bookended by monumental events—the two revolutions that coincided with Ukraine's two most prominent spectacles of global pop visibility, its Eurovision Song Contest victories in 2004 and 2016—but I will also attend to the interstices of revolutionary crests and wartime troughs, when hopes for the future took creative form and gained momentum as emergent social imaginaries.[9] To pursue such hopeful formations, I introduce the analytic of *sovereign imaginaries*: expressions of citizens' desires for ways of life that are enabled by particular forms of governance. My notion of sovereign imaginaries is rooted in the anthropological argument that the form of hegemonic power known as sovereignty is constituted through sociocultural practices. By invoking the phrase "ways of life" (life in community according to social norms and practices), I follow Caroline Humphrey's critique of Giorgio Agamben's "somewhat pallid" understanding of ways of life as "merely the habitual activities of politically and judicially defined groups." Humphrey points out that ways of life "have their histories and their modes of governmentality.

They do not simply acquiesce to the menace of sovereignty but interpose a solid existence of their own that operates collaterally or against it" (2004, 420).[10] This means that such ways of life—such practices of sovereignty—order how citizens conceive of themselves as subjects (personal sovereignty) who consciously attach to—while leaving space to contest and reimagine—the political sovereignty of the state. In this sense, political sovereignty can be rethought not just "as a set of political capacities but as a formation in society that engages with ways of life that have temporality and their own characteristic aesthetics" (421). What, then, can ways of life that are sensory, acoustic, musical—with their history, temporality, and "characteristic aesthetics"—tell us about emergent conditions of sovereignty?

Through musical ways of life, citizens negotiate histories of representation, transmuting Wildness from a diminishing term of otherness into a source of power. But these expressions of Wildness are not purely hopeful: they also bear the historical burdens of Ukrainian "backwardness," and the contemporary fatigue and disappointment with the failures of postmillennial revolutions. The wild music I investigate throughout this book can be roughly classified using the capacious post-Soviet Ukrainian genre term *etno-muzyka* (ethno-music), which emplaces local sonic markers (*etno-*) within global popular music styles (rock, hip-hop, and so on).[11] The "wild" sounds of *etno-muzyka*—which typically index an internal Ukrainian *etnos*—forge solidarities through shared recognition.[12] Within the large and diverse space of the Ukrainian state, "wild" sounds take many forms—the *trembita*'s signal blurt, the sung cries of elderly *babushkas*, the modes and ornaments of traditional Crimean Tatar songs, and so on. These "wild" sounds often relate to each other in delicately negotiated patterns of nested otherness. Yet when the heavy, often painful histories of exoticism are refigured and redeemed, citizens bond themselves to each other and to the state in part through the webs of signification spawned through these sounds. Publics are formed through shared interpretations of sounds made meaningful through performance. I understand this process as a branch of sensory citizenship that I call "acoustic citizenship."[13] Acoustic citizenship, a term I will elaborate on at the end of this book, naturalizes forms of belonging within the space of the state through shared experiences of listening, sounding, or being *listened to*. This study therefore explores the various "audible entanglements" (Guilbault 2005) of music with the politics of citizenly attachment to the state, even when the state is weak, corrupt, and fractured.

The historical and present-day resonances of Wildness, and its representation in various forms of wild music, allow us to consider how Ukrainian musicians and audiences attempt to bring certain ways of life into being. Since these ways of life are mediated through the apparatus of the state, the Wildness of wild music opens the space to rethink sovereignty and citizenship. This is especially critical in a state as fragile as Ukraine, but the ramifications reach well beyond the case study at hand. Ukraine's present geopolitical conundrum reveals the "fragility of state sovereignty" on a global scale (Wanner 2014, 430),[14] even as far-right nationalist movements that are often predicated on maintaining the state's unassailable sovereignty have risen to power around the world.

Arjun Appadurai memorably wrote that the nation and state are locked in "a battle of the imagination" (1990, 14). A sovereign imaginary, as I define it here, holds the potential for broadening this battlefield beyond the nation or state, toward emergent logics of rule. José Muñoz, following Ernst Bloch, might identify the sovereign imaginary as an "anticipatory affective structure" (2009, 3) in its ability to bring to light personal-political desires that are "not-yet conscious." In Muñoz's terms, it is a "concrete utopia," one that may be "daydreamlike, but [represents] the hopes of a collective, an emergent group, or even the solitary oddball who is the one who dreams for many" (3).[15] How, for example, do "state-less people" such as the Kurds or Roma appeal to existing logics of the nation-state? How will the new diaspora of Syrian refugees conceive of themselves in the aftermath of the war that ravages Syrian territories? What is the obligation of a state to provide a minority or Indigenous population with the right of self-determination? Ten years after the global financial debt crisis, is the Greek state sovereign, or merely subject to the neoliberal policies of the European Union? The analytic of the sovereign imaginary allows us to observe how sovereignty might be concretely territorialized (that is, "the Palestinian state"), but it also permits the object of sovereignty to be a "hyperreal" abstraction (that is, the "West" or "Europe," with its hegemonic connotations of order and civil society) (Chakrabarty 2000, 27). These imaginaries may privilege precolonial or nostalgic networks of belonging (Indigenous communities, former empires, diasporas) that can be nested within or stretch beyond a modern state's borders. Sovereign imaginaries, then, often cull from different sorts of sovereignties, redirecting the disenchantments of the present toward the future. It is in their futurity, in fact, through which sovereign imaginaries develop the potential to collide with the potentiality of Wildness contained in wild music.

A note of caution: I do not mean to overstate the transformational potential or utopian promise of music with regard to emergent sovereignties. As Lila Ellen

Gray has recently written, "For scholars of music, aesthetics, and politics in an era of social media and protest, one challenge is how to investigate imaginative aesthetic practices engendered in globally interlinked processes and technologies of protest and uprising while steering clear of the traps of thinking music, mobility, social media, and politics through the frame of only utopic promise (with 'democracy' and 'aesthetics' particularly vulnerable in this respect)" (2016, 69). What Gray identifies as these "traps of thinking" in contemporary popular music extend, as I see it, from nineteenth- and twentieth-century ideologies of Western art music centered on the belief that (elite) music could suspend rationality, transcend the base and worldly constraints of human existence, and universally ennoble all human subjects (see Taylor 2007 for a critique of this narrative). Vladimir Lenin, in fact, reportedly stated that listening to classical music "affects your nerves, makes you want to say stupid nice things, and stroke the heads of people who could create such beauty while living in this vile hell" (quoted in Nelson 2004, 1). Despite this, portraits of a brooding Lenin listening intently to Beethoven's "Appasionata" sonata "hung in almost every Soviet music school and conservatory" (Levin 2002, 195; see also Skinner 2003). All of this to say: such utopian ideas about music are potent and entrenched.

But, as ethnomusicologists have long argued, imaginaries of musical transcendence are, at root, ideological. They fail to account for the varied cross-cultural strategic and quotidian uses of music: to make a livelihood, to facilitate or accompany rituals, or to act as a lubricant that enables specific kinds of socio-musical participation (see, for example, Turino 2008; DeNora 2000). Such ideologies also fail to account for the unstable significations of musical sounds, those obscured by persistent assertions of the universal "language of music," despite decades of anthropological studies of music that undermine this reductive formulation.[16] Ethnomusicological studies since the 1980s, instead, have asserted the deeply contextual meanings of musical sound, advocating for understandings of how music not only reflects but also produces meaning in society. I reiterate these disciplinary truisms in part to warn against overemphasizing the curative potentiality of musical aesthetics, and also to underscore the potency of the ideological apparatus that supports notions of aesthetic autonomy, of music as a sphere apart from the debased world of politics.

I also wish to note the irony of claiming that the Wildness of *etno-muzyka* has the potential to project futurity in the context of a post-Soviet state, with its legacy of Soviet cultural policies that mandated that music must *always* speak for the (glorious proletarian dictatorship of the) future. Lenin's famous dictum that artworks should be "deeply implanted in the very thick of the laboring masses" (Nelson 2004, 220), in tandem with the socialist realist aesthetic norms codified under Stalin, demanded that Soviet artworks take inspiration from peasant and working class "folk" forms to generate the music of the socialist future. What is clearly different in this twenty-first-century scenario is that Ukrainians making *etno-muzyka* today conjure sovereign imaginaries without an ideological imperative from above (even if, as some of my examples show, some of the techniques by which sounds are utilized for political ends are similar to those used in the Soviet period).

Contemporary musical practices of *etno-muzyka* have afforded Ukrainians the opportunity to at once re-litigate the past while still projecting creative future paths forward. In the decade framed by two revolutions, sovereign imaginaries morph and multiply. In their Wildness, the inflamed rhetorics of post-Soviet ethno-nationalism splinter and enable new ideologies of affiliation, such as the pragmatic patriotism that has been most vocally supported by the small but growing middle and creative class of urban and cosmopolitan Ukrainians. For example, by the end of the revolutionary decade circumscribed in this book, a sovereign imaginary exists that centers on the ambiguous but powerful trope of "dignity" that became key to the rhetoric of the Maidan Revolution, also known as the "Revolution of Dignity."

What dignity means, and how it maps onto the idealized liberal transcendental subject of European history, remains hotly disputed within Ukraine. But what is striking is that such a sovereign imaginary is not predicated on any of the traditional ideas associated with nationhood, such as ethnolinguistic unity, common culture, or shared history. Rather, it is premised on the inclusion of citizens deserving of dignity, who happen to be contained within the somewhat arbitrary sovereign borders of contemporary Ukraine. In this case, instead of exclusionary nationalist ideas of who deserves dignity and sovereign protection, Ukrainians are developing imaginative strategies through which affective ties can be generated across class, racial, ethnic, religious, linguistic, and gendered experience. What interests me is how such sovereign imaginaries are articulated through musical expressions of Wildness. This becomes apparent in the following example, when Ukrainian citizens at risk of losing their citizenship voiced emergent solidarities by wilding the national anthem.

WILDING THE ANTHEM

In 2014, in the destabilizing aftermath of the Maidan Revolution, I witnessed a performance of the Ukrainian national anthem—which bears the rather uninspiring (and, in 2014, dispiritingly apropos) title "Ukraine Is Not Dead Yet"—where the communal embrace of discursive and relational Wildness enabled this most staid of song forms to resound with fresh political possibilities.

That summer, my husband, infant daughter, and I attended the ArtPóle (АртПоле) festival in a tiny Western Ukrainian village located approximately sixty battered kilometers from the nearest city of Ivano-Frankivsk. ArtPóle was held on the territory of a decommissioned Soviet *kolkhoz* (collective farm) turned festival space, picturesquely situated above the shore of the Dniester River, about a fifteen-minute walk from the small cluster of rural homesteads that comprised the center of the village. On festival weekends, Unizh, population 156, swelled to the low thousands. The festival ran for five days in July and featured musical groups from Finland, Turkey, the Czech Republic, Russia, Poland, and the UK, as well as Ukrainian acts from Kyiv, L'viv, and Crimea. Theatrical presentations, film screenings, children's programs, and master classes filled out the schedule. That summer, the Ukrainian "land art" summer festival was in its twelfth and, unbeknownst to the organizers, last iteration. The ambiance that summer was noticeably subdued, with much smaller crowds than previous ArtPóle festivals that I had attended. When I inquired in casual conversation as to this apparent shift in mood, one of the organizers told me that this muted atmosphere was by design. In a year when, as she put it, "the entirety of Ukraine is depressed by the political situation," it had felt wrong to stage the usual exuberant, large-scale event.[17] In this context, the intermittent rain, which disrupted programming and further dampened the mood of organizers and attendees throughout the week, seemed especially fitting.

The previous year in Ukraine had been especially chaotic: the boisterous Maidan Revolution spilled over from the winter of 2013 into 2014 and turned violent, culminating in the murder of over one hundred protestors in central Kyiv by state forces and the abdication of the democratically elected president, a corrupt figure heavily indebted to the Russian government. The Russian mediasphere decried the uprising as a fascist takeover of the Ukrainian government, while most US and European media outlets breathlessly reported on the Ukrainian citizenry's "revolution of dignity" (революція гідності).[18] The spring brought the loss of Ukrainian territory to the Russian Federation: first, with the swift annexation of the Crimean peninsula, and later, through Russian-backed separatist violence in the eastern border regions (the violent conflict there remains ongoing in 2019).[19] The rapid deterioration of the political situation—from the euphoric highs of revolutionary possibility to the miserable lows of wartime—reverberated across all corners of Ukrainian society: the state was exposed as vulnerable, its sovereign borders indefensible against Russian aggression, its military embarrassingly under-equipped and understaffed. In Simferopol, Crimea, a Crimean Tatar friend—one of the Sunni Muslim Indigenous minority of the peninsula who were generally pro-Ukrainian—told me, "We understand now just how powerless we really are . . . and how vulnerable all of Ukraine is. We are abandoned by our state, and our state is abandoned by our world" (personal communication, June 14, 2015).

By the summer of 2014, the illegal annexation of Crimea appeared entrenched, at the very least, as a "frozen conflict" (Dunn and Bobick 2014; see also Charron 2016). In the eastern borderlands, Russian-backed "separatists" had announced the secession of the Donetsk and Luhansk "People's Republics" from the Ukrainian state.[20] Russia welcomed these "new Russian" provinces into its orbit, depicting the separatists as heroic anti-fascist crusaders. Everyone I encountered that summer seemed preoccupied with the slow-boiling war at Ukraine's borders. Even the youth-oriented music and culture festivals that had defined summer revelry in twenty-first-century Ukraine were not immune from the unfolding crisis.

At Artpóle in Unizh, the stated theme of the 2014 festival was "ornaments." The press release—though ambiguous—lent itself to political interpretation:

> Borders are lines. Lines delineate space. Lines connect points in space. Points and lines create ornamental patterns. Geometry borders on art. Your movement in space, a path, a line, is designated to imprint your movement (press release, 2014).

There was no question that Ukraine's vulnerable borders motivated some of the programming for the festival, particularly on the festival's Sunday evening program. The night was billed as an "Authentic Program" (Автентична Програма) featuring music from Crimea and the Carpathians, two borderland regions of Ukraine that loom prominently in Ukrainian imaginations of its internal Wildness. The evening featured back-to-back performances of two groups from these distinct regions. The first group were Hutsuls, the same population who inspired Ruslana's "Wild Dances," and who occupy the space of the Herderian ür-folk of Ukraine, with colorful traditional costumes, lively music, and a unique cosmology. The Hutsuls were followed by a trio of Crimean Tatar musicians, upon whom many ethnic Ukrainians and Russians project racialized Orientalist stereotypes (especially of a capacity for violence) due to their historical link to the Ottoman Empire and to the fact that they are neither Slavic nor Christian (with some few exceptions).[21] The Crimean Tatar trio had traveled through the blockaded border to perform—illegally, in the eyes of the Russian state that now controlled the peninsula but had not yet forced them to surrender their Ukrainian passports.

By juxtaposing two "authentic" borderland musical traditions from extremely different parts of Ukraine with different present-day statuses vis-à-vis citizenship, the festival organizers asked the audience to engage with those performances as parts of one whole—a coherent Ukrainian state with its sovereignty intact—despite the bitter reality that this whole had been so recently broken. At 8:00 in the evening, the Hutsul collective (actually an amalgam of musicians from various Hutsul bands who performed under the name Hutsuls that night) began to play on one of the outdoor festival stages, a makeshift amphitheater fashioned out of the ruins of a building.[22] Their up-tempo tunes, played on the iconic instruments of the Hutsuls—sopilka (wood flute), tsymbaly (hammered dulcimer), bubon (bass drum with attached cymbal)—resounded through the post-Soviet rubble. After about ten minutes, their set was interrupted by a pelting downpour. The festival organizers hurriedly steered both musicians and audience into one of the bunker-like "gallery" spaces. In the smaller space, the acoustic instruments boomed, electrifying the crowd, who danced energetically. As the musicians played the well-known Hutsul men's circle dance called the "Arkan," I was pulled into the dance with my daughter in my arms, as young and hip festivalgoers mingled with local villagers in a jubilant approximation of the acrobatic folk dance.

The downpour ended as abruptly as it began, and when the Hutsuls finished their set, the audience filtered back out into the now-muddy festival field. The crowd reconvened at the outdoor stage, where Taraf, the trio of Crimean Tatar musicians—a violinist, accordion player, and percussionist—were setting up for the second set of the avtentychna prohrama. As they began to play, it became clear that the crowd had retained their high-octane energy from the Hutsuls' musty indoor set. Audience members scaled and then danced on the crumbling stone walls of the makeshift amphitheater as a bright moon shone in the night sky. After a medley of fiery qaytarma—the iconic 7/8 dance genre of the Crimean Tatars—the violinist spoke into his microphone: "Ukraine is united." The crowd erupted in cheers. Deep in the set, the trio performed an arrangement of the faux-baroque composition known as "Albinoni's Adagio." I recognized the mournful tune from my fieldwork in Crimea in 2008–2009 as one of the melodies that Crimean Tatars have adopted to commemorate their traumatic twentieth-century deportation and exile under Soviet policy.[23] The Crimean Tatar trio then continued their set with a spirited instrumental performance of the Ukrainian national anthem.

The unusual choice to include the national anthem in such a festival performance, and then its creative rearticulation using Crimean Tatar musical gestures, reanimated "Ukraine Is Not Dead Yet." An archetypal "anthem-as-hymn" (Daughtry 2003, 45), the performance of the song that night was unusually intimate, stripped of its pomp and revitalized with wild feeling. Because the trio performed instrumentally, the audience supplied the lyrics, creating a shared energy between performers and the audience that encircled them, some singing from high atop the crumbling walls of the improvised amphitheater. The melody of the anthem was elaborated with Turkic ornaments from the violinist and supported by the tonally varied sounds of a *doumbelek* goblet drum. This uncharacteristic mix made the anthem feel less militaristic, more lush in its melody and contoured in its rhythms. Instead of standing solemn and still, audience members moved their bodies in time with this new anthem and used their voices to howl and cheer when it concluded. The performance and its reception dislodged the anthem from its typical nationalistic setting by channeling it through an improvisatory Wildness. This Wildness did not rest purely on the anthem's "Crimean Tatar-ization" but arose relationally, in dialogue with the Hutsul group who had inspired the Crimean Tatars toward this improvisatory expression of solidarity, and with the festival audience who elevated the performance with their effervescent appreciation.

What I perceived as the relational impetus for this articulation of Wildness was clarified for me the next day, when I asked one of the Crimean Tatar instrumentalists of Taraf whether the Ukrainian national anthem was part of their standard repertoire. He replied that it was not. But, he explained, given the circumstances of the ongoing political instability, the spirited festival crowd, and after hearing the Hutsuls play, they wanted to reassert their claim as citizens of Ukraine and chose to enact that claim spontaneously, through musical means. This gesture of goodwill emerged in response to, but also in solidarity with, the performance of the Hutsuls. The Hutsuls made no overtly patriotic gestures; yet they spurred the Crimean Tatars to overt patriotism through a gesture of musical solidarity in a creative, collectively realized rearrangement of the national anthem.

FIGURE INTRO.2 The Hutsul collective soundchecks at the ArtPóle festival in Unizh, 2014. Photo by Maria Sonevytsky.

FIGURE INTRO.3 The Crimean Tatar group Taraf performs after the rainfall at ArtPóle in Unizh, 2014. Photo by Maria Sonevytsky.

On that Sunday night at ArtPóle, Ukrainians came together in a "spirit of conviviality" to make sense of a world that seemed to be falling apart. Paul Gilroy's idea of convivial culture is helpful here to explain how I interpreted the evening—not, to borrow from Gilroy's lexicon, as a triumph of tolerant multiculturalism, but as a solidarity borne from "radical openness" (2006, xv). This was a wild solidarity that promised new, yet unanticipated modes of affiliation and ways of being—of reimagining, in this case, what it is to be "Ukrainian" when the nation-state is no longer intact.[24] The ruins, a monument to Soviet communal agriculture, contributed to the wild possibilities of the night, calling to mind Ann Laura Stoler's question about "how people live with and in ruins . . . to the politics animated, to the common sense they disturb, to the critiques condensed or disallowed, and to the social relations avidly coalesced or shattered around them" (2008, 196). Stoler asks that "we might turn to ruins as epicenters of renewed claims, as history in a spirited voice, as sites that animate new possibilities, bids for entitlement, and unexpected political projects" (232). The rain-soaked ArtPóle amphitheater did, in fact, become an epicenter for a renewed claim to—and an expression of the broad desire for—Ukrainian political sovereignty. In wilding the national anthem, the concert expressed the potentiality of emergent politics articulated within the fractured space of an imperiled state.[25] Pleasure, sociality, spontaneity, and the *deus ex machina* effect of a temperamental bout of weather merged to foster this kind of ecstatic space. Thus, the festival night resembled a "temporary autonomous zone" (Bey 1991 [1985]), with acts of symbolic remaking akin to what Alexei Yurchak (1999) identified in the fleeting utopian promise of post-Soviet raves.[26]

In Unizh, the performance of the Ukrainian anthem gave voice to an emergent "intimate public" of festival participants (Berlant 2008; see also Shank 2014). Here, as festival attendees swayed and sang the words of the Ukrainian national anthem, the political became foregrounded and interwoven with the sociality and pleasure of the festivalgoing experience. As the seated attendees joined those standing to stomp their feet, clap, and hoot following the anthem, the performance achieved, in Benedict Anderson's terms, "unisonance"—the selfless feeling of simultaneity and solidarity through which the "imagined community" of the nation is conjured (1991, 145). What interests me here, however, is how this unisonance was diverted from the idea of nationhood and toward an idea of statehood—of the integrity of sovereign borders and the power of the state to enact protections for the ways of life enclosed within those borders.

Since it declared independence from the Soviet Union in 1991, Ukraine has tried and failed to conform to European liberal democratic models that presume an isomorphism between nation and state. Begoña Aretxaga memorably dismantled logics of the nation-state by pointing out its "untenable hyphen" (2003, 396); Ukraine offers some proof of how ill-fitting that conjunction really is. A nation, at least in its idealized form, is generally defined through its shared history located on a distinct territory, with a common language and expressive culture. Ukraine confounds these criteria.[27] First, Ukraine was partitioned and repartitioned among numerous imperial powers (including the Russian, Ottoman, and Austro-Hungarian Empires, the Polish-Lithuanian Commonwealth and, if one advances the belief that the USSR operated in Ukraine as a quasi-imperial formation, the Soviet Union).[28] Second, language usage in Ukraine is a contentious subject since Ukraine functionally—though not legally—has two national languages, Russian and Ukrainian, and a widely utilized hybrid form of those two languages called *surzhyk*.[29] Third, Ukraine is and has always been multiethnic and multinational. Though its population is majority Slavic (including people and groups that may identify as ethnic Ukrainians, Russians, or Poles, or more localized forms of affiliation such as Hutsuls, Polissians, Rusyns, and others), it also has significant numbers of protected minority groups (Greeks, Armenians, Germans, Bulgarians). Then there are the Muslim-majority Crimean Tatars, whose post-Soviet struggle for human rights has largely been predicated on gaining recognition as "Indigenous people" (in Ukrainian, корінній народ; in Russian, коренной народ), a status mediated in large part through the United Nations Permanent Forum on Indigenous Issues.[30] In the period of post-Soviet independence, and especially since the 2004 Orange Revolution, reductive yet tenacious narratives of a Ukraine split in two along an East-West axis have characterized media representations and many academic analyses of Ukraine (Portnov 2013, 242). As I write in 2019, Ukraine's sovereign borders remain disputed.

In the performative wilding of the national anthem at ArtPóle, instrumentalists and audience members voiced a collective wish for a sovereign state that could protect its citizens across the lines of identity that were present in that moment. This suggests an awareness of power in "its capillary form of existence," at "the point where [it] reaches into the very grain of individuals, touches their bodies and inserts itself into their actions and attitudes, their discourses, learning processes and everyday lives" (Foucault 1980, 39). The metaphor of the capillary, however, also suggests circulation. This begs the question: How do individuals agentively tap into and instrumentalize this power as it trickles into their bodies, voices, actions, and attitudes? How do they redirect its flow, or allow it to pass through, in order to animate new ways of life? Giorgio Agamben (1998) critiques Foucault on similar ground in the opening pages of *Homo Sacer*.[31] I propose that if we hear the Wildness in this national anthem as a collective and creative expression of a wish for sovereignty, then we also witness how "technologies of the self" link to the "political techniques of the state" *through* musical practices (cf. Agamben 1998, 5).

A core premise of this study is that citizens not only desire, but demand the state's sovereign power. Even when its institutions are weak and corrupt, the state form endures as a modern "screen for political desire" (Aretxaga 2003, 394). Citizens dream of the sovereignties that would best suit the state they inhabit and attempt to bring such potentialities into being. This claim therefore positions this study in productive tension to the broad literature that documents how people have historically resisted, been silenced by, or refused the coercive forces of state power (Scott 2009; Mbembe 2003; Simpson 2014). But here, rather than document the violent and necropolitical effects of sovereign power, I center on the *potential* of the sovereign state to enact policies of care for its citizens, who, in Ukraine, creatively voice their wishes for such care through Wildness and its historically freighted, imaginative, and revolutionary potentials. The musical articulations of Wildness that interest me most circulate widely and destabilize entrenched nodes of power, elevating instead the peripheral and seemingly inconsequential ways of life that offer alternative models of citizenship and belonging.[32]

Apprehending Wildness in this way, of course, presupposes that citizens *can* harbor sentiment for institutions, infrastructures, and bureaucracies—perhaps easier to imagine when we consider how the refusal of institutions and bureaucracies to succumb to the demands of powerful leaders can actually thwart or block corruption.[33] Beyond the state's monopoly on violence, or the well-studied quasi-theological power its sovereign power exerts to discipline its polity and protect its borders (Schmitt 1985 [1935]), a state, of course, maintains its legitimacy by providing stable governance for its citizens. The often under-emphasized formulation of Max Weber's idea of the modern "state as enterprise" is helpful here to understand how a modern state's entrepreneurialism—its pursuit of certain strategies aimed at the betterment of the quality of life for its subjects—is key to maintaining the state's legitimacy (Anter 2014, 206).[34] Put simply, the state is the guarantor of the ways of life desired by citizens, as well as the formulator of their desires. In 2018, we see such desires for renewed sovereignty articulated in care-giving terms both in global superpowers such as the United States (where attacks on "globalism" are core tenets of Trumpist populism) and in vulnerable states such as Ukraine (where these desires take various defensive forms).

An important distinction lies embedded in the chasm between the *possibility* that a state would act with care and compassion on behalf of a citizenry and the *reality* of the violent and exploitative mechanisms through which state power is typically consolidated (that is, the better-known components of Weberian state theory). I do not intend to paper over this reality, nor over the specific and egregious inadequacies of the modern Ukrainian state. In fact, since its independence from the Soviet Union in 1991, the Ukrainian state has repeatedly proven its untrustworthiness, incompetence, and disregard for its non-elite subjects. In the post-Soviet period, with the influx of foreign aid and business, the growing population of migrants from Asia and Africa, and the rush of consumer items into a starved marketplace, a kleptocratic regime emerged along with stark socioeconomic inequalities that forced the vast majority of Ukrainians into conditions of poverty. The brutal conditions wrought by neoliberal capitalism might also explain why many Ukrainians today harbor nostalgia for aspects of Soviet life, or—in extreme cases such as those pro-Russian separatists in the eastern borderlands—desire Russian state power.[35] Ukraine's political-oligarchic class has been compromised through the influence of both Russian and Western governmental entities. The state is deeply in debt to Russia and to the International Monetary Fund. Its bureaucracy is penetrated by corruption at all levels. The nascent middle class of urban Ukrainians, those who came of age in the late and post-Soviet eras, tend to have a profound mistrust of the state as it exists, but they also often harbor little nostalgia for the USSR, and nurse no delusions about the injustices and crises that face liberal democracies in Europe and North America. Many Ukrainians across socioeconomic categories suffer from revolutionary fatigue, having lived through many cycles of social collapse, revolutionary hope, and eventual disappointment.[36]

It should also be noted that the Ukrainian state has recently sanctioned violence against its citizens. During the Maidan Revolution, for example, the government of then-President Yanukovych enlisted snipers to assassinate street protestors who are now memorialized as the "Heavenly Hundred" (Небесна Сотня). Further, Maria Mayerchyk and Olga Plakhotnik (2015) have argued that as war erupted in the eastern borderlands in the aftermath of the Maidan, the Ukrainian state prioritized the defense of its political sovereignty over protecting the citizens ensnared in a war zone. With respect to the post-Maidan political climate, they write,

This new precarity has been ideologically legitimized by a new rhetoric of Othering . . . which divide[s] the population into more valuable and less worth[y] groups on the basis of national consciousness. People from Donbas are constructed as "improper Ukrainians": their so-called *lack of national identity* is associated today with the label of Soviet, as if this part of [the] population did not "grow up," [was not] "developed," "emancipated" from the Soviet past. They are contrasted with the apparently "nationally conscious" citizens of the other parts of Ukraine, whose national consciousness makes them valuable for the state and the nation in contrast to the people from Donbas.

As the authors outline some of the tragic realities of the postrevolutionary period through the lens of postcolonial and feminist critique, they underscore the failures of the modern, ostensibly democratic Ukrainian nation-state to care for all of its citizens. The authors draw on Victoria Hesford's work on "feminist time" versus "nation time," where "nation time" blurs with the "emergency time" of late capitalist societies who are in "perpetual war." This "emergency time" emphasizes a present that is "at once both empty and full—empty of historicity and full of a mythical future" (Hesford and Diedrich 2008, 174). It does so "at the expense of a 'historicizing, futuritial consciousness'" (193). Mayerchyk, Plakhotnik, and Hesford are in agreement that, to combat this present-oriented emergency time, "thinking matters, especially in a time of war. Speculative, non-instrumental thought, experimental approaches to the present, and a skeptical, historicizing self-critique become acts of resistance in the emergency time of war where action, myth and amnesia become the drugs of certainty" (Hesford and Diedrich 2008, 183).

This is where wild music stands to intervene in the future of sovereignty. Music, an ensemble of social practices that comprise ways of life—enables precisely such "speculative, non-instrumental" thought that might shift the emphasis of a dominant temporality toward the future, even as it draws on historical legacies in order to remake the past and channel desire for the continued existence of a state form in the present. This speculative and non-instrumental capacity of music to be transformational in an expanded political sense is core to the aesthetic philosophy of Jacques Ranciere (2013). Recently, in a Rancierian vein, the ethnomusicologist Gavin Steingo has written that music has the potential to "double reality, or to allow [individuals] to imagine and even experience a world that does not yet exist" (2016, 9). In this Ukrainian context, the imaginative agency of musicians and audiences who conjure and fleetingly experience such emergent worlds is always informed by a reconceptualization of the contested pasts of Ukraine.

And so, returning to the crumbling amphitheater in Unizh, I ask: When the standard criteria for nationhood do not hold, when the nation is uncoupled from the state, who then has the right to claim a song such as the national anthem—and which sonic-aesthetic-bodily-poetic techniques may be used to trouble conventional senses of ownership? These are not only narrow Ukrainian questions. We see their resonances in the symbolic forms of recent historical struggles in the United States, such as Jimi Hendrix's legendary rearrangements and distortions of "The Star-Spangled Banner" at the Woodstock festival in 1969. Or in the raised fists or kneeling bodies of African American athletes affirming their personhood through a "sovereignty of quiet" while the anthem plays (Quashie 2012). Or when immigrant-rights activists protesting then-President George W. Bush's assertion that the anthem "ought to be sung in English" (Holusha 2006), translated the lyrics into Spanish and sang it in the streets. That episode prompted Judith Butler to suggest that "certain ideas of sensate democracy, of aesthetic articulation within the political sphere, and the relationship between song and what is called the 'public'" had to be reconsidered when citizens adopt such a "performative politics" (Butler and Spivak 2010, 62–63). If we hear this anthem sung in Unizh as a spontaneous articulation of a new form of "sensate democracy" that coalesced around a community of citizens brought together through sensory—and chiefly acoustic—means, we can apprehend this music for its Wildness, as it refuses a status quo and enacts a mode of hopeful thinking about the future. This wild anthem—one situated example of what I mean by wild music—reveals the interdependence of sovereignty, citizenship, performance, and sound.

EVIDENCE AND ABSENCE

Science is observational and evidentiary. Please accept this
wild bouquet of evidence I have collected.

Samantha Hunt, *Queer Theorem*

Wild Music assembles its "bouquet of evidence" from a variety of sources. I draw first on my decade-long ethnographic engagements in Ukraine. This fieldwork is supplemented with archival research conducted in Western Ukraine and Crimea, as well as ongoing conversations with musicians (often conducted online, through email, text message, and social media). I also address widely circulated media artifacts (YouTube videos, studio recordings, television programs, and

Eurovision performances). I strive to connect these ubiquitous digital objects of internet public culture to the thickness of situated ethnographic research. Sherri Ortner, who in 1995 warned of the "thinning" of ethnography that occurs when ethnographic specificity is compromised by taking on deterritorialized objects of study, has more recently asserted that "the study of 'media' or 'public culture' should not be some niche subfield of anthropology, but rather an aspect of almost any ethnographic project . . . [A]s long as the study of public culture is not purely a study of texts, but is rather about their production, circulation, and consumption—their interaction with social and political life on the ground" (quoted in Unger 2017).[37] Following in the trail of recent exemplary ethnographic studies of media and public culture (see Bickford 2017; Fisher 2016; Kunreuther 2014; Larkin 2008; Meintjes 2003; Novak 2013), I attempt to privilege local knowledge frameworks and to make interpretive moves derived from long-term ethnographic fieldwork even when the ostensible topic of concern is a media text like the Eurovision festival or an online music video.

I wish to clarify here some of the ways in which this study offers a partial view. First, it does not account for most of the commercially successful music that was produced in Ukraine between the Orange and Maidan Revolutions, much of which is not *etno-muzyka*. I would not be surprised if some Ukrainian popular musicians and audiences—fans of Ukrainian rock bands like Okean El'zy, not to mention many *estrada* (light entertainment), pop, and hip-hop artists—find the frame of Wildness distorting, though I would argue for its presence even in many cases when tropes of exoticism are not foregrounded in obvious ways.[38] Second, I do not account for a broad spectrum of political positions, and I especially fail to account for those Ukrainian citizens who are enthusiastic about Russian state power—the examples I chose to write about largely conform to political positions embraced by the makers and fans of *etno-muzyka* to whom I had access. There are a few reasons for this: one is my politicized subject position as a Ukrainian American, which made it difficult to engage in productive dialogues with pro-Russian citizens, as I described in the preface. Another is due to my initial focus on Hutsuls and Crimean Tatars, where strongly pro-Russian voices were simply not audible in 2008–2009. Finally, personal and professional reasons prevented me from traveling to the war-torn regions of the east after 2014, though I was able to return to post-annexation Crimea for a short visit in 2015.

There is also a deliberate conceptual silence in this book that deserves to be explained, which is my treatment of the topic of nationalism and how it relates to wild music. There are two primary reasons that I de-emphasize nationalism.

First, because I am committed to the project of decolonizing ethnomusicology, and because I believe that this entails a reassessment of the traditional theoretical investments that mark our discipline, this extends, in the present study, to the inherited assumption that modern musical cultures relate primarily to the nation—and, by extension, to nationalism. Music's relationship to nationalism has been a foundational concern of music studies, since the very notion of "folk music" was core to Johann Gottfried Herder's understanding of national spirit, identity, and history, as I have already mentioned (Herder 2017; see also Bohlman 2004; Taruskin 2001). Benjamin Teitelbaum's (2017) vital work on the relationship of music to radical white nationalism in Sweden pursues this theme into the contemporary era. Yet, despite the numerous studies that deepen our understanding of music and its ability to "perform the nation" (Askew 2002; see also Olson 2004; Sugarman 1999; Bohlman 2010), music's relationship to the state remains under-examined. Moreover, ethnographers of music have yet to engage with sovereignty, having prioritized instead questions of how music is governed through various "micropractices" (Guilbault 2007) or "administered" through state policies and (mutable) ideological mandates (Tochka 2016); how musicians adapt through transitional political-economic orders (Buchanan 2006); or how cosmopolitanism operates within the space of the nation (Turino 2000).[39] I am deeply indebted to all of this work. In this project, however, I attempt to invert the flow of power that is usually presupposed in these studies by prioritizing how the musical practices of citizens that comprise cultural "ways of life" contribute to emergent political sovereignties.[40] ↗ IMPORTANT

The second reason I do not center discussions of nationalism in *Wild Music* has to do with the fact that Ukrainian nationalism has been overdetermined by the narratives of others—Russia, Europe, the United States—while Ukraine's emergent twenty-first-century patriotism—exemplified in episodes such as the night at ArtPóle—has been largely overlooked. Therefore, I largely sidestep the nation and the problems of nationalism (which I define here as an ideology of superiority and exceptionalism) in favor of examining the operations of patriotism (loyalty and appreciation for one's ways of life).[41] This rationale has particular salience for the perennial underdogs of global geopolitics whose "nationalisms" are depicted as threatening and suspicious rather than the stance of ennobled patriotism bequeathed to the victors of geopolitics (Von Hagen 1995).[42] Though nationalism has operated as a pernicious ideology used to justify violence at points in Ukrainian history, the trope of "Ukrainian nationalism" as it is deployed in the current information war waged by Russia demonstrates how the narratives of a

NATIONALISM vs PATRIOTISM

regional superpower flatten or distort the actual threat of Ukrainian xenophobia. During the Maidan Revolution, for example, Russian media narratives decried the rise of a threatening ethno-nationalism in Ukraine, labeling the revolution a fascist coup, even as many Ukrainians celebrated the inclusivity of (especially the early) Maidan protests. Though scholars of Ukraine are doing important work to study the role of right-wing nationalists in escalating violence during the Maidan Revolution (Ishchenko 2016) and those who continue to operate in militias in the eastern border conflict with Russia (Risch 2015), nationalist groups in Ukraine continue to hold little electoral power and possess effectively no formal governing authority in Ukraine at the time of this writing (unlike far-right groups in Hungary, Poland, Brazil, and the United States). Nonetheless, the narrative of rabid Ukrainian nationalism is a key weapon deployed in the informational warfare waged by Russia on Ukraine.[43]

By circumventing these tropes of Ukrainian nationalism, then, *Wild Music* takes up a challenge set forth by postcolonial and decolonial theorists to provincialize the master narratives of history (Chakrabarty 2000, 41). Alexei Yurchak, in his project to "rehumanize Soviet life," asserted that "in the case of socialism, especially in Russia, the object of 'provincializing' would not just be 'Europe' but, more specifically, 'Western Europe'" (2005, 9).[44] In Ukraine, however, where even the premodern myths of Russia and Ukraine are bound together through shared sites and figures such as Saint Volodymyr/Vladimir the Great, the urgent need to de-provincialize Ukraine hinges first on its relationship to Russia.[45] By provincializing Russia, then, one can glean something of how Ukrainians deploy wild music to reimagine the layered imperial and neo-imperial histories that inform contemporary discourses of Ukrainian sovereignty (cf. Fowler 2017, 11).

The unexpected outcomes of the Maidan Revolution have led Ukraine into a seemingly perpetual condition of "war without war and occupation without occupation" (Dunn and Bobick 2014, 405). Despite this, the prospect of a better future is being actively and creatively reimagined by an internet-savvy generation of activists, creators, and performers, who are attached to the idea of Ukrainian statehood and are finding new ways to make and amplify political claims through wild music. This generation tends to reject the creeping authoritarianism of Vladimir Putin's Russia, but they also do not fully embrace faltering European models of nation-statehood. They are suspicious of voracious capitalism and understand the dangerous precedents of "actually existing socialism." These actors take the Ukrainian past and present seriously on its own terms by attempting to decenter master narratives from both European and Russian perspectives,

FIGURE INTRO.4
Graffiti of the word
"Revolution" in Independence
Square in Kyiv, 2014. Photo
by Franz Nicolay.

decoupling nation from state, and privileging patriotism over nationalism. This affords the possibility to consider that, while the Ukrainian state may be considered "fragile" or even "failing" (by some outside metrics and by the account of many of its frustrated, alienated citizenry), it nonetheless remains at the center of the sovereign imaginaries that its citizens are conjuring in wild music.[46]

The six body chapters of *Wild Music* elaborate on such sovereign imaginaries through examples that reveal the situated knowledges and mediated forms of Wildness that permeate various musical and social contexts of contemporary Ukraine. The following two chapters center on the representation and reception of Western Ukrainian Hutsuls in the Ukrainian mediasphere: first through Ruslana's "Wild Dances" (Chapter 1) and then through the remediated video of the "freak-cabaret" collective known as the Dakh Daughters (Chapter 2). I then move to analysis of *avtentyka* singers who compete on the popular reality TV singing competition called *Holos Kraïny* (Voice of the Nation). Here, I examine how the politics of undisciplined vocal timbre reject logics of success according to the standards of reality TV "democratainment" (Hartley 2004). Their untamed singing remakes failure as an act of refusal of the limited musical forms that dominate Ukrainian media and an assertion of the ungovernability of Ukrainian rural expression. Chapter 4 focuses on the liminal sovereign imaginaries of Crimea as they relate to the "Eastern music" that was branded and broadcast by Radio Meydan, the Crimean Tatar radio station that operated in Simferopol from 2005 until 2015. I demonstrate how the presence of "Eastern music" in the semipublic spaces of microtransit motivated competing sovereign imaginaries among distinct Crimean populations, including the Crimean Tatar Indigenous minority. In Chapter 5, I interpret the sounds of "ethno-chaos" in recordings by the group DakhaBrakha, whose commercial success in the North American and European world music markets positioned its members to speak as "Ambassadors of the Maidan" to the world. In this chapter, I introduce the idea of "soundmarks of sovereignty"—sonic markers of history, territory, and temporality, embodied and subjugated knowledges, and postcolonial reclamation—and examine their relationship to emergent citizenly solidarities. The conclusion develops the idea of acoustic citizenship and explores it as a form of volitional, and therefore limited, citizenship that may have particular salience in imperiled states.

Despite the embattled status of Ukraine and its citizenry during the era that this book examines, I hear many expressions of tentative hope for the future in this wild music. Ortner recently questioned how one might balance an "anthropology of the good life" against the "dark anthropology" that tracks power and inequality in daily life: "How can we be both realistic about the ugly realities of the world today and hopeful about the possibilities of changing them?" (2016, 60). Many of my interlocutors—like the musicians who create wild new forms of *etno-muzyka* but do not fight to defend Ukrainian sovereignty with weapons of war—point out the potential futility of *any* music to *do anything*. I do not dispute that music has little power against bombs, or BUK missiles.[47] But I also assert that the study of music cannot be consigned only to our study of "the good life" since it is so prominently enmeshed in systems of capital, and therefore in the operations of power, and—importantly—because it also holds the affective power to captivate imaginations, move bodies, and support political actions. The politics and aesthetics of wild music allows us to investigate how the good life is imagined in dark times.

ONE

Wild Dances

Ethnic Intimacy, Auto-Exoticism, and Infrastructural Activism

In the very heart of Europe in the majestic kingdom of the Carpathian
Mountains there live an ancient people, the Hutsuls. Their riches are
unique mystic rituals, mountainous rhythms and dances. Ruslana visited
them and revealed their mystery. Europe will learn about . . . Ukrainian
ethnic originality, brightness of the highlander's rhythms mixed with the
modern music of the youth . . . Ruslana is experimenting with genres.
There is no right name for it, but it could be either called Hutsul rap or
kolmiyka's hip-hop. In any case . . . you are reminded that even though
"Wild Dances" come from ancient times, they are still the product of
the 21st century. DJ dance mixes on the songs of the album make you
feel like at the dance floor in night club . . . Ethnic motifs with electronic
elements of house and drum-and-bass make the music sound fantastic.
And it also makes us think that hundreds of years ago the progressive
young people were dancing to the same beat [sic].

www.ruslana.ua/en, accessed April 28, 2005

Provoked to curiosity by the rhetoric of the pop star Ruslana's press materials,
I embarked to reveal the mystery of the majestic kingdom of the Carpathian
Mountains for myself. It was a hot day in July 2005, and my small entourage was
nearing the end of a long journey to a village represented as the end point of a

slender serpentine line on my large road map of Ukraine. We were en route to Kosmach, a village in Hutsulshchyna, the southwestern mountainous region of Ukraine that borders the northern edge of Romania. Despite earlier journeys on equally remote and similarly pockmarked dirt roads in this region of the world, a feeling of naïve expectance overcame me as the car lurched toward our destination. That morning, I had revisited the press materials first released at Ruslana's "Знаю Я" ("Znaiu Ya," or "I Know") *etno-muzyka* video premiere in the chic Western Ukrainian capital of L'viv in 2002, where I was fortunate to be in attendance. That event kicked off her "Hutsulian Project" and featured a music video that was touted as a history-making *megaklip* (rather than a *klip*, the term for an average music video). The *megaklip* had been filmed largely in the village of Kosmach. The press materials told the story of how Ruslana had traveled "high in the mountains, where the people live in [a] different time and dimension," to find her "source of inspiration." Familiar with the long history of Hutsul romanticization by L'vivan urbanites, and as someone who thinks of herself as allergic to exoticizing rhetoric, I nonetheless briefly entertained the possibility that maybe, somehow, this would be "the place," as the press release boasted, "where you find true Ukrainian exotics!"

As my friend negotiated the unpaved mountain roads in his small tank-like Soviet Lada, I sat in the back seat and imagined that Kosmach might actually be different from scores of other Hutsul villages that I had visited earlier that week and on previous trips—it was, after all, the *end* point of the thin, snaking line on the map. After hours passing through scenic mountain vistas and roadside villages, we finally rolled into Kosmach, where a large Ukrainian Orthodox church and a few small cafés framed the center of town. As it started to drizzle, we ducked into the only café that appeared to be open. Inside, three teenagers—two girls and a boy—sat sharing a Snickers bar and text messaging each other with their cell phones from across the table. In my field notes, I jotted the observation that, while Kosmach was geographically remote, its isolation did not preclude such technologically sophisticated—if also technologically alienating—forms of modern teenaged flirtation.

We introduced ourselves, and I shared that I had come to Kosmach to investigate the source of inspiration for Ruslana's brand of *etno-muzyka*. One of the teenagers, Lida, who was also the daughter of the café's proprietors, leaped forward with an opinion that was echoed with differing degrees of intensity, but a notable amount of consistency, by the majority of the Kosmach villagers with whom I spoke later that week. She explained, "Ruslana came in with a huge crew;

it went well. We dressed up in our folk costumes for her and staged a wedding. Everything was fine. But I can't say that people are happy about it—especially about the name of the project, *Dyki Tantsi* (Дикі Танці, meaning Wild Dances).[1] How, in what way, are we wild (дикі)?" My video footage from that summer cuts from Lida to a scene that followed just a few minutes later: a wedding band called Kosmats'ka Pysanka (Kosmach Easter Egg)—composed of many of the same musicians Ruslana had hired for her project—led a wedding procession through the center of town. They waved at us, an invitation to join the parade of partygoers in festive, but not folkloric attire. I fell in line and spent the next two days at the wedding party gathering their perspectives on Ruslana's representation of their village in her Hutsulian Project.

Now to the Eurovision Song Contest (ESC) held in Istanbul one year earlier. In 2004, Ukraine was the tenth country to take the stage at the ESC, a forum that "notoriously mingles kitsch with geopolitics" (Heller 2007, 199). Ukraine was thought to be in a statistically unfavorably placement, sandwiched between Albania and Croatia in the middle of the competition. It was also one of the two newest participating countries in the 49th annual ESC, having entered for the first time in 2003. Over one hundred million viewers in thirty-six countries were reported to have taken part in the 2004 televised contest, making it the biggest televoted contest in world history at that time. As described in the introduction to this book, Ruslana gave an energetic performance of her song "Wild Dances," which drew on familiar sonic and visual gestures of Hutsul exoticism, repackaging them as a message of Wildness with a European-facing aspiration. After all of the thirty-six participant national broadcast companies reported their countries' televoting results, Ruslana and her squad of Wild Dancers were proclaimed victorious. The win rocketed Ruslana to heights of international stardom unprecedented for a post-Soviet Ukrainian pop musician in the early twenty-first century (see Fig. Intro.1).

In addition to the specifically Hutsul stereotypes of "wildness" represented in "Wild Dances," the performance also trafficked in generic tropes of exoticism. In some cases, it blurred the lines between what was supposed to index Hutsuls specifically, and exoticism globally. This was most evident in how Ruslana's sartorial choices were perceived. In the aftermath of the competition, her aesthetic was compared frequently to Xena the Warrior Princess, the protagonist of the popular fantasy television show of the mid-1990s. Xena's violent, ambiguous, and kinky sexualized presentation has been noted (Morreale 1998); Ruslana was careful to distinguish the pacifism of her Wildness: "Ruslana—who has always maintained her work is entirely innovative and original—admitted she could see the parallels between her 'Wild Dances' costumes and those worn by US TV character, Xena the Warrior Princess. However, she maintained that unlike Xena, the 'Wild Dancers' are not hostile, merely 'wild in style'" (Eurovision press release, 2004).

Other connections to Ruslana's depictions of Wildness were made after the competition. One effect of the attention given to the discursive presence of Wildness in Ruslana's "Wild Dances" was that it persistently configured Hutsuls in relationship to discourses of Wildness through musical performance in complex ways that muddled the global and local. In some ways, the song simply revived old discourses of the archaic Wildness of Hutsul music, making those discourses accessible to fans of Eurovision who had never considered Ukraine as a space of such enticing exoticism before the ESC. In other ways, it diluted the specificity of Hutsul positionality and their unique history of being represented as "wild."

Ruslana's capitalization on Wildness—as it echoed generic conceptions of "otherness" and as it was negotiated in daily use as a result of her numerous "wild projects"—is one theme of this chapter. I examine, in turn, Ruslana's initial musical experiments exploiting tropes of Hutsul Wildness, the reception of this Wildness by the Hutsul community that bears the stigma of a deep history of objectification as the "wild folk" of Western Ukraine, and then Ruslana's shifting ideas about and politicization of Wildness in recent years. This chapter, then, provides an overview of how one celebrity musician's wild music exploited different tropes of exoticism for the benefit of different audiences in order to make different political claims over the span of a decade bracketed by popular revolution.

The force of Ruslana's celebrity and her widely circulated depictions of Wildness also offer some insights on emergent sovereign imaginaries between the Orange and Maidan Revolutions. After the ESC, Ruslana's new visibility as Ukraine's premiere pop cultural export endowed her with authority as the promoter of what she called "the Ukrainian image" for international audiences, a role in which she reimagined the meaning of Wildness and its relationship to Ukrainian-ness in accordance with shifting visions of Ukrainian statehood between the Orange and Maidan Revolutions. When Ukraine plunged into political turmoil with the start of the Orange Revolution in late 2004 following rampant electoral fraud in the contest for the presidency, Ruslana allied herself with the pro-Western reform candidate Viktor Yushchenko, who was eventually elected to the presidency. In the winter months during which Ukrainian state activities were effectively frozen due to the enormous protests that paralyzed the Ukrainian capital, Ruslana performed "Wild Dances" and other hits on the revolutionary stage that was erected in central Kyiv.

After the Orange Revolution, Ruslana was appointed to be Ukraine's first Goodwill Ambassador by the United Nations Children's Fund (UNICEF) in 2005. In March 2006, she was elected to the Verkhovna Rada, the Ukrainian Parliament, as a representative of President Yushchenko's Nasha Ukraina (Our Ukraine) coalition (a position she relinquished in June 2007).[2] Meanwhile, she became the spokesperson for the Organization for Security and Cooperation in Europe's (OSCE) campaign against female trafficking in Europe, appearing in television commercials in Ukraine and throughout Europe. In 2008, she premiered what she called the "social single" titled "Not for Sale," which she composed as the anthem for the anti-human-trafficking league based in Vienna, Austria. She also used it to tease her new album, *Wild Energy*, which featured Missy Elliott and T-Pain, two prominent US hip-hop artists, as guests on two tracks. In recent years, Ruslana has been photographed with former First Lady Michelle Obama, and has performed for audiences throughout Europe, North America, and South America. Along with other post-Soviet musical luminaries, Ruslana has been a judge on the popular televised reality TV singing competition in Ukraine known as *Holos Kraïny* (Voice of the Nation), which I take up in Chapter 4.

During the 2013–2014 Maidan Revolution, she sang the Ukrainian anthem nightly to motivate protestors through the cold winter nights, and played John Lennon's "Imagine" on the upright piano (painted yellow and blue, the colors of the Ukrainian flag) that had become a symbol of that revolution's somewhat quirky creative energy (see Figure 1.1). Billing herself as a "humanitarian pop star," Ruslana has never again reached the meteoric heights of fame that accompanied her 2004 ESC win, yet she remains a permanent fixture at the nexus of Ukrainian cultural policy, activism, and popular music.

From her first success as a "wild dancer" influenced by the traditions of the Hutsul minority of Western Ukraine, to her later rebranding as a social activist invested in "wild energy," the "wild projects" mirror contemporaneous changes in Ukrainian coalitional politics, as earlier post-Soviet ideologies of ethnonationalism gave way to new ideas about citizenly belonging within the state, including—in some corners of Ukrainian society—an emergent idea of civic nationhood (Plokhii 2016). Early in her career, as Ruslana reconfigured the source of her Wildness from a concrete local language attributed to Hutsuls to an aspirational category that dissolved specifics and let a more inclusive notion of Wildness stand in, Wildness morphed from a term of ethnic intimacy, to

FIGURE 1.1 Ruslana Lyzhychko plays the blue and yellow Maidan piano during a concert organized for Maidan activists. Photo by Sergii Kharchenko/ NurPhoto/Sipa USA via AP Images.

marketable auto-exoticism, to one of eco-conscious infrastructural and civic activism. This transformation maps onto broader Ukrainian political concerns following the Orange Revolution, as revolutionary fatigue and disenchantment with the revolutionary government's failures paved the way for the emergent civic-oriented and pragmatic sovereign imaginary that would eventually come to motivate the Maidan's politics of dignity.

This chapter follows Ruslana's transformation from a marginal figure of post-Soviet Ukrainian *estrada* to a global "ethno-pop" (*etno*-pop) star, and then to a political activist with ambitions to transform state policy and redefine Ukrainian futurity. I observe this transformation through an examination of three songs that mark this trajectory: "Znaiu Ya" (Знаю Я / "I Know") (2002), the ESC winner "Wild Dances" (2004), and "Wild Energy" (2008). However, rather than represent three disjunct nodes in this pop star's career arc, I elucidate how the hybrid influences present in "Znaiu Ya" and "Wild Dances"—despite the discourse of ethnic purity that marked them—anticipated the project of civic belonging announced by "Wild Energy" by drawing together diverse national myths, including those of Scythian primordialism and post-Soviet categories of femininity. This chapter also returns questions of representation in Ruslana's Hutsulian Project to Hutsuls themselves, allowing them to evaluate Wildness on their own terms.

In this chapter, I introduce the term "ethnic intimacy" as a minor variant of Michael Herzfeld's influential coinage "cultural intimacy," in part to emphasize that the utilization of Hutsul motifs represents a regional collective space that overlaps with ethnic identification but bleeds across state borders; this distinguishes it from the nationally bounded collective space within which cultural intimacy is articulated. In this example, Hutsul ethnic intimacy is nested within the national imagined space of cultural intimacy, though it also exists in latent tension to the state's political sovereignty, since Hutsuls also inhabit villages in modern-day Romania. Like cultural intimacy, the space of ethnic intimacy is also one in which stereotypes operate as the identifying codes of communities. In the Ukrainian case, the historical uses of "Hutsul-ness" have particular resonance as a kind of post-Austro-Hungarian imperial formation of the "authentic folk," and therefore have little in common with other regions of Ukraine that were shaped through different imperial regimes. That said, Hutsul-ness becomes deployed as a form of (national) cultural intimacy—when the borderland "folk" became elevated to the status of national symbol, as happened in Ruslana's "Wild Dances" performance on the Eurovision stage.

This chapter assesses how Wildness has been defined by Ruslana in shifting post-Soviet sovereign imaginaries that draw upon nested and varied histories of postcolonial representation and geopolitical affiliation. Through Ruslana's controversial use of tropes of exoticism, we observe how Wildness becomes metonymic for shifting sovereign imaginaries between the Orange and Maidan Revolutions, that is, Wildness *as* sovereign imaginary. First, Wildness is represented in the service of a vision of Ukrainian statehood rooted in ethnonationalism (drawn in particular from the exotic representation of Hutsuls and later exported to both domestic and international audiences). Then, in a later iteration, Wildness becomes a trope of wilderness and eco-activism rooted in a civically minded pragmatic patriotism. Through her wild music, Ruslana, the pop-star-cum-political-activist, dreams of distinct visions of statehood. She enacts these visions of statehood in part upon her own body as she toys with self-representations in extreme gendered, sexualized, and cyborgish modalities. The *etno*-pop celebrity's public and commodified body, then, becomes a generative site through which the sovereignty of a body becomes bound to broader political sovereignties.

To begin, I return to the premiere of the 2002 *megaklip* of the song "Znaiu Ya" ("I Know").

IN THE KNOW

In 2002, Ruslana's guests to the newly renovated downtown cinema in L'viv were treated to back-to-back screenings of the five-minute *megaklip* of "Znaiu Ya" ("I Know"), the first single released as part of her Hutsulian Project (and later, the first track on the 2003 Ukrainian-language album *Dyki Tantsi*). The evening also included a live performance by a trio of Hutsul musicians who had traveled from the mountains that day, a performance by Ruslana herself, and speeches by local politicians and tastemakers. Attendees were told that the evening marked a trailblazing achievement by Ruslana and for Ukraine: as the biggest budget endeavor to date in Ukrainian popular music at the time, the "Znaju Ya" video brought in two hundred fifty specialists from seven companies in four countries (Ukraine, Russia, Belarus, and Finland), who utilized state-of-the-art camera and special effects. The video was the first Ukrainian cinematic product filmed on color 35 mm film in high definition and adhering to the sonic standards of Digital Dolby. The project included a fleet of ten helicopters, and at least one Hummer. Scenes were filmed in the Carpathian and Crimean Mountains, and in Belarus. In the village of Kosmach, the team filmed a "folk" Hutsul wedding. (The press release noted that it is "interesting, that the Hutsuls, their costumes, and the wedding itself are real," though of course the locals I spoke to disputed this account.) Press highlighted Ruslana's daredevil stunts (scaling rocky crags to get an "unparalleled vista") and sense of innovation (such as the rock concert stage built into a waterfall, where Ruslana performed "without any security"). One thousand people reportedly traveled to witness the concert-on-the-waterfall.

Years before her victory at Eurovision, the hullabaloo around the advent of the Hutsulian Project marked a substantial shift in Ruslana's status among the pantheon of post-Soviet Ukrainian popular musicians. Born in 1973 in L'viv, Ruslana Lyzhychko completed her studies in classical piano and conducting at the Lysenko Academy of Music in L'viv. In 1996, she was awarded first place at the Slavic Bazaar music competition in Belarus with the performance of the folk song "Oi Letily, Dyki Husy" (which was made famous throughout the Soviet world in the 1970s folk-pop rendition performed by Nina Matvienko). Ruslana's first album, *Myt' Vesny* (*A Moment of Spring*, released in 1998) contained small ethnic gestures such as melodies played on *sopilka* (wooden recorder), but mostly aligned itself stylistically with the saccharine aesthetic of Soviet *estrada* pop ballads. It was not until 2002, with the release of "Znaiu Ya" and her Hutsulian Project, that Ruslana differentiated herself from scores of other singers reared on Soviet-style popular forms.

The hit single "Znaiu Ya" has a clear and seductive message: Ruslana has uncovered the secret wisdom of Hutsul culture, and now she earnestly wants to share what she knows with you, the audience. The video opens with a crackling campfire. Fireside, Ruslana sits with a computer in her lap. She types in "The Lost World" (in English), and the computer begins "searching . . ." as she gazes into the distance. She then types "Znaiu Ya" (in the Cyrillic alphabet). When she presses "enter," the scene dissolves into a cosmic panorama, which zooms out to reveal the end of a *trembita*, played by a man, soft focus, in folk dress.[3] Another *trembita* blares in response. Winds rustle through mountain grass as the frame widens onto trees, forests, and sweeping mountain vistas. Ruslana enters the frame, dressed in a modest leather pantsuit, and sings lyrically, in Ukrainian, of a "beautiful land, that flies in the stars." The rubato introduction culminates in the words "Znaiu Ya," and the song revs into a propulsive rhythmic groove reminiscent of traditional Hutsul dance tunes. A *sopilka*, the Hutsul wood recorder, features prominently in the mix. The lyrics enumerate all of the knowledge that Ruslana has derived from the high mountains ("There is no real love in the valleys . . . only on the peaks," and "You don't know how the wind sings for us . . . but I know!"). The video proceeds by juxtaposing symbols of ancientness and rurality against emblems of modernity: Ruslana on horseback, hitting a weathered tambourine; Ruslana splashing through a mountain stream at the helm of a Hummer; elderly women washing laundry in the river; Ruslana white-water rafting in a colorful inflatable vessel; a traditional wedding; men circle dancing around a raging, flickering bonfire; an elderly Hutsul woman puffing on a pipe; Ruslana gesturing as she sings with a traditional *bartka* (ceremonial ax) used by male carolers to mark time as they sing; Ruslana firing a pistol into the sky; then, a rock concert on the river with fuming, glittering pyrotechnics.

At the *megaklip* premiere in L'viv, Ruslana's affirmations that "I know" expanded to place the audience, to borrow an English-language colloquialism, "in the know." It appeared to me that this well-heeled audience, who were impressed with the technical achievements of the video and also attracted to the mystique of Hutsuls, felt secure in their shared intimacy with Ruslana and her Hutsulian Project. Grounded in the territorialized identities of the Hutsuls, the song invited this Western Ukrainian audience to share in the special kind of knowledge that Ruslana had unlocked. The staged wedding, theatricalized as it was during the Soviet period, is key to the narrative of "Znaiu Ya" and rehearses images of the authenticity of rituals in this community that were quite distinct from the Hutsul weddings that I attended in Ukraine.[4] Equally important for "Znaiu Ya"'s claims about knowledge, however, are the various icons of modernity utilized by Ruslana, who was depicted as a twenty-first-century rock star. Demonstrating repeatedly that she is someone who lives in the contemporary world, in the video Ruslana expertly mediates between the local knowledge of Hutsuls and the world of the urbanite, the tourist, the outsider whose portal to knowledge is, after all, the internet.

The song lyrics, some of which were cited earlier, further suggest that anyone to whom the lyrics are intelligible is now in the know about the ethnically intimate space of the Hutsuls. This allows Hutsuls to recognize themselves in the caricatured depictions of their traditions, but also gives non-Hutsul Ukrainian speakers the privilege of feeling in the know. Thus, the ethnic intimacy of a particular group is expanded outward, aligning with Lauren Berlant's observation, "Intimacy poses a question of scale that links the instability of individual lives to the trajectories of the collective" (1998, 283). In "Znaiu Ya," the pop star makes her treasured knowledge of a historically exoticized ethnic borderland group stand synecdochically for the shared knowledge of a larger collectivity—one that is Ukrainian. In other words, she attempts to refigure ethnic intimacy as cultural intimacy.

I interpret "Znaiu Ya" and this iteration of the Hutsulian Project as an initial attempt to elevate the Hutsul exotic as a form of postcolonial Ukrainian national culture, demonstrating how "the peasant (or subaltern) perspective may be assimilated into a national discourse that portrays 'the peasant's world' as representative of an idea of national culture" (Bhabha 1990, 297). In the earliest iteration of her Hutsulian Project, Ruslana's appeal was made to a domestic public, one that would pridefully recognize and embrace the particular Western Ukrainian rusticity of Hutsuls as their own. In situating her first articulation of Wildness in the predominantly Ukrainophone and nationalist-leaning west of Ukraine, the project reified the link between the cosmopolitan cities of the former Hapsburg Empire and its isolated villages inhabited by picturesque "folk." The project depicted a community based on qualities of essentialized Wildness but exclusive of other groups prevalent in Western Ukraine, many of whom also endure histories of objectification (this includes Jews, Roma, Poles, Armenians, and others). Therefore, "Znaiu Ya" lines up with a kind of vision of nationhood premised on theories of *etnos* that, as Serguei Oushakine notes, "became . . . a major analytic device for conceptualizing the continuity of post-Soviet nations . . . at the turn of the twenty-first century" (2009, 83). Some of the Hutsuls who would later reject Ruslana's Eurovision depiction of Wildness could still manage to embrace this early iteration pridefully, since it fit into a sovereign imaginary that validated their ethnic identity at its core.

Just as the press releases on opening night predicted, the "Znaiu Ya" video sparked massive interest among viewers on Ukrainian television. The success of the "Znaiu Ya" single led to Ruslana's signing with Comp Music, the Ukrainian affiliate of the global music label EMI. This was followed by an invitation to produce an album of songs from her Hutsulian Project at Peter Gabriel's Real World Studios in England, a famous locus for hit "world music" albums. The *Dyki Tantsi* album recorded there consists of ten original songs with an additional remix version of the hit single "Znaiu Ya." Most of the songs incorporate token Hutsul sounds such as the iconic *trembita* (alpine horn), *tsymbaly* (hammered dulcimer), *drymba* (jaw harp), and a variety of wooden flutes and recorders (*sopilka, floiera, telynka, dentsivka*). Many songs use the scansion and declamation associated with the Hutsul song form known as *kolomyika*.

On the album *Dyki Tantsi*, the lyrics are exclusively in Ukrainian and marked by Ruslana's urbane, L'viv-based pronunciation, though she stresses well-known Hutsul tropes by pronouncing key terms in dialect, or by dropping the ends of words (as is the convention in village-style performance). Rhythmically, the songs emphasize syncopations associated more with male Hutsul foot-stomping dances than the regular *oom-pah* played by Hutsul *bubon* drummers, though the rhythmic dimension of much of the album evokes a generic "tribal" world music quality more than anything specifically Hutsul. Less than six months after the album was released in June 2003, it reached platinum sales in Ukraine, breaking another record for Ukrainian commercial music. The commercial success of the album led to Ruslana's nomination to represent Ukraine at Eurovision, thus giving Ruslana access to new international audiences, for whom the ethnic intimacy of Wildness would resonate differently. Just as intimacy "may be protected, manipulated, or besieged by the state, framed by art, embellished by memory, or estranged by critique," so does Ruslana's Wildness accrue new meanings once it is made salable to diverse international audiences on the Eurovision Stage (Boym 2000, 228).

THE EROTIC AUTO-EXOTIC

Two years after the "Znaiu Ya" premiere, Ruslana released the album *Wild Dances* (a direct translation from an earlier Ukrainian-language release, *Dyki Tantsi*). On the heels of her 2004 Eurovision victory, the album topped the charts in Belgium, Greece, and Cyprus, and made it to the top ten in many other European countries. In the course of these two years, the pop star also reinvented herself as a pop icon whose unrestrained sexuality and ferocity drew upon ancient Slavic and Soviet archetypes of femininity.

The Eurovision-winning titular song "Wild Dances" is sung half in English, half in Ukrainian. The lyrics feature a recurring "Hey!" (in the studio version, the booming "Hey!" comes from a field recording of Hutsul highlanders), and also the prominent use of Hutsul vocables such as *shydy-rydy-dana*:

> Just maybe I'm crazy,
> The world spins round and round and round.
> *Shydy-rydy-dai, shydy-rydy dana.* (2x)

> I want you to want me
> As I dance round and round.
> *Shydy-rydy-dai, shydy-rydy dana.* (2x)

> Forever and ever—
> Go, go, go wild dancers!

> (Refrain)
> *Dai-na, dai-na*, wanna be loved,
> *Dai-na, dai-na*, gonna take my wild changes,
> *Dai-na, dai-na*, freedom above,
> *Dai-na, dai-na*, I'm wild 'n' dancing!

> Гей! (Hey!)
> Напевно даремно, (Surely for nothing,)
> Була я надто чемна (I was too polite)
> *Shydy-rydy dai, shydy-rydy dana.* (2x)

> Для тебе, для себе, (For you, for myself,)
> Застелю ціле небо. (I will make a bed of the whole sky.)

Гей! (Hey!)
Shydy dai, shydy-rydy dana. (2x)

Без жалю запалю, (Without sorrow, I'll start the fire,)
Go, go, go, wild dancers!

(Refrain)

Dance forever, come and be mine!
Dance together till the end of time!
Dance together!
Go, go, go wild dancers!

(Lyrics reprinted from Pavlyshyn 2006, 473; translations
from Ukrainian are my own.)

In reference to this song, literature scholar Marko Pavlyshyn has suggested that "the lyrical 'I' . . . identifies her as 'wild': her condition is one of pre-civilizational naturalness, perhaps of noble savagery." Pavlyshyn argues that this association with wildness acts as "Ruslana's . . . refutation of the Orientalist stereotype. By association with the wild beast, she has strength, and it is strength that inflects her attitude toward love" (2006, 474). Pavlyshyn elaborates on the European Enlightenment ideals espoused through Ruslana's confident assertion of herself as "wild," arguing that her "wildness" operates as a form of "European-ness." But I think another interpretation is possible: instead of a confident reversal of the Orientalizing gaze, the text of the song may also be heard as an expression of postcolonial desire, as a yearning for inclusion. Ruslana sings, "I want you to want me," and one can hear it as aspirational allegory or as a formulaic attempt at seduction through popular music, instead of as an empowered solidarity with European values. By rehearsing some of the clichés of Orientalism—including the eroticizing of the mysterious "other" (here, the Hutsul)—Ruslana's auto-exoticism in "Wild Dances" attempts to slake the European public's thirst for the exotic at its eastern borders.

Ruslana thus refashions the ethnic intimacy cultivated for the Ukrainian public through *Dyki Tantsi* into a strategic and erotic auto-exoticism for the benefit of an imagined European public. Was Ruslana's auto-exotic strategy unique in the context of Eurovision? Arguably not, since, as Janelle Reinelt writes, "Eurovision

. . . annually constructs the collective memory of European cooperation while dramatizing the impossibility of escaping the borders and boundaries of nation and culture, gender and sexuality, self and other. Participating countries are united less by geography than by media space. Otherwise, the contest serves as a consolidating cross-cultural discourse, situated squarely in the popular domain, wherein the struggle over European identity plays out" (2001, 386). With regard to Turkey's winning entry in 2003, when pop star Sertab invoked stereotypical musical and visual gestures evocative of "Turkey" (including the *arabesk*, the harem, and the Turkish baths), Thomas Solomon points out that "trading on, and taking advantage of, familiar orientalist tropes and Europe's fascination with exotic Turkey was . . . shrewd marketing, however politically incorrect it may seem from progressive and Europeanist Turkish points of view" (2005a, 8). In "Wild Dances," Ruslana's ambition was to combine the language of Eurovision kitsch with a claim for Ukraine's legitimacy as a European state through a marketing language of Wildness that at once romanticized the object of her research while firmly asserting its location in Europe.

Ruslana's auto-exotic representation of Hutsul culture as representative of the whole of Ukraine doubles as a bid for European identity, albeit one filtered through the unique, kitschy sensibilities of the Eurovision Song Contest.[5] Between the *Dyki Tantsi* and *Wild Dances* albums, as her primarily Ukrainophone domestic audience expanded to an international (primarily European) public, Ruslana's persona also underwent a radical shift, as the guileless post-Soviet *estrada* singer metamorphosed into an "Amazonka."

From its first iteration in 2002, Ruslana's Hutsulian Project was marketed with flamboyant language, positioning Ruslana as a uniquely skilled curator tasked with the mission of "popularizing" the ancient traditions of the Hutsuls for the modern consumer. Due to the international ambitions of Ruslana's Hutsulian Project, even early press releases were made available in multiple languages, including English: "The colors of Hutsul music, fiery rhythms, dance that pulls you into its circle—that's the energy that lights a fire in the soul! The music of Ruslana stores this fire. She brought the rhythm of the mountains to the stage and made it modern, cultish [sic]" (press materials, 2002).

In the lead-up to the Eurovision performance, Ruslana's marketing language became even more ostentatious: "Without giving [the] audience an opportunity to take a breath from the impression, here we see wild and sexy, hot and dangerous, mystic and knowledgeable about all the secrets of Carpathian *mol'fars* (shamans) mountain Amazonkas. Fur and leather, ethnic weapons, dangerous games and unique meditations all of this charms and entertains you, gives shimmering in the heart [sic]" (press materials, 2004). This heightened pitch of her marketing language corresponded to the increased sexuality in Ruslana's self-presentation and self-identification: whereas the Ruslana of "Znaiu Ya" was modestly dressed in a tailored full-body leather suit, a shoulder-length bob, and an unassuming grin, the Ruslana of *Wild Dances* emerged as an "Amazonka," predatory and stern, with an expansive mane of gnarled hair and an innovative wardrobe of bikinis, microskirts, and studded leather accessories.

Ruslana's identification as an Amazonka was first and foremost a nationalist allusion, referencing the ancient Scythian warrior women who inhabited parts of modern-day Ukraine (the Crimean peninsula and the "wild field" (*dyke pole*) to its north, but not modern-day Hutsulshchyna) in antiquity. Famously described in Herodotus's *Histories* as archetypal barbarians, these Amazon warrior women battled on horseback, and were reputedly willing to amputate their right breasts to facilitate shooting arrows (2003, 276–79). Ruslana knowingly drew on this history as she reconstructed her persona as a fierce and wild woman, even releasing a 2004 music video to the song "Oi, zahrai my muzychen'ku" (originally included on the album *Dyki Tantsi*) filmed in Crimea, where she is depicted as a horseback-riding free spirit who viciously beats up her cheating boyfriend on the shore of the Black Sea.

Ruslana's erotic auto-exoticization—predicated initially as it was on the image of Hutsuls—became a contentious source of debate for scholars, critics, and Hutsuls themselves, especially as the image of Ruslana-as-Hutsul-woman became conflated with Ruslana-as-Amazonka. Ruslana justified the change as an outgrowth of her prolonged ethnographic study of Hutsul culture, legitimized by her cooperation with ethnomusicologists from her alma mater, the Lysenko Academy of Music in L'viv. Ruslana's turn toward this reputed institution historically devoted to the systematic study of rural folklore was significant as a legitimizing step in the reinvention of the material (despite the fact that some of her consultants later distanced themselves from the work), and as a brace against accusations of exploitative exoticism. Emphasizing the "exotic" and "ancient" aspects of Hutsul culture as truisms ostensibly observed during Ruslana's own field expeditions, she validated her license as an artist to exploit these facts. Pavlyshyn explains that "just as the music of *Wild Dances* was publicized as the fruit of Ruslana's own ethnomusicological research in the Carpathians, so the costumes were explained as the outcomes of the meticulous collection and study of ethnographic data" (2006, 481–82). This explanation, however, did not pass the muster of Hutsuls themselves: in the course of my fieldwork, it was repeatedly pointed out to me that traditional Hutsul dress for both females and males is quite modest (if extremely colorful), and always covers the body. The traditional wardrobe is composed of painstakingly embroidered shirts; ornate woolen vests embellished with vibrant embroidery, mirrors, and leather piping (*kozhukhy*); overcoats (*serdaky*); men's pants and thick leather belts (*cheres*); skirts (*zapaska*, for women); and elaborate headwear: colorful hats for men (*krysania*), and meticulously wrapped head scarves (*khustky*) or headbands (*namitka*) for women.

Ruslana's bodily palette of leather, metal, and bare skin suggested, to many onlookers, a kinkiness that directly opposed the traditional conservativeness of Hutsul female self-representation. This was partially demonstrated in Ruslana's integration of Scythian imagery in her Hutsulian Project, which she repackaged as modern sexuality: "In these clothes, we felt ourselves to be true Amazons—at once sexual and warlike" (quoted in Pavlyshyn 2006, 481). Pavlyshyn read the "sado-masochistic attributes with which the costumes were replete" as a comment on the strong female voice represented in the song, one defined by power and the defiance of quotidian norms (481). This interpretation is valid, but does not account for the diversity of interpretations and the robust debate about meaning that followed Ruslana's 2004 Eurovision victory, in which her erotic auto-exoticism meant many different things to different publics. As a representation of Ukrainian femaleness within Ukraine, Ruslana's body became inscribed with the weight of internal national discourses of Ukrainian sexuality and femininity; as the representative of Ukrainian femaleness outside of Ukraine (on the Eurovision stage), her message communicated an ethno-national wildness vis-à-vis unbridled female (understood as some combination of Hutsul or Amazon) sexuality.

As the anthropologist Sherri Ortner (1974) famously argued, the female voice and body are recurrent tropes of the nationalist myth cross-culturally, where femininity is conflated with the sphere of "nature" that is counterposed to the rational, masculine sphere of "culture." In the Slavic world, the nation has, "since time immemorial," been depicted as female (Goscilo 1996, 32). In Ukraine, where a gargantuan Soviet-era statue of *Rodina Mat'* (Motherland, called the *iron baba* with ironic affection by locals) towers over the city of Kyiv, the cradle of Slavic civilization, the symbolic position of the female protector and mother in the Slavic imaginary is manifest physically, in massive quantities of steel. The ancient archetype of the female *Berehynia* (protector of the hearth of the nation) has recently been rehabilitated as a prevalent trope in Ukrainian notions of femininity, referenced by prominent politicians such as Yulia Tymoshenko, radical feminist groups such as FEMEN, and in revival festivals celebrating pre-Christian fertility (Bilaniuk 2003, 54; Helbig 2011; Zychowicz 2011).[6] In its reinvention, the *Berehynia* has been repurposed to express a range of stereotypical feminine qualities, from nurturing to mysterious to hysterical. Ruslana's self-sexualized presentation also evokes Western postfeminist discourses that, among other things, mark a "shift from objectification [of the female body] to sexual subjectification" (Gill 2009, 101). Thus, Ruslana fused an emergent brand of post-Soviet Ukrainian femininity onto the canvas of her celebrity body, one that culls from nationalist and Soviet discourses of female aggression and freedom, Western postfeminist discourse, and the ancient archetype of the Amazonka.

Ruslana's manipulation of such Indigenous tropes—of both femininity and rurality—and her savvy branding of them as a uniquely Ukrainian kind of "world music" on the Eurovision stage, suggest that her strategy of auto-exoticism was enacted in part to subvert the power structures inherent in acts of exoticizing.[7] Yet, her method stands in contrast to other notable examples of such subversions on the ESC stage, such as the controversial Russian pop duo t.A.T.u.'s performance in 2003. Dana Heller has suggested that the duo's faux-lesbian shtick and poo-pooing of Eurovision norms presented a "challenge to the hegemony of the West" and "indifference to the 'assumed rules of the globalization process'" (2007, 204). Heller interprets this as revealing of the deeply entrenched hostility felt by Russians toward Europe.

In contrast, Ruslana's 2004 performance appears to be a dedicated endeavor to appease Europe by perfecting the Eurovision aesthetic that blends catchy global pop with essentialized national self-presentation. Ruslana's celebrity body, adorned in the primitivist drag of Amazonian/Hutsul fantasy, is surrendered to the crude exigencies of the Eurovision machine in order to make a claim about Ukrainian political desire. Thus, the pop star's body is put on display in what might be called a pop "ritual of sovereignty," in which Ukraine's European-facing desires for political sovereignty in line with the values of liberal democracy are expressed through deference and submission (cf. Bernstein 2013b).[8]

In its tactics, the appropriation of Hutsul elements into this Ukrainian popular music rehearses themes prominent in the scholarly literature on globalization and the world music industry: the reproduction of hegemonic relations between cities and villages (Taylor 1997), the masking of compensation mechanisms (Meintjes 1990; Feld 2000), the denial of modern subjectivity to peoples on the margins of power, and, less cynically, the "intimate entanglement of sounds and bodies in music and dance underpinned at the ideological level by an 'all out relation-ism' and 'empathetic sociality'" (Stokes 2004, quoting Erlmann 1999, 177). But the interpretation of "Wild Dances" as an attempt to subvert marginalization through strategic auto-exoticism is further complicated by the complaints that were voiced by many of the very people that Ruslana constructed as the Ukrainian subaltern: the villagers of Kosmach and other villages in Hutsulshchyna. For some Hutsuls, the shame of being called "wild" outweighed the fact that Ukraine had won, as many put it, "the attention of Europe." Segments of the community stereotyped as the "exotic other" attempted to resist the tropes of othering that were thrust upon them through the rhetoric of Ruslana's press releases and the branding of her product. This attitude exposes a tension predicated on the power of postcolonial representation, here rendered as the wish for affiliation with legitimizing discourses of civilization that are mostly, but not always, opposed to discourses of Wildness. For some Hutsuls, the rejection of Wildness was demarcated strenuously, as an explicit alignment with the sovereign imaginary that desired inclusion in the European Union and that would finally shed the burdens of exoticism that mark Hutsul modernity.

PRIDE, SHAME, AND *SHAROVARSHCHYNA*

In 2009, I asked Mykhailo Tafiychuk, the patriarch of the Tafiychuk family of musicians, for his opinion on Ruslana's Eurovision-winning "Wild Dances" as we sat in his kitchen in the isolated Hutsul village of Bukovets'. His initial reply was a shrug. After a pause, he added that he didn't "understand her jumping around. She behaved badly." Further, he said, "she really offended us by calling our culture wild." I asked him what he took this "wildness" (дикість) to mean. He answered that it implies that "we are not smart" and then added, "animals are wild, not people." At this, his wife Hannusia, who had been quietly sitting by and listening, weighed in, "Ruslana put on some underwear and a Hutsul *kozhukh* [traditional decorated vest] and danced on television . . . it was not very nice [гарно]." To the Tafiychuk family, Ruslana's labeling and selling of her aesthetic as "Hutsul" was taken personally, as an insult and a denigration of their own integrity and sophistication.[9]

In the months following Ruslana's ESC victory, some Hutsuls lobbied their local district parliament to censor sales of the *Wild Dances* disc for their strong objections to the representation of their culture as "wild" in an international arena. Ivan Mykhailovych Zelenchuk, a historian and ethnologist based in the

FIGURE 1.2 Mykhailo Tafiychuk in his instrument workshop. The unfinished body of a *lira*, a hurdy-gurdy, is visible in the foreground. Photo by Alison Cartwright Ketz, 2011.

FIGURE 1.3 Father and son demonstrate the sound of newly completed horns in front of their home as other members of the Tafiychuk family look on. The *trembita* is the elongated horn played by Mykhailo Tafiychuk. Photo by Alison Cartwright Ketz, 2011.

town of Verkhovyna, told me about the misunderstanding and bitterness that local people felt when they saw Ruslana's representation of the deeply entrenched stereotype of Hutsuls as "wild people":

> Ruslana harmed us in this regard, because instead of calling them "fiery dances" [запальні танці], she was looking for a word, and someone must have suggested wild [дикі] . . . if she had called them "Fiery Dances," she would have hit the mark [попала в точку] and become a national hero. But someone must have suggested—this—"wild" and she went with it—and *wild* has many meanings, a few different aspects. The word *dyki* literally means primitive . . . implies that someone is primitive. People understood in its most direct meaning, and so, there were some incidents . . . people did not accept it, but then it passed, all of that. (personal communication, January 20, 2009)

A local historian based in the village of Kryvorivnia expressed another view on Ruslana's impact. He commented on the fact that "wildness" is a pervasive and potentially insidious stereotype of his culture, but that it can be read multiply, as evidenced through varied reactions of Hutsuls to Ruslana's depiction. (His village, Kryvorivnia, had spearheaded the attempt to boycott the album in Ukraine, expressing outrage at the term "wild" in the album title, though he was not directly involved.) As we talked about trendy representations of Hutsuls in popular music and historical representations in ethnographic studies, he shared a nuanced position: on the one hand, it's good to raise awareness of our existence; on the other hand, we don't deserve slander (personal communication, October 19, 2009). Many others voiced such ambivalent reactions, acknowledging that while Ruslana may have raised the profile of Hutsuls internationally and helped stimulate tourism to the region, it came at the price of disgrace and through the reinforcement of negative stereotypes.

While shrugging ambivalence and unfavorable reviews of Ruslana's chart-topping *Wild Dances* were common among Hutsuls in many regions of Hutsulshchyna, some evaluated her work more positively. One young Hutsul violinist told me, "Ruslana brought glory to Ukraine" (interview, January 29, 2009). During my fieldwork, many Hutsuls would simply laugh about the dispute, repeating a canonical joke such as, "What is a Hutsul? He is a Ukrainian, but wild!"[10]

Debate about *Wild Dances* in Hutsulshchyna arose in many social situations, including the quotidian practice of locals gossiping about each other. On January 7, 2009 (Christmas Day by the Julian Calendar), I trudged through the snow to the Sergei Parajanov Museum in Verkhovyna with my host Oksana, her friend Svitlana, two visiting tourists from Kyiv and Sweden, and my Russian American friend, who had come to visit me. In the two-room Parajanov Museum, located in the humble Hutsul house where the Georgian-born, ethnically Armenian film-maker lived while directing the internationally acclaimed Soviet-era film *Shadows of Forgotten Ancestors,* tour guide Pani Halyna recited her guide's monologue and then opened the small floor to questions. As the formality of the tour-guide-to-audience relationship relaxed, she shared a story concerning Ruslana and her reception since "Wild Dances" had won Eurovision. Following a devastating flood in the Verkhovyna region, which destroyed many homes in isolated villages in July 2009, Ruslana sent provisions via Hummer and helicopter, and also wanted to stage a concert to "lift the people's spirits." The people, however, were not all receptive. Pani Halyna and Oksana discussed:

HALYNA: My godmother [*kuma*] was involved in the *Dyki Tantsi* project. Maybe you remember, in the first video ["Znaiu Ya"], there were three ladies, and they're all standing, and they show their fingers—do you remember? It was a short fragment. And so she came to me and said, "Did you see Pani Marijka on the television?" And I hadn't seen it yet . . . She was so offended! Even now when there were the floods, she [Ruslana] loaded up a whole truck with provisions and sent it up to [the village of] Zamagora—

OKSANA: Yes, that's true—

HALYNA: Okay, I heard all of this from my godmother; I don't ask these questions myself! [Laughs] And so this lady said, "She made a joke of me to all of Ukraine, this humiliation, and now I'm supposed to take her macaroni too?" I laughed so hard!

OKSANA: [Speaking to me] See, our people are stubborn as rams!

MARIA: Did she know they were making a film?

HALYNA: Yes, but, you see, they said for what? Why turn the cameras to show our fingers? Like we don't wash! . . . They were so mad, even that one fellow Futivsky, he said it was really not good, said they made us into clowns, with horns . . .

OKSANA: No, well, the thing is that there is progress! She couldn't have just given us the same old thing—then it wouldn't be her song! Let the *troisti muzyky* (traditional trio ensemble) set up and play; that's one style and hers is a different one—

HALYNA: That's what I'm saying—this is modernity [сучасність]!

OKSANA: But I think we made an important project! And the fact that people get so upset about these *Dyki Tantsi*, I tell them, "Good people, we should be proud that we're *dyki*, that our nature here is wild, so let us be wild in that sense, as in primordial [первозданними]! But our people, they say, "We're not wild, we're like this, we're like that." But why should we be ashamed? . . . See, and even now, she's so proud, she'll die of hunger before she takes macaroni.

Oksana articulated another viable interpretation of Ruslana's Wildness, in which it stands as a trope of resistance to the commercial, urban industrialized world (even as "Wild Dances" is made significant due to its commercial success). For Oksana, Wildness emphasizes the obvious fact that Hutsuls live in rural conditions, or as Ruslana would have it, in "wild nature, high in the mountains" (press materials, 2005). Later in the same conversation, Oksana pointed out that the women featured in the video should not be ashamed of having the dirty fingernails and weathered hands of a farmer or shepherd, since the traditional values and lifestyles that Hutsuls take so much pride in maintaining are based on agrarian, subsistence living.

The local *mol'far* (shaman) Mykhailo Nechai articulated a position similarly sympathetic to Ruslana's depiction of Hutsul Wildness. As a public figure in his own right (known for being the "Last Living Carpathian *Mol'far*"), he acted as a spiritual consultant to Ruslana when she was developing her original Hutsulian Project, and remained a trusted advisor until his tragic death in 2011: "She took the strength of Hutsulshchyna and showed the whole world! Beautiful women, outside and inside, Hutsuls' wild and active dances. She was in seventy countries of the world, and she showed the artistry of our Hutsuls, that the whole world watched and marveled, not only those seventy countries of the world, but even more. So she's a woman deserving because, you understand, she showed the history of our Hutsulshchyna" (personal communication, February 2, 2009).[11]

Outside of Hutsulshchyna, some accounts of Ruslana's "Wild Dances" re-hearsed romanticized notions of Hutsul "wildness" in celebratory, sometimes naïve terms. One Western Ukrainian reviewer rhapsodized that "Wild Dances" was "an attempt to touch the soul of the people, which has always been in harmony with the universe. Consciously or not, Ruslana has brought to life a deep, strange layer of genetic memory [. . .] that is able, ultimately, to explode with revelation: yes, I am a Ukrainian, these are my lands, my mountains, my people" (Koval', quoted in Pavlyshyn 2006, 482).

Perhaps it is no surprise that the kitschy nationalistic pageant of Eurovision would cultivate such prideful feelings in Ukrainians who saw Ruslana's depiction as embodying a deeply entrenched truth about their culture. Yet such attempts to draw the line from a conceptual and essentialized Ukrainian Wildness through the Indigenous Hutsuls to Ruslana's polysemic *Wild Dances* resulted in a variety of reactions from Hutsuls whose intrinsic Wildness was purportedly being represented on the global stage. Why? In part, because at the heart of this debate over Wildness lies the perennial question about affiliation in Ukraine, a nation forever occupying a liminal position as the historical crossroads and battleground of empires, and now the borderland between the exclusive European Union and Russia. By activating the stereotype of Hutsul Wildness for the benefit of the Eurovision-consuming public, Ruslana's "Wild Dances" provoked anxious discourse among Hutsuls about whether Ukraine could be taken seriously as a "European" state if it portrayed itself as a cradle of ancient, primitive expressive culture. To many of my Hutsul interlocuters, "Wild Dances" represented an obstacle on the path to Ukraine's integration into the European Union.

Many Ukrainian intellectuals echoed this critique, bemoaning the fact that Ukraine's most visible post-Soviet cultural export to date came ensconced in leather and metal, hyping ethno-kitschy *popsa* (попса) (the genre term used, often as a pejorative, to describe low-brow popular music). Once Ruslana's "Wild Dances" became known internationally, her exploitation and reinvention of folk symbols represented, to many intellectuals, an embarrassing public display of post-Soviet Ukrainian cultural intimacy. (Imagine, as an analogue, that the Eurovision Song Contest entry from Greece featured choreographed plate-smashing or a prideful song about sheep-stealing, to borrow from Herzfeld's famous examples.) In Ukraine, these critiques were often articulated by invoking the Ukrainian slang term *sharovarshchyna* (шароварщина).

Sharovarshchyna can be defined as the mixing of regional symbols and caricaturing of folk culture that was originally made manifest through Soviet cultural policies. (*Sharovary* refers to the billowing red pants that became the official costume for male Ukrainian folk dancers in Soviet times.) Critiques of frivolous or cynical reappropriations of Soviet-era symbols are often framed as *sharovarshchyna*, though, in the post-Soviet era, the term has become shorthand that merges a Ukrainian critique of "world music" postmodern banality with specific reference to the Soviet institutionalized culture regime that dominated Ukrainian expressive culture for most of the twentieth century.

An article on *sharovarshchyna* by Vlad Trebunia (who is also known as "Mokh," the impresario behind the Hutsul-punk band Perkalaba) in the erudite Western Ukrainian online journal *Halytskyi Korrespondent* opened with the following definition of the term:

> The term *sharovarshchyna* has a negative meaning. That's the term we apply to culture of a low quality, which speculates on national motifs. It was especially active in developing and being cultivated by the government in the Soviet times. The motivations of the regime were understandable: on one hand, complete control over creativity, on the other—throw a bone to those who still want to hear, see and create his or her native art . . . Today's times are different. Ukraine is independent, there is no control over creativity. Nevertheless, *sharovarshchyna*, as the unprincipled Hutsuls sing, "lives and flourishes" [жие й процвітае]. (Trebunia 2010)

The ending phrase—"lives and flourishes"—is a rich and sarcastic double entendre, an example of the shift in "authoritative discourse" that characterized late socialist speech, which privileges formulaic structures over literal meaning (Yurchak 2005). To Ukrainophone ears, the phrase "lives and flourishes" rings with Soviet slogans that endlessly celebrated the enduring socialist revolution, the Communist Party, or Lenin's immortality (cf. Yurchak 2015). This bloated rhetoric is partly undermined, however, by the dialect form of the verb "to live": in literary Ukrainian, this would be *zhyve* (живе); the author's rendering (*zhye* / жие) is in rural dialect, and acts as a tragicomic suggestion of how sell-out ("unprincipled") Hutsuls might utter the phrase. Trebunia criticizes the way that money and resources are diverted to support projects tainted by *sharovarshchyna*. He continues with a provocative question: "But, then again, if the development of pseudo-Ukrainian culture hadn't been organized in Soviet times, then would artists have had the opportunity to create and develop at all? It was at least a chance to step onto stage, in front of an audience."

The remainder of Trebunia's article consults with "experts"—writers, public intellectuals, musicians—to assess whether there are any benefits to the "pseudo-Ukrainian culture" called *sharovarshchyna*. Of these experts, the analysis most relevant to our discussion of Wildness came from Yurko Izdryk, a well-known poet and essayist based in the Western Ukrainian town of Kalush. He wrote about *sharovarshchyna* as a particularly Ukrainian iteration of a broad cross-cultural "identifying code": "Though so-called '*sharovarshchyna*' belongs to culture, it is not itself a full-worth cultural phenomenon. It is, rather, a cultural code, an identifying code. This is the code that puts a substantial part of identity on the nation-bearer and performs a representative function—it is an original calling card of the nation for emergence into the world. In this sense, '*sharovarshchyna*' is no different from similar codes of other nations—'*tsyhanshchyna*,' 'Russian matryoshka-caviar-vodka,' 'Argentine tango,' 'French chanson,' 'Latin lovers,' etc." (Trebunia 2010, italics in original). However, Izdryk believes that the Ukrainian "identifying code" is in a "sorry state" due to its contamination by previous generations of folklorizing discourse. He bitterly identifies Ruslana as the current paragon of what he sees as a lamentable trend:

> The only shame is that *sharovarshchyna* absorbed only the totally poor assortment of *oblmuzdramteatriv* and odious societies like "Prosvita." The trouble is not that *sharovarshchyna* begs poorly stylistically; the trouble is that it unsatisfactorily performs the identifying function. I don't know how it seems to the miner from Donetsk, but to me, for example, it is very hard to identify myself with the pederastic youth in raspberry-colored pants, with their sado-mazo bracelets, their *oseledets'* flapping in the wind, doing some cosmopolitan dance move in the background of the national deputy to Ukraine, the winner of some kind of Eurovision, Ruslana Lyzhychko. Now then, here's the definition: "*Sharovarshchyna*—this is a kind of *lyzhychka*."[12] (Trebunia 2010)

Izdryk cleverly manipulates the pop icon's rarely used last name, Lyzhychko, into a neologistic synonym for *sharovarshchyna*. By equating the most prominent contemporary purveyor of Ukrainian *etno-muzyka* with *sharovarshchyna*, Izdryk shrewdly eulogizes the state of popular expressive culture in Ukraine in the twenty-first century.

To critics who accused her of tokenizing and exploiting the historically exoticized Hutsuls, Ruslana denied that her project succumbed to the banality of *sharovarshchyna*. She responded to critics by explaining that "We turned to *etnos*, not to *sharovarshchyna* [. . .] I am a contemporary singer with ethnic interests who has seen [ethnic material] through fresh eyes" (Koskin, quoted in Pavlyshyn 2006, 480). Still, after the success of Eurovision and "Wild Dances," Ruslana's interests largely shifted away from the specificity of her "ethnic interests." As she toured internationally, and took on the roles of Goodwill Ambassador for UNICEF, the anti-trafficking spokesperson for the OSCE, and member of the Ukrainian parliament, she reinvented herself as an infrastructural activist who championed Ukrainian renewable energy as the path to future state security and prosperity. With the introduction of post-Soviet environmentalist rhetorics into her press materials and songs, she reframed the Hutsul *etnos* as a more generic "ecologically noble savage" whose proximity to wilderness assumes a special Indigenous knowledge (Ellingson 2001, 357). Thus, she again re-signified Wildness, no more as a term of ethnic intimacy or auto-exoticism, but toward the future-oriented metaphor of "wild energy."

WILD ENERGY AND INFRASTRUCTURAL ACTIVISM

In 2008, Ruslana released the album *Wild Energy*, which was marketed as a science fiction sequel to the *Wild Dances* project. It aimed to reach new, English-speaking audiences, as evidenced in part by the inclusion of two African American hip-hop celebrities, T-Pain and Missy Elliot, as hired guests on two tracks.[13] According to a press release on Ruslana's website, her *Wild Energy* project "takes us into a future city which experiences a global energy crisis, far more threatening than lack of oil and gas. The cyborg inhabitants of the synthetic city are lacking their will for life, their energy of the heart—the 'fuel for people.'" The project was developed in collaboration with Ukrainian science fiction authors Sergiy and Maryna Diachenko beginning in the spring of 2006. The protagonist of the concept album is Lana, a bleach-white-skinned, platinum-blonde-haired girl who is "a synthetic." Lana, like all the other synthetics in the city, depends on a daily dose of electricity, transmitted through wires, to charge her life. However, she is aware that "in the city, there are others" who feed their energy needs through "wild rhythms," though the "energy police" do everything in their power to keep the "synthetics" away from these "other people." (The "others" are depicted in earth tones, cavorting to the sounds of hand drums and soaring around the postapocalyptic landscape on giant bat wings.) In the closing line of the opening monologue in the music video for *Wild Energy*, Ruslana (as Lana) says, "Today, I will seek this wild energy, and I will find it . . . or die." As the music begins, Lana breaks free from the wires that sustain, but also constrain her. She evades the energy police, and encounters the crew of non-synthetic "other people." Like Michelangelo's representation of the mortal fingers of Adam approaching the divine touch of God, a non-synthetic man energizes the wan cyborg Lana through a touch of the hand, thus propelling her into "real life."

The *Wild Energy* video was released in conjunction with OSCE-sponsored television commercials to raise awareness about female trafficking. Summarized by the slogan "People are not products" and the image of a hand with a barcode on it, the campaign called attention to the dehumanizing sex trade industry that, in the mid-2000s, enslaved forty thousand Ukrainian women annually. By repeating the image of a barcode-inscribed hand throughout the commercial, and showing the image of a naked woman's body transported in a box marked "Leather: Made in Ukraine," the manufactured nature of the enslaved human as "product" underscores the "synthetic" nature of the industry. In the powerful gesture that concludes the commercial, Ruslana's hand touches the hand of a young woman who is rescued from her future of sexual enslavement as the glass wall between them shatters. The hand-touching gesture would be familiar to viewers who had seen the *Wild Energy* video elsewhere, where the culminating moment depicts a non-synthetic man's hands reaching out for Lana's, creating a rupture that prevents the synthetic future from coming into existence.

Ruslana's *Wild Energy* project also doubled as an activist campaign in which the pop star reinvented herself as Ukraine's most prominent environmentalist, invested in Ukrainian statehood through the creation of new energy infrastructures. This garnered her some attention in the US media. On April 7, 2008, in a segment titled "A Ukrainian Pop Star's Would-Be Revolution," radio host Dan Charles introduced Ruslana on the National Public Radio (NPR) program *All Things Considered* as follows:

Like a Brazilian soccer star, Ruslana gets by with just one name. And everybody in Ukraine knows it. In her music, you can hear echoes of Ukrainian folk songs. But nobody is going to call Ruslana a folk singer. Her live shows are spectacles, with fire, smoke, dancers and costumes. In the middle of it all, there's Ruslana, tossing her hair, stamping her feet, and usually not wearing very much—a small bundle of unbridled energy. That image is why she originally decided to call her new stage show *Wild Energy*. (Charles 2008)

In the interview, Ruslana described her new show as a way to viscerally communicate the importance of Ukraine's need for renewable energy, energy independence, and the dangers of global warming "with dazzle and a driving beat." The radio program describes her as someone whose main motivation to agitate for Ukrainian renewable energy is born of a desire to emancipate Ukraine from its dependence on Russian resources:

Ukraine is not a rich country, but it burns coal and gas as if it were . . . Most of Ukraine's energy, especially natural gas, comes from Russia. And every so often, Russia threatens to cut Ukraine off. In fact, that's a big reason why Ruslana got interested in this issue. She's a Ukrainian nationalist. She joined street protestors that brought down a government in 2004, and took a seat, briefly, in Ukraine's parliament . . . She's pushing for greater independence from Russia, including energy independence. "Ukrainians should know that they are not as dependent on the natural gas as they think they are," she says. (Charles 2008)

The NPR story presents the difficulties that Ruslana's campaign has faced in engaging young Ukrainians in environmentalist concerns when they are "too busy hanging on as their country continues its wild ride from Soviet socialist republic into capitalism." The radio segment concludes that in money-hungry post-Soviet Ukraine, Ruslana's assertion that "[energy] is the most valuable currency" may be too symbolic a rallying cry.

Yet I disagree that Ruslana's activism can be reduced to the position of a "Ukrainian nationalist." While the US media represented the campaign behind *Wild Energy* as a move for energy independence from Russia, Ruslana's own press materials made the geopolitics of her campaign implicit rather than explicit, advocating for the cultivation of Ukrainian energy drawn from within the sovereign borders of the state—without additional comment. In one sense, Ruslana resurrects an old trope of Ukraine as a fertile heartland, familiar from Soviet times when it was considered the "breadbasket" of the USSR. She is also drawing on a contemporary anxiety of Ukrainian citizens, as desirable Ukrainian farmlands have been subject to "land grabs" by foreign corporations (Visser 2011). In the social campaign attached to the *Wild Energy* project, Ruslana recontextualized Ukraine's potential for productivity in the vernacular of contemporary eco-activism: she proselytizes about "green" and renewable energy, and warns of the threats of global warming. In the music video and song narratives, she conjured a bleak future inhabited by enslaved cyborgs as a means to agitate for innovation and development. By campaigning for energy independence, Ruslana's activist rhetoric shifted the vision of Ukrainian futurity from one grounded in a romantic notion of (Western) Ukrainian rurality and wilderness as the source of national strength, toward one rearticulated in the language of eco-activism, where the sustainable development of Ukraine's natural resources will drive the state's security, development, and prosperity on its own terms.

To summarize my argument to this point: in "Znaiu Ya," from the original Hutsulian Project, Wildness operated as a term of ethnic intimacy, drawn from rehashed representations of a Sovietized "folk"; in its intermediate and most widely consumed iteration, as the Eurovision-winning "Wild Dances" Wildness became an auto-exotic way to elevate Western Ukraine's internal others to the status of aspirational "European" nationhood; in *Wild Energy*, Wildness becomes a metaphor for the potentiality of care-giving state power, as Ruslana lobbies for the development of renewable energy infrastructures. (Indeed, in February 2018, Ruslana announced on her Instagram feed that she was renewing the *Wild Energy* campaign. The photo she posted featured her in an outfit of chain mail, with wind turbines in the background.)

Alternate interpretations of the change in the discursive utility of Wildness are possible. Ruslana's rhetorical shift away from Hutsuls may betray nothing so much as naked ambition: as she crafts a more generic redefinition of Wildness, the material becomes easier to market outside of an ethno-national framework (certainly, the presence of US hip-hop artists on *Wild Energy* suggests aspiration for the US music market, where Ruslana has not broken through). Or, perhaps, this inclusive new manifesto of Wildness worked as a salve to quiet the protestations of those Ukrainians who took issue with such blunt stereotyping of Hutsul culture in *Wild Dances*.

However, Ruslana's choice to revisit and transmute the term itself—steering Wildness away from Hutsul particularity toward a more generic concept of wild energy as absolute power—is telling in the ways that it allows for echoes of earlier Wildness to resonate. While Ruslana's comments at the premiere of the video stressed "the complete originality" of *Wild Energy*, as the total transformation of the *Wild Dances* aesthetic "into a futuristic, electronic sound with no ethnic samples," there are undeniable moments of sonic and visual continuity between the two projects. The idea of "wild rhythm" sounding via hand drums that are not indigenous to Ukraine, for example, is imported from *Wild Dances*; visually, the "wild" non-synthetics of the *Wild Energy* music video are dressed similarly (in leather and metal) to the "Wild Dancers" of Eurovision fame. Most significantly, the climactic moment of the video, when Lana reaches out for the touch of a "wild" man, foregrounds an iconic sound associated with Western Ukrainian Hutsul rurality: the *trembita* (see Figure 1.3). The video culminates in a moment that draws together these disparate modes of Wildness in the scene where Lana's hands are outstretched. As the music pauses dramatically, we see the image of a non-synthetic, "wild" Ruslana crouched and breathing deeply on an oversized drumhead. The suspense is interrupted by a brief sample of *trembitas*, an undeniable sonic call back to the opening sounds of "Wild Dances." The sonic gesture emphatically re-territorializes the otherwise unmarked dystopian sci-fi landscape of "Wild Energy," but newly contextualized—by now, this iconic sound of *trembitas* had become a globally commodified "identifying code" of Ukraine—it resonates as a gesture of broad inclusion rather than essentialized ethno-nationalism.

The sonic-aesthetic techniques here reinforce the message that is narrated visually through the two bodies of Ruslana present in this video: the pallid cyborg dependent on the grid for nourishment, and the vital, earth-toned character whose strength comes from her inner Wildness. Ruslana's two bodies offer an allegory of political sovereign desire: if we invest in the ethnic and energetic resources housed within the territory delineated by our sovereign borders, we can renew what it means to be Ukrainian.

TOWARD A PATRIOTISM OF PRAGMATISM

In this chapter, I have sketched three stages of development in the career of the figure who was one of Ukraine's most internally and internationally prominent pop stars between the Orange and Maidan Revolutions. My interpretation hinges on the claim that her messaging, especially as she became legitimized as a player in both domestic and international political organizations, mirrors the growing disenchantment that followed the 2004 revolution, when President Yushchenko attempted to "turn Ukraine into a European country [by] trying to recast it as an ethno-nationalist state" (Gessen 2010). To many critics, Yushchenko's rehabilitation of controversial figures such as the World War II–era nationalist guerrilla warrior Stepan Bandera undermined his credibility as a representative of *all* of Ukraine, not just its nationalist-leaning West (Snyder 2010).[14] Even Yushchenko's strong approach to commemorations of the Holodomor, the Soviet famine that decimated the Ukrainian peasantry in the early 1930s, was polarizing for the way that it portrayed the famine as a genocide enacted by Soviet rulers to subjugate the Ukrainian people (Portnov 2013). To Ukrainians who did not believe in the evil intent of Soviet rule, the anti-Soviet tenor of Holodomor commemorations was deeply alienating. Yushchenko was elected to the Ukrainian presidency in 2005 on a wave of revolutionary zeal. His failures of governance—his inability to excoriate entrenched corruption or to substantially improve the lives of average Ukrainian citizens, and his non-inclusive approach to redefining Ukrainian statehood—ultimately and improbably led to the election of Viktor Yanukovych (the same oligarch accused of orchestrating the electoral fraud that sparked the Orange Revolution, and who later served as prime minister under Yushchenko) to the presidency in 2010, until he abdicated his position during the ferment of the Maidan Revolution in 2014.[15]

Ruslana's influential albums from the period up to and following the Orange Revolution—*Dyki Tantsi, Wild Dances,* and *Wild Energy*—sketch an arc from the decorative, the folkloric, and the romantic attributes of exclusive forms of ethno-national belonging, toward hardheaded and future-oriented hopes for Ukrainian prosperity that dissolve ethnic specificity and replace it with a desire for the development of infrastructure, articulated in the trendy language of twenty-first-century eco-activism. Instead of the "patriotism of despair" that Serguei Oushakine (2009) identifies as the glue that bonded disparate peoples in the post-Soviet Siberian city of Barnaul, I interpret this as a move toward a "patriotism of pragmatism" that displaces ethno-nationalism in favor of a sovereign imaginary predicated on civic inclusivity and incremental change. *Wild Energy* anticipated a newly sober approach to state-building that was fulfilled by the post–Maidan Revolution ascent of chocolate-magnate-turned-politician Petro Poroshenko, who was widely believed to be a "strong manager," and therefore the most pragmatic choice for the presidency following Ukraine's second dramatic post-Soviet revolution (Coalson 2014).

As I have described it, Wildness can be understood as a core representational strategy for Ruslana, and one elastic enough to encompass a time period marked by seismic shifts in Ukrainian culture and governance: as the ethnic intimacy that addressed an ethno-nationalist domestic public morphed into a tantalizing auto-exotic display for international consumption, and finally into the pragmatic patriotism that motivated the Maidan Revolution. Conceptually, as it cut across and yet bound together contested desires for rational governance, the iterations of Wildness in Ruslana's wild music amplified the "beautiful, countermythologizing grammars of madness" that marked a confusing and clamorous decade of Ukrainian revolution (Halberstam 2014, 147). Drawn out of the "epistemic murk" (Taussig 1987, 127) where geopolitics meet pop music kitsch, Wildness proliferates: as a problem of representation, as a symptom of postcolonial desire, or as the citizen's wish for the fragile state to make bold and reparative investments in its territorial resources.

TWO

Freak Cabaret

Politics and Aesthetics in the

Time of Revolution

> Would it be better to think of revolutions not as specifically definable events,
> but instead as subtle shifts in language, imagery, and limits of the thinkable?
> W. J. T. Mitchell, *Occupy: Three Inquiries in Disobedience*

What happens when musicians who profess "apolitics" suddenly, in the heat of an intensifying revolution, reorient their aesthetic projects toward the political? In November 2013, the self-described "freak cabaret" known as the Dakh Daughters performed on the Maidan Revolution stage. Following that performance, they were described by the *Guardian* as "Spice Girls with Molotov Cocktails" (Culshaw 2013), though their art director, Vlad Troitsky, preferred to compare them to "Pussy Riot—with good music." I first encountered their performance on the revolutionary stage online, in the form of an edited video that cut the Dakh Daughters together with scenes from the unfolding revolution, which had not yet turned deadly. I tracked the video as it accrued "likes" and comments on social media and various video-sharing platforms. Most platforms framed the video as a fierce pro-revolution performance (sometimes underscoring that the freak cabaret was composed solely of women), but soon I noticed that it was being remediated on video-sharing platforms as evidence of the neofascist tenor of the revolution.[1]

This chapter investigates how this video performance by the Dakh Daughters—a group that publicly disavowed the political until the moment they took part in the Maidan—became quickly co-opted into opposing narratives of the revolution.[2] I examine how, in this performance, their merging of a Hutsul women's narrative resilience transmuted by their "freakish" aesthetics embodied a form of revolutionary wild music. In order to parse the complex entanglements of the aesthetic with the political in this case, my analysis will primarily focus on two issues.

First, I evaluate how a sudden reorientation toward the political lends itself to contested interpretations, especially among online publics, and especially when the aesthetic project itself is rooted in pastiche. In the case at hand, the exaggerated and lightly humorous mash-up of symbols—of Indigenous femininity and revolutionary feminism, Western Ukrainian (Hutsul) rurality, urban experimental theater—triggered opposing reactions from pro-Ukrainian and pro-Russian audiences online. As I pull apart strands of this semiotically rich performance, which occurred in the midst of a complex war of media representation, I

FIGURE 2.1 A collage of screenshots from the YouTube video titled "Dakh Daughters Band Euromaidan 2013." Used with permission by Anton Baibakov.

Freak Cabaret **59**

attempt to limn the various interpretive moves that could make it possible for the Dakh Daughters' performance to be interpreted either as "hipster rebellion" or "neofascist agitation."

Second, witnessing how these artists who claimed to be "apolitical" reframed their music as political in a time of crisis, I seek to investigate how bourgeois strategies of "aesthetic distancing" (Bourdieu 1984, 34) fail in precarious states such as Ukraine, where daily life is often unstable. Artists may embrace apoliticism for a variety of strategic reasons: to assert plausible deniability when the right to freedom of speech is not guaranteed; to avoid having to subscribe to a particular politics as dictated by the state (something especially resonant in post-Soviet spaces trying to distance themselves from the legacy of politicized aesthetics in the USSR); or to voice an alliance with those parts of the world (such as the "West") where discourses of musical autonomy correlate with models of artistic integrity (and, often, economic viability) that many artists aspire to achieve. I argue that the Dakh Daughters—whose songs often theatricalize explicitly political themes with a winking, oblique humor—publicly disavowed the political for some combination of the reasons just enumerated, until the drama of revolution pushed them to take a political stand. At that moment, the Wildness embedded in their sound, performance style, visual display, and song arrangements took on an explicit political charge. This wild music, directed toward supporting the protests that were still known at the time as the Euromaidan, made ambiguous political claims by refiguring a contested past as a claim on the future.

As the Dakh Daughters repurposed their aesthetic project for the revolutionary cause, they participated in the "creative recoding" of sounds and images in order to undermine contemporary Russian state media narratives of the Maidan as a fascist coup (Gerasimov 2014; cf. Carroll 2014). Simultaneously, they redirected their political ambivalence (their stated apolitics, but also their winking engagement with topical and political themes) in service of an emergent inclusive sovereign imaginary that was taking shape during the revolution. Contrary to Western media narratives that depicted the Maidan solely as a "pro-European revolution," or the Russian narratives that depicted it as a "fascist coup," a member of the Dakh Daughters stated her desire for the articulation of Ukraine's future as not *either* Western *or* Russian, but as *something else*.[3] Anti-Maidan remediations of the Dakh Daughters' Maidan video, however, insistently worked to reframe their performance in terms of the conventional binary politics that they had previously publicly disavowed by conflating pro-revolution Ukrainians with fascists, thereby pitting them against Russia.[4]

Occurring nearly a decade after Ruslana's Hutsulian Project, the Dakh Daughters performance I examine also draws on Hutsul motifs. In contrast to Ruslana, whose pop represented Hutsuls in a quasi-ethnographic and essentializing way, the Dakh Daughters draw together influences from a variety of sources in this and all of their other works. So, unlike in Ruslana's "Wild Dances," the Dakh Daughters did not intend to conflate Hutsuls with ethno-nationalism—though it was interpreted as such by pro-Russian audiences, who often made a further interpretive leap to equate this performative Hutsulness with fascism, as I will describe later.

COUNTERCULTURE HIPSTERS TO REVOLUTIONARY HEROINES

Originating in Kyiv, the Dakh Daughters came together under the aegis of the influential cultural impresario Vlad Troitsky, the founder of the art space known as Theater Dakh.[5] Troitsky also founded GogolFest, one of Kyiv's premier annual arts events, where the Dakh Daughters premiered in 2012. The act grew out of one of the performer's fantasy of an absurdist Parisian cabaret theater. The group is composed of seven women who play (and often trade roles on) some fifteen instruments, including accordion, keyboards, upright bass, flute, cello, and a variety of percussion instruments. Its members are trained actresses and musicians, and all seven alternate at center stage in performance. Many of the performers are also members of other prominent Ukrainian musical and theatrical acts. The seven multi-instrumentalists are Natalia Halanevych, Nina Haranetska (also of DakhaBrakha), Tanya Hawrylyuk (Tanya Tanya), Ruslana Khazipova (formerly of Hutsul-punk band Perkalaba), Solomia Melnyk, Anna Nikitina, and Natalia Zozul (known simply as Zo).[6] In October 2013 (one month before the Euromaidan protests began), GogolFest and the Dakh Daughters were touted by the *Economist*'s "Prospero Blog" as evidence of Ukraine's emerging "hipster counterculture." That report portrayed Troitsky as frustrated by the inevitable association of creativity and artistry in Ukraine with political motives. Talking about GogolFest, Troitsky is quoted as saying, "This is not supposed to be a political event, yet in the end it is political" ("Signs of a Hipster Rebellion" 2013).

Troitsky has professed ambivalence toward the role of art, theater, and music in the political processes of the state, and this position has become a defining characteristic of the influential musical acts with which he is associated. As part of this "hipster counterculture," political ambivalence emerged as an option for

FIGURE 2.2 The Dakh Daughters "freak cabaret" performs in Paris in 2016. Sadaka Edmond/Sipa via AP Images.

musicians and performers who had naturalized the idea of being career musicians (that is, being compensated for making art in the neoliberal marketplace) without feeling obliged to be defined as "Ukrainian" musicians (and thus serving the agendas of particular actors within the state, or shouldering the burden of representing Ukraine).[7] The possibility of expressing ambivalence over the embeddedness of the political in the sonic and performative dimensions of popular music was a privilege, a relatively new phenomenon for musicians like the Dakh Daughters, who effectively denied politics while engaging with and theatricalizing inherently political aspects of Ukrainian identity.

The consistent toying with and public disavowal of political messages in politicized tropes characterized the Dakh Daughters' first breakout piece, which became an online sensation through its widely watched video in June 2013, five months before the Euromaidan protests began. This original composition, titled "Rozy/Donbass," presents a mash-up of Shakespeare's accusatory 35th Sonnet with a traditional Ukrainian song and the menacing repetition of a semiotically dense word: "Donbass."[8] Donbass, conventionally transliterated as "Donbas," refers to the industrial coal-mining region of Eastern Ukraine that was the political home and stronghold of the former president Viktor Yanukovych (who became the target of the Maidan Revolution and fled to Russia after one hundred citizens were shot to death in central Kyiv at his command). Donetsk, the monumental capital city of the Donbas region, was known in the USSR as the "city of a million roses"—a rather unlikely nickname, given the city's otherwise austere style. Thus, the composition's title simultaneously alludes to the Soviet moniker for the urban capital of Donbas, and to the opening metaphor of the Shakespearean sonnet. (It is also the area that remains, in 2019, mired in largely stagnant conflict, with occasional outbursts of deadly violence between Ukrainian troops and Russian-backed rebels.)

The "Rozy/Donbass" video garnered over a quarter of a million views in its first two months online: enough that it registered as an "online sensation" among Ukrainian internet users (Desiateryk 2013).[9] In it, the Dakh Daughters are dressed monochromatically. Their lips are painted with bright red lipstick. They wear short white dresses cinched at the waist, white tights, and powder-white faces that conjure associations with the French mime Marcel Marceau. They complete the look with accents of black and white lace. They are stone-faced. The piece begins with a flat, unison declamation of Shakespeare's sonnet, delivered in accented English against a simple chord progression played on the piano. After some time, Ruslana Khazipova, playing bass in this composition, interjects with a gravel-filled utterance of "Donbass!" She repeats it after lines of sonnet text until she aggressively utters, in German, "*Fantastische* Donbass!" This pronouncement acts as a rupture, propelling the piece forward rhythmically, dramatically, and lyrically. Fragments of Ukrainian folk songs float in, sung by different performers in both a monotone declamatory style and the village style associated with Central Ukraine. Khazipova offers percussive vocalizations reminiscent of Hutsul vocables (similar to those used by Ruslana in her "Wild Dances" hit). The composition returns to an arrangement—now harmonized—of the Shakespearean sonnet. From there, it escalates into a frenzied repetition of the word "rozy" (рози / roses), with singers reaching into higher octaves. The piece gathers a manic energy until it ends, suddenly, and the video fades to black.

Despite the aggressive manner in which the word "Donbass" is uttered throughout piece, the group denied that the term had any political significance for them. In a television interview given in August 2013 (just three months before the Euromaidan protests began), Dakh Daughter Solomia Melnyk said, "It's not political, it just sounded good and fit in the rhyme scheme."[10] A journalist writing, in English, for the trilingual (Ukrainian, Russian, English) magazine called *Day* summarized the appeal of the composition's invocation of Donbas as follows:

> Formerly Donetsk was called a city of million roses. That was one of numerous Soviet mythologem [sic] which wrapped the entire region into a comfortable cocoon. Today, by whim of destiny, the Donbas became for Ukrainians not just a geographic or political notion, but an ontological concept, as kind of myth, too. Unsmiling, with histrionic pathos a la German band Rammstein, all possible expression, and mocking irony, the girls with their yells and dances show the entire wild, fantastic (fantastische Donbass) and inexplicable absurd that is reigning around us. Namely for this reason "Rozy" has taken the lead.[11] (Desiateryk 2013)

Yet Troitsky, commenting on the song in the same article, acknowledged that while it was not the group's "best" composition, the topicality of Donbas made the composition seem relevant and appealing to Ukrainian listeners. Like many of their pieces, the exaggerated gravitas of their stony-faced performance is juxtaposed against potent texts and symbols, producing a hybridity that is deeply ambiguous. Online commenters vigorously debated the degree to which irony, sincerity, or satire was intended in the piece and its performance.

All of this ambiguity took on new meaning when the Dakh Daughters performed on the Maidan Revolution stage framed by EU and Ukrainian flags.

Described in Western media as "heroines of the Revolution" for their performances as well as their other activities (including food preparation and volunteer organizing), the Dakh Daughters shifted from a stated apoliticism to a critique of the received notion of the political as defined either with or against Russia and the West.

STREAMING THE REVOLUTION

November 30, 2013, marked the first special police (Беркут / Berkut) crackdown on what was then called the "Euromaidan" and later became referred to simply as "Maidan." The violent assault on protestors provoked growing numbers of citizens to flock to Kyiv's Maidan Nezalezhnosti (Independence Square), the central node of the unrest. Reporters and locals streamed video of that day's protest. The following Sunday, December 8, was designated as the "March of a Million" by Euromaidan organizers. Reports from that morning's *Kyiv Post* live Twitter feed described metro trains clogged with protestors en route from the city's peripheries to its center ("Euromaidan Rallies in Ukraine—Dec. 8"). Protestors came from various class positions, generations, education levels, and political convictions to unite in opposition to the rampant corruption of then-President Yanukovych's regime. By midafternoon in Kyiv, thousands of protestors had blocked the entry to the Cabinet of Ministers building, expanding the footprint of the Maidan's occupation of central Kyiv. Media reports at that time estimated that the crowd had swelled to one hundred thousand people. At 6:15 p.m., protestors toppled a monument of Vladimir Lenin that stood at one end of Kyiv's central promenade, kickstarting the "Leninopad" that brought the felling of Lenin statues throughout Ukraine.[12] That evening, the *Kyiv Post* reported that the rally's atmosphere was "festive, with protestors seen singing and dancing."[13]

The fall of the Lenin monument in Kyiv was met with mixed reactions. Notably, the pop star and activist Ruslana (Lyzhychko), whose participation in the Euromaidan protests figured heavily in November and December, warned against participating in such "barbaric acts." In a blog post written for the independent Ukrainian newspaper *Ukrainian Pravda*, she wrote, "We judge acts of vandalism, wildness [дикості], violence, and all that can divide and split Ukrainians. No monument should be worth the fate of the Maidan. We do not want to be far from European standards and humanistic principles . . . We must act civilized! We do not want for this Creative Revolution to turn into a riot" (http://blogs.

pravda.com.ua/authors/ruslana/52a4c2e3b8b13, accessed November 18, 2013, original in Ukrainian).

In her post, the pop star invokes wildness—the very term she branded (and rebranded) as a source of strength and resilience—as a synonym for barbarism. Though Ruslana offers another—perhaps more canonic—meaning for the term in the heat of the revolutionary moment, I return to it in an expanded discursive sense when I read the theatricalized "freakishness" of the Dakh Daughters as an iteration of Wildness, one deployed in the service of overcoming binary sovereign allegiances to either "Europe" or "Russia."

Like so many others watching the revolution from afar, I sat hostage to my computer, gripped by unfolding events. Unable to fly to Ukraine, I consumed the revolution primarily through the web streams of intrepid reporters, or through fragments of radio stories, articles, and internet memes that flitted across my digital screens. One evening in mid-December, as my infant daughter settled into sleep, I finally clicked "play" on the eleven-minute video that had been cluttering up my social media feeds that day.

At the beginning of the video, which was edited by Anton Baibakov, the Dakh Daughters prepare for a performance. One musician, speaking to someone on her cell phone, tearfully reports that the last existing Lenin monument has been toppled in central Kyiv. In a theater's dressing room, a group of performers apply their signature pantomime makeup—white faces, rouged cheeks, severe eye makeup, painted black brows, vermilion lips. They reflect on the climate of the revolutionary moment. Gazing into the mirror as she applies white paint to her face, Dakh Daughter Solomia Melnyk says, "What people need now is love and movement [рух], you understand, not these aesthetic and intellectual trivialities [штучки] of ours." The women laugh, exchanging quips about being "slightly disturbed" women, Ukrainian freaks, and Melnyk adds, "Right now everything that happens is a provocation . . . you think you're making a joke; it's a provocation." Others murmur in agreement. Another member of the group explains that she is going to perform because she supports her friends who support the Maidan, distancing herself from her own political commitments. Though they would later be cast as "heroines of the revolution," the Dakh Daughters portrayed in this video hardly seem to be the group of hardened radicals agitating to overthrow the governing regime.

The camera follows the performers, now fully costumed, through the Kyiv Metro to the Maidan Nezalezhnosti (Independence Square), ground zero of the Euromaidan Revolution. About three minutes in, the video cuts to the stage erected in the center of Kyiv, where a blue backdrop hangs with a slogan in large yellow script. It reads, "For a European Ukraine" (За Європейську Україну). A European Union flag and a space heater are visible in the frame as Ruslana Khazipova straddles a bass drum in the front and center of the stage. She, like the others, wears a typical Ukrainian woman's patterned head scarf that covers her stylish short hairdo. The flamboyant flowered pattern of the scarf accentuates her powder-white face. The performers are outfitted in enormous woolen overcoats that allude to (and comically exaggerate) the traditional overcoats worn by rural Western Ukrainian mountaineers, or Hutsuls. One of the other performers, outside of the shot, suddenly exclaims, "Let's go to the mountain valley!" (Гайда на полонину) in Hutsul dialect into the microphone. As Khazipova negotiates with the stage's sound engineer to amplify the bass drum, which she beats steadily, she mews into the microphone as if caricaturing the high-pitched, lilting speech associated with Hutsul women. Without warning, Khazipova begins the performance by launching into a monologue voiced from the perspective of an elderly Hutsul woman. The crowd is rowdy. Audience members call out to her, and she responds by flirting, cajoling, and sticking out her pierced tongue between lines of text; she modulates expertly between the persona of the Hutsul grandmother and the urban freak-cabaret performer.

Against the regular thump of the bass drum, Khazipova mimics the voice of a Baba Hannusya from the mountains, a woman whom Khazipova's former spouse met and recorded during a field expedition to Hutsulshchyna (personal communication, July 8, 2015). Khazipova narrates a typical, almost formulaic lament: it is late in her life, she is alone, with no surviving children or close family, sustained in part by the kindness of strangers (чужі). Her husband died, "he was too weak." This is a line that Khazipova and the Dakh Daughters return to emphatically later in the piece. When she was well enough, she kept livestock. She receives a small pension: it is not enough, but at least something to live on. There were very poor times in her life, when she was not well; many things happened, war. There were times when she was eating "all kinds of nothing . . . but . . . I survived!" (тай вижила). Following this declaration of perseverance, Khazipova voices the refrain to this piece, known as "Hannusya," exclaiming Glory to Jesus Christ! (Слава Ісусу Христу). This typical greeting among Hutsuls is met by an enthusiastic roar from the crowd. Khazipova then continues by crying out the typical response to such a greeting: Glory to God for eternity! (Слава на віки Богу). The full band enters suddenly with a driving tempo, augmenting the solo drum and voice act with a rich instrumental palette—keyboard, cello, bass. The performers holler in unison on the syllable "Yo" in a vibrato-free village style—one singer breaks from the unison to improvise a traditional lament-style descant. ("Yo" is also a common greeting among Hutsuls.)

An elderly Hutsul woman's voice—extracted from the mountain village, channeled on the revolution stage, and filtered through the sensibility of the freak cabaret—became a rallying cry in this heightened political context. Baba Hannusya's litany is thematized as the nation's victimhood and resilience. Amplified through the voice of a young woman freak-cabaret performer to the crowd of thousands who have gathered for revolution, Baba Hannusya's words seem to resonate with the protestors, who respond enthusiastically to specific repeated lyrical tropes: I am cold, I am hungry, I am disenfranchised, but I will endure. Departing from the languid feel of the opening, the "Hannusya" composition becomes propulsive, with Khazipova narrating on the edge of a scream, shifting from the voice of Baba Hannusya to a grittier, less dialect-inflected, punk-rock scream. The instrumental accompaniment is spare yet active as the keyboard arpeggiates a four-chord progression against a heavy downbeat. The narrator declares, "I have no fear, achoo! [She sneezes performatively] . . . my husband died, he was weak; I can not, I can not" (Я не годна, я не годна).

"Hannusya," the piece performed by the Dakh Daughters on the Euromaidan, uncannily evokes a "Baba Hannusya from the mountains" while doubling as a narrative of twenty-first-century revolutionary defiance. Such acts of voicing may index specific subjects yet misrepresent those subjects as "unified entities" (especially when Western notions of personhood are ascribed to non-Western subjects); through processes of mediatization or in contexts of performance, the representational content of a voice that is speaking or singing is not fixed (Weidman 2015, 238; cf. Kunreuther 2014). Daniel Fisher names this "the vocal uncanny . . . a power at once deeply familiar but, as the nodal point of at times competing interests, also a site of defamiliarization, struggle, and unease" (2016, 9). As the voice of Baba Hannusya becomes transmuted through the vocal performance of Ruslana Khazipova, the elderly Hutsul woman's voice takes on the significance of an unfolding political struggle, simultaneously reintroducing and reconfiguring the meaning of "Hutsul" in the Ukrainian public sphere.

Just as the pop star Ruslana's appropriation of Hutsul sartorial and instrumental motifs worked as a code for Ukrainian revival and Wildness in 2004 as described in the preceding chapter, the Dakh Daughters draw from the same well of signification in calling upon Ukraine's quintessential internal folk as an index for something quintessentially *ours* yet simultaneously *other* (an über-volk of the Western borderlands, a metonym for survival). Why, then, did the Dakh Daughters ventriloquize the voice of a Hutsul, the long-exoticized and overrepresented *etnos* that provided so much raw material for post-Soviet Ukrainian popular music? Khazipova's own relationship to Hutsul materials offers part of an answer: as a long-standing member of Perkalaba, the "Hutsul-ska-punk" band based in Ivano-Frankvisk, a city on the foothills of the Carpathian Mountains, Khazipova had spent considerable time in Hutsulshchyna, and contributed to the hedonist spectacle that characterized that band's output.[14] Another reason was offered obliquely by Vlad Troitsky, the group's director, in an interview with a Kyiv-based newspaper, where he also enumerated the layers that comprise the piece: "'Hannusya' [is] a kind of Ukrainian spiritual based on the words of a grandmother from the mountains—and the 'Testament' [Заповіт] of Shevchenko, which they yell, and it's not *stiob*.[15] There is irony—on the one hand, and on the other—maximum sincerity and openness, truly dramatic music. Here, between that Scylla and Charybdis, we are trying to pass."[16]

The life story of the elderly woman from a remote village is cast alongside the narrative of Ukraine's nineteenth-century poet-hero, inflating the extraordinary ordinariness of a Hutsul woman's experience to compete with one of the most iconic anti-imperial statements of freedom in the Ukrainian literary canon. That Baba Hannusya's narrative is juxtaposed against fragments of poetry taken from Taras Shevchenko's 1845 poem "Testament"—one of the most celebrated and overtly patriotic Ukrainian poems—endows the composition with a weightiness that forces it to creak under the absurdity of its own representational overdetermination.[17] The effect is a hybridity that teeters on the brink of self-seriousness and utter absurdity.

As the group's performance was rearticulated explicitly in the context of revolution, its political content came into focus, charged with intense layers of meaning. As a constellation of features, Baba Hannusya's hard femininity, rurality, and age convey a particular Ukrainian narrative associated with resilience and anti-imperialist patriotism. Such charged meanings provoked discourse around past and future sovereign imaginaries of the Ukrainian state, especially in the video that culled footage from the events of the revolution and orbited through different clusters of internet users. On the Euromaidan, the Dakh Daughters' "Hannusya" became redefined as a protest song beyond the "essentialized stylistic categories" that often mark protest songs (such as, in the American context, a refrain that allows for easy group participation); rather, it became a kind of "resistance music" defined in terms of its "musico-political processes: its articulation within larger projects of social change" (McDonald 2013, 5). As the song and accompanying video became coded as protest music, the political content became available for interpretation in the terms of the unfolding revolution. To some, the Dakh Daughters became "heroines." To critics, the invocation of Hutsuls in general, and Hutsul women of a certain age in particular, suggested a link from World War II–era anti-Soviet resistance to contemporary neofascism.

In knowingly recontextualizing this Hutsul woman's voice as a feminist incitement for revolution on par with the famous (masculine) poetry of Shevchenko's "Testament," the Dakh Daughters activated complex historical narratives of national belonging while simultaneously toying with the propagandistic allegations of fascism levied against Euromaidan activists by the Russian media (Struve 2014). Baba Hannusya, by virtue of being a *baba* (grandmother), is someone who lived through and survived the brutalities of Soviet rule (war, hunger, and so on), which she partially enumerates in her monologue. As someone who survived her "weak" husband, she is characteristic of the generation of women who experienced the decimation of the male population in the midcentury due to war, imprisonment, or Soviet industrialization experiments (see Brown 2004). As a Hutsul, Baba Hannusya stands in for the notoriously self-reliant yet picturesque folk of Western Ukraine who were also closely identified with nationalist guerrilla warriors during World War II—as the USSR was trying to assimilate it as Soviet territory. By serving as the conduit of voice for an elderly, female, and Hutsul figure, the Dakh Daughters drew together historically contested symbols and generated new meanings around generation, gender, and *etnos*.

As Khazipova delivers Baba Hannusya's monologue, the video cuts between footage of the Dakh Daughters' performance on the Maidan stage and shots of the revolution: the idealistic faces of protestors huddled against the cold; menacing police activity; nationalist graffiti inscribed on the base of the fallen Lenin statue; a pianist draped in the Ukrainian flag playing the iconic Euromaidan upright piano; the building of improvised barricades; a Dakh Daughter with black makeup streaming down her face. The performance ends with the Dakh Daughters leading a chant: "If not now, when? If not us, who?" (Коли як не зараз, і хто як не ми). The video concludes as one of the Dakh Daughters, her face scrubbed clean, looks directly into the camera and repeats the protest chant in a hushed, earnest tone.

In the days following the December 8 "Leninopad," the eleven-minute video of the Dakh Daughters performing "Hannusya" on the Euromaidan stage was posted on the video-sharing sites YouTube ("Dakh Daughters Band Euromaidan

2013") and Vimeo ("Dakh Daughters Hannusya Euromaidan 2013," with French subtitles). As it circulated on social media, the original YouTube post quickly accumulated over one hundred thousand views. A week after it was initially posted, it was reposted on YouTube with the title "Banderite group Dakh Daughters on the Maidan" (Бендеровская группа Dakh Daughters на майдане [sic]), recasting the performance as one by rabid Western Ukrainian nationalists, and drawing on an emerging feminine archetype of the Maidan Revolution: the *Banderivka*, a warrior woman associated by many with World War II–era Ukrainian guerrilla warriors (Phillips 2014). (This video also featured a variety of pop-up ads for the user with headlines such as "Find out the terrible truth about the Maidan," and "For YOU: Best videos of Putin.")

ON FEMINIST FASCISTS

Scholars of gender in post-Soviet Ukraine have mapped a variety of broad trends in Ukrainian feminism since the fall of the Soviet Union that also highlight different feminine archetypes. Sociologist Alexandra Hrycak (2006) has critiqued the elite "foundation feminists," who, in attempting to bridge the gap between Western NGOs and local women's organizers in the post-Soviet era, ended by alienating grassroots associations. Hrycak and literary scholar Maria Rewakowicz (Hrycak and Rewakowicz 2009) describe various "Indigenous feminisms" exemplified, in part, by intellectuals such as the writer and public intellectual Oksana Zabuzhko, as well as by the rise of academic centers in Kharkiv and Kyiv devoted to the study of gender. Key figures in Ukrainian public life typify other varieties of Ukrainian feminisms, as I have mentioned previously: former prime minister Yulia Tymoshenko's "two bodies" (the impeccably coiffed and polished politician, and the tortured prisoner) that represent differing ideas and ideals of Ukrainian femininity (Zhurzhenko 2014); the Eurovision-champion-cum-activist Ruslana Lyzhychko (see Chapter 1); and the radical "sextremist" group known as FEMEN, whose exhibitionistic and sensationalist acts have stirred controversy within Ukrainian feminist circles (Mayerchyk 2010; Zychowicz 2011).[18] Tracking how both feminine and fascist discourses have operated on the Maidan and in Russian state media representations of contemporary Ukrainian revolutionaries adds further complexity to the ways in which online publics received the Dakh Daughters' video of "Hannusya."

By indexing Hutsul femininity and defiance, the Dakh Daughters constructed a symbolic link to an emergent gendered archetype of the Maidan, albeit one with deep historical roots: the *Banderivka*. Unlike other feminine archetypes of female defiance, like the "Amazonka" introduced by the pop star Ruslana after her Eurovision Song Contest win, this archetype emerged as a direct response to Russian propaganda that portrayed the Maidan as a fascist revolution. Born of the history of the controversial World War II–era Ukrainian national liberation movement that was led by Stepan Bandera (his followers were known as *Banderivtsi*, or *Banderovtsi* in Russian; *Banderivka* is the feminine form of that term), the *Banderivka* became an important term of reclamation for some feminist activists on the Maidan (Phillips 2014, 417). If the Dakh Daughters' performance of "Hannusya" on the Maidan is a musical performance that subverts and recasts current Russian propaganda with Soviet roots, it also draws on other national stereotypes linked to indigeneity, spirituality, and the nation-state. The category of "Hutsul" cuts across archetypal notions of Soviet and post-Soviet femininity, lending itself to multiple interpretations, including the self-consciously defiant reappropriation of the *Banderivka* by Ukrainian feminists during the Maidan Revolution.

The *Banderivka*, in particular, sits at the nexus of feminist and (anti-)fascist discourse; the resonance of this deeply contested term points to the broader context of dispute over the ongoing conflict between Russia and Ukraine. This conflict has been defined to a large degree by the propaganda campaigns of the Russian and Ukrainian states as well as ideologically charged representations in various European and US media outlets. "It is crucial," Alexei Yurchak wrote, "to refuse all reductionist diagnoses of the current situation, whichever side they come from. An example is the term 'fascism' constantly used to describe one or the other position in this conflict" (2014b). Yurchak calls attention to the incendiary allegation of "fascism" from multiple sides of the conflict: the Russian state has consistently portrayed the Maidan protestors and new political leadership of post-Yanukovych Ukraine as fascists and neo-Nazis; Ukraine and the West have drawn facile comparisons between Putin and Hitler, equating the encroachment on sovereign Ukraine to Hitler's incursion into the Sudetenland. Within Ukraine, the term "Putler"—a portmanteau of Putin and Hitler—emerged as a common nickname for the Russian president.

Contemporary Russian allegations of Ukrainian fascism stem from the role of the Ukrainian national liberation movement that fought to defend Ukraine from all foreign invaders during World War II.[19] The most controversial aspect of this history has to do with the various alliances that were often temporarily forged with Nazi forces against the Soviet Red Army (a fact that, if anything, underscores the degree to which drawing clear moral judgments in the simplistic binary of "good" or "evil" is impossible in the current conflict, as Yurchak suggests). Stepan Bandera, the radical leader of OUN (Organization of Ukrainian Nationalists), became closely conflated with the history of Nazi collaboration on the part of Ukrainian nationalists, despite the fact that he was imprisoned in a Nazi camp until 1944.[20] The Ukrainian nationalist battle against Soviet occupation persisted in some areas of Western Ukraine into the early 1950s, especially in remote regions inhabited by Hutsuls.[21] In response to this militarized resistance movement, Soviet propaganda returned at crucial historical moments to the latent threat of Ukrainian fascists on the Soviet border, and inhabitants of Western Ukraine (including Galicians, Lemkos, Rusyny, Boikos, and Hutsuls) became associated with the term *Banderivtsi* or Banderites—the followers of Stepan Bandera.

Baba Hannusya's story bears much in common with another well-known Hutsul *Baba*, Teodosia (known as Odosia) Plytka-Sorokhan from the village of Kryvorivnia, with whom I visited several times during my fieldwork in 2008–2009. Sentenced for ten years of hard labor (including five that she spent in the notorious Gulag camp known as "Kolyma" in the Russian Far East) for her activities as an OUN partisan during the 1930s and 1940s, Plytka-Sorokhan's story has become famous throughout Ukraine as an allegory of Hutsul female resilience and patriotism that resonates closely with Baba Hannusya's story in the Dakh Daughters composition.[22] The exceptional and public biography of a figure like Plytka-Sorokhan highlights how average Hutsul women—who were not usually themselves members of the World War II–era nationalist guerrillas so much as individuals who protected and supported them—could elide with the figure of the nationalist militant in the Soviet imaginary.

So while Hutsuls did not often join the ranks of Ukrainian nationalist militants themselves, they did frequently provide support and shelter to soldiers. Subsequently, Hutsuls and nationalist soldiers shared a figurative space in Ukrainian narratives of twentieth-century Western Ukrainian resistance. After the Orange Revolution, Hutsuls invested in rewriting the history of Ukrainian nationalist resistance (the same history coded as fascism by Soviet historians) to include their prominent roles. During my fieldwork in Hutsul villages in 2008–2009, the role of Hutsul villagers—particularly women—in giving safe haven to UPA (Ukrainian Insurgent Army) soldiers was told and retold. In the important market town of Kosiv, a museum to UPA soldiers was opened in the center of town. In Kosmach, villagers proudly spoke of how they resisted Soviet forces until

FIGURE 2.3 The author pictured with Odosia Plytka-Sorokhan in her home in Kryvorivnia. Photo by Oksana Susiak, 2011.

1953, largely due to the villagers' cooperation with UPA soldiers. In numerous Hutsul villages, locals proudly pointed out the places where *kryiivky* (криївки) had been, the underground bunkers where UPA soldiers hid in the 1940s.

In post-Soviet propaganda, and concurrent with the rehabilitation of the image of the UPA in Western Ukraine following the 2004 Orange Revolution, the semantic meanings of "Banderivtsi" and "fascists" further blurred (Marples 2006; Snyder 2010; Portnov 2013). Despite the fact that the Euromaidan protests were initiated on social media by an Afghan-born, Kyiv-based, cosmopolitan journalist, and that the first few casualties from the Ukrainian side were not ethnic Ukrainians, Putin's media depicted the Euromaidan from the outset as the takeover of the Ukrainian government by xenophobic radicals, reactivating the panic of "fascism" held over from a previous century, as detailed by historian Kai Struve:

> [Russian media's] central motif is that the Euromaidan and the change of government in the end of February 2014 in Ukraine were a "fascist coup" and, in a way, a recurrence of the German invasion of the Soviet Union in 1941. The evil, hostile forces from the West, now mostly the EU and the United States, took over power in Kiev, as in 1941, with the support of the extremely brutal and cruel Ukrainian "fascists," the *banderovtsy*, from Western Ukraine. When

they tried to extend their brutal regime of suppression and murder to the eastern parts of Ukraine the "people" began a heroic fight against them. (2013)[23]

In contemporary Ukrainian discourse, as an April 2014 *Kyiv Weekly* interview with a historian from Donetsk—whose name is not given beyond the initials "Y.Y."—describes, the term *Banderivets* has come to be synonymous with "enemy" for residents of the Donbas region in the post-Maidan era (Ivanov 2014). In response to the journalist's question of whether Donbas residents have a historical justification for fearing Western Ukrainian "banderivtsi," the historian responds by saying that "there are some reasons, but they are greatly exaggerated":

> For example, my grandfather fought in the Western Ukraine, he had personal reasons to dislike "banderivtsi." But he worked at the mine, in his brigade there were people from Western Ukraine (at the time it was a regular practice). And all of them were called "banderivtsi," because it was typical for Donetsk, but behind such nickname there was no implication. Now the word "banderivets" means "enemy," and then it simply meant "stranger," nothing more. People treated them as outsiders, but they were trusted in the mines, everyone knew nothing bad would happen. There were some common myths—for example, that one cannot speak Russian in L'viv, but no one was able to confirm such information. (Ivanov 2014)

The convergence of "banderivtsi" with "enemies," in other words, can be understood as a long-term effect of the dominant Soviet historical narrative that reduced the politics of World War II into a simple binary of heroic anti-fascists (Soviets) and enemy fascists (*Banderivtsi* and Nazis), thus erasing the lived experiences of those Ukrainians who feared or resisted Soviet power, but who did not embrace fascist ideology.

In response to Russian media representations of Ukrainian protestors as Banderites/neo-Nazi fascists, Maidan activists actively reappropriated "Banderite" to mock the conflation of the term with "fascism." T-shirts and images that were mass-produced and circulated on social media announced, "I am a Banderite," "Jewish Banderite," and "Crimean Tatar Banderite." Some feminist Maidan activists, fearing the "retraditionalization of gender ideals," reacted by militarizing women's participation and creating social media spaces dedicated to repurposing the revolution "in a manner that contributed to overturning patriarchal discourses"—and thus stoking the image of the *Banderivka* (Phillips 2014, 417). A 2007 painting by the artist Ihor Pereklita, made to look like Soviet propaganda, was printed onto stickers and posters. It depicted a sexy Ukrainian woman in "national costume with a machine gun. In one hand she holds a grenade, and in the other, a bough of snowberries . . . The picture has the text, 'I am a *Banderivka*. I am a Ukrainian. Death to the Muscovite Occupiers'" (Buryechak and Petrenko, cited in Phillips 2014, 417). This provocative image was one of many of Ukrainian female partisans that circulated on the Euromaidan.

The *Banderivka* projects a kind of femininity that links Ukrainian nationalism, the subversion of Russian propaganda, and militarization, but the Dakh Daughters' Hannusya is anything but a militant. Though she asserts her will to survive, she does not resort to political slogans, nor does she confess to any particular political orientation; rather, she speaks of her community, her homestead, and her ability to subsist as her source of strength. In this, she evokes another archetypal femininity: the domestic figure of the *Berehynia*, the pagan goddess of the hearth, who became popularized in post-Soviet Ukraine as the mother and protector of the nation (Rubchak 1996).[24] Through Baba Hannusya, Khazipova voices a rich parable of female heroism, albeit as an example of intimate, domestic, mundane endurance. Therefore, despite the seeming incompatibility of the radicalized warrior women with the domestic hearth goddess, the performance of "Hannusya" opens a syncretic space for these disparate modes of femininity. By recasting a narrative of lament as one of resilience and revolutionary potential, by resituating the utterance from a setting of rural domesticity to a public urban stage, and by re-voicing the elderly speech and dialect of a Hutsul woman as a punk scream, the Dakh Daughters demonstrate the continuities between the *Banderivka* and the *Berehynia*, and open a new space for feminine expression that merges national stereotypes with bold new assertions of feminine power.[25]

While I concede that pro-Russian online publics may not have apprehended the specific Hutsul qualities of the Dakh Daughters' performance—they may have just understood Hannusya to be Western Ukrainian—the figure of the Hutsul has circulated widely since Soviet times as iconic of a particular form of prideful Ukrainian identity. Therefore, the interpretive moves that could lead someone to construe Khazipova's performance of Baba Hannusya as stereotypically (Western) Ukrainian and therefore Banderite do not require a great deal of imagination. That their performance had such unintended consequences as the video traveled across the internet is also perhaps not surprising, since in the campaign of media destabilization that is part of Russian hybrid war strategies, nearly every cultural and political object is filtered through a paranoiac sensibility. Yet I assert that something else remains when the Dakh Daughters' stated apolitics make a sudden turn to explicit revolutionary politics, which makes the polysemy of their aesthetics especially potent for political ideologies on opposing sides of the revolution.

AESTHETICS AND POLITICS
IN THE TIME OF REVOLUTION

The Dakh Daughters video described in this chapter is, in many ways, a typical digital artifact of the Maidan Revolution. Social media was pivotal in the revolution, where it incited the groundswell of protest that eventually led to the abdication of power by President Viktor Yanukovych, who fled for safe harbor to Russia after ordering government troops to open fire on citizen-protestors. Much like the 2011 "Arab Spring" (Hounshell 2011), this Ukrainian revolution was live-tweeted, shared on Facebook, streamed on various media sites, and witnessed, often in real time, by a global community of interested watchers, such as myself (see also Pinkham 2014). Key moments, images, and sounds from the Maidan—violent clashes between protestors and police, public art installations, and musical performances on the stage erected in downtown Kyiv—became viral internet phenomena. Videos of popular musical performances, including "Hannusya," became digitally remediated through acts of re-titling, re-posting, and editing. As part of the broad social contest over meaning that has characterized the Ukrainian Maidan, the Crimean annexation, and the ongoing war in Ukraine's eastern borderlands, online communities often interpreted such texts in dialectically opposing ways, engaging in bitter feuds over the meanings of politically charged tropes on the comment boards of websites and social media feeds, each side accusing the other of propagandizing on behalf of either Putin's Russia or the United States and European Union.[26] This polarized battle over interpretation often mirrored the entrenched discourse over Ukraine's liminal geopolitical position.

Yet the Dakh Daughters' participation in the revolution was also remarkable in that it represented the somewhat reluctant involvement of a group of cosmopolitan artists whose political stance had been, up to the moment of their revolution performance, avowedly apolitical. Here, I return to the Dakh Daughters' public rejection of the political in favor of a *l'art pour l'art* stance—at least, before the revolution—as assuming a privileged stance of political ambivalence, which I treat as a particular form of "aesthetic distancing" performed by musicians. Such bourgeois notions of pure aesthetics, or ontologies of the autonomous artwork, were also, of course, reviled and censored by Soviet ideologues.[27] Therefore, the embrace of an "art for art's sake" position might also be understood as a way to reject that art was made to serve the state in the not-too-distant past.

Ukraine's 2004 pro-democratic Orange Revolution further intensified the link between music and politics in a variety of ways, most of all through the staging of that revolution as a music festival (Klid 2007; Helbig 2006). Therefore, the post–Orange Revolution, post-post-Soviet generation of cosmopolitan, internet-savvy popular musicians began to reject this new post-Soviet iteration of the politicization of music, in which ideology was no longer the controlling factor, but in which making music in Ukraine was inherently conceived of as a political act (that is, "Ukrainian musicians"). Finally, the volatile political climate of post–Orange Revolution Ukraine made it risky for musicians to voice explicit critiques of the oligarchic class that controlled Ukrainian media and cultural industries (in addition to the energy sector). Once Viktor Yanukovych, the Donbas kleptocrat, was elected to the presidency in 2010, the line between oligarchy and the government blurred to an even greater degree. Therefore, some musicians made strategic choices to be "apolitical" to avoid offending the ruling class, who also had the potential to stall or ruin their careers.

I see the Dakh Daughters' initial embrace of this bourgeois ideal of musical autonomy as part of a trend that was characteristic among a small but influential demographic of young, urban, cosmopolitan Ukrainian popular musicians for the decade leading up to the Maidan. During this period, interviews and television appearances given by various Dakh Daughters were marked by outward denial of political intent in their artistic work, even as they drew on charged political tropes (such as in their first hit, "Rozy/Donbass"). In other words, their privileged stance of political ambivalence emerged as a reaction to the late and post-Soviet generation of politicized popular music, when being a Ukrainian making music was always perceived in politicized terms. Importantly, while such an ideology of pure aesthetics came to signify freedom from the political carnival and corruption of the Ukrainian state, I also interpret this as an investment in the notion of creative work—of artistic practice—as a dignified form of labor that would be recognized as such in the kind of state that the Dakh Daughters hoped a lustrated Ukraine would become. In this sense, the ontological autonomy of artworks becomes linked to legitimate forms of labor in imaginary elsewheres. While, as those who study the effects of neoliberalism on the precarious livelihoods of musicians are well aware (Abe 2018; Garland 2012), this may truly be an

FIGURE 2.4 A statue of the mythical founders of Kyiv—Kyi, Shchek, Lybid', and Khoryv—holding a Ukrainian flag and draped with a banner that reads "Lustration," one of the slogans of the Maidan Revolution. Photo by Maria Sonevytsky, 2014.

imagined more than actually existing reality, I see it as mapping onto the kinds of values that were folded into the broader Maidan campaign for "dignity."

The autonomous "musical work"—along with the fetish of the masterpiece and its author, a (usually male) composer—has been usefully historicized and dismantled by numerous scholars who have diagnosed how the archetype of the musician-as-artisan shifted to the notion of the musician-as-artist in elite European society (Taylor 2007; Satie 1996; cf. Williams 1983, 40–42). In *Music and Capitalism*, Timothy Taylor outlines how earlier ideologies of meritocracy (success attributed to those rare artists who rise to the top of a "pool of talent") gave way, with the full penetration of neoliberal capitalism into society in the late twentieth century, to an ideology of "genius" defined more by an artist's success at shaping and satisfying the demands of a constantly mutating market (2016, 17).[28]

In ethnomusicology, a common belief is that the bourgeois ideology of pure aesthetics seeks to obscure its politics by invoking the autonomy of the art object (or by fetishizing the creative genius who created the art object), but that the art object is nonetheless inescapably shot through with the social and the political. Gavin Steingo launches a vociferous critique against the so-called critical music scholar for defaulting to such a Bourdeusian interpretive modality (2016, 5) in which music acts only as a cipher for categories of social distinction to the detriment, he warns, of serious engagement with the potentiality of "musical autonomy," or how aesthetics can "double reality" (xi). His study of South African kwaito—largely panned as an "apolitical" genre—argues for a revitalized politicized aesthetics that hews closely to Ranciere's views on aesthetics and politics. Steingo also argues for a Marxist theorization of the political that is free of ideology (and Adorno) (20–21). I am sympathetic to Steingo's argument that by setting aside projects of "demystification," we stand to observe something of how "music can generate or recover nonnormative sensory relations to the world" (19). (Indeed, this notion animates the analytic of acoustic citizenship that I develop at the end of this book.) But I find Steingo's attack on the "critical music scholar . . . [who] believes that she or he knows the correct way to perceive sounds and rails against any deviation from that 'proper' mode of perception" (6) difficult to accept as a generalization.

Perhaps I take umbrage at this formulation because I do not see the interpretive work that I do throughout this book, and especially in this chapter, as some attempt to "unmask" the hidden politics that were always latent and waiting to be revealed by the expert scholar. Nor do I seek to trap the Dakh Daughters into a genre identification beyond their own "freak-cabaret" descriptor. Rather, here I seek to emphasize how the exigencies of daily life in an imperiled state often appear to *demand* an articulation of politics by musicians, and I bear witness as musicians who had claimed apolitics suddenly feel compelled to pivot toward a more explicit politics—one closely tethered to ideology—in a moment of social crisis. My aim is to bring the reader along on the interpretive moves that opposing wartime internet publics were able to make as they decoded these newly politicized aesthetics. But this does not mean that other forms of sensory and somatic engagement are impossible.

Of course, a key distinction should be made between the kind of "apolitics" that has been referred to by South African politicians and media to define and disparage kwaito, and the "apolitics" initially embraced by the Dakh Daughters. While, according to Steingo, South African kwaito musicians do not merely appropriate a "degraded bourgeois ideology" of aesthetic freedom imported from Western Europe, the Dakh Daughters do align themselves with the set of revolutionary principles that were grounded in a notion of "European values" and principles of "dignity." Their early refusal of politics on the grounds that their work was purely aesthetic can be interpreted within those systems of value. This suggests that the legacy of elite European aesthetic ideology plays a larger role for these Ukrainian musicians than for those South African musicians about whom Steingo writes.

The analysis I offer here, of the Dakh Daughters' video and its interpretation by both friendly and hostile internet publics, underscores the unanticipated political resonances of their aesthetic gestures, whereby the aesthetics of their performance could be slotted back into the conventional binary politics that plague Ukrainian political history. This was enabled, I believe, in large part by the ambiguous semiotic content of their aesthetics in tandem with their publicly stated apoliticism leading up to the revolution. When a pastiche-based music is reoriented toward the political in the heat of revolution, does the gap in what Ranciere calls the "distribution of the sensible" (2013) change in form or character? Does the transformative potentiality of aesthetics increase or diminish in an urgent time of crisis?

To many online commenters, and to the Dakh Daughters themselves, the performance represented a creative outpouring of solidarity with the early ideals of the revolution, articulated as a performance of theatrical Ukrainian *etno-muzyka* that merged ambiguous and somewhat absurd performative and sonic gestures with a genuine ambivalence about Ukrainian national politics. This political ambivalence became spotlighted by the dramatic conditions of revolution. By taking part in the revolutionary action, this ambivalence—this refusal to make a restricted choice in favor of imagining a different future—fed into an emergent sovereign imaginary that searched beyond the nation and its geopolitical position for a future. Once they joined the revolution, the Dakh Daughters actively participated in the formation of this wild binary-defying sovereign imaginary, as articulated by one of the band members in an article reported in the *Guardian*. In it, Tanya Hawrylyuk (the group's pianist and accordionist) rejected Ukrainian ethno-nationalism but also described the revolution as attempting to escape the "lack of joy" present in both "the puritanism of the west and repressiveness of the east" (Culshaw 2013).

This wild sovereign imaginary that circulated during the early phases of the Maidan Revolution was oriented toward an inclusive Ukrainian civic society, and marked a significant departure from the politics that governed the Orange Revolution, during and after which ethno-nationalism became central to rebuilding the Ukrainian state (Gerasimov 2014). Key to this new model of revolution, Ilya

Gerasimov argues, was the appropriation and "creative recoding" of historical tropes, including the practice of recasting Russian accusations of fascism as a source of revolutionary solidarity among diverse Ukrainian citizens: "They are creatively minding their own business, inventing a new country for themselves and when they have to respond to outside pressure, they frame the response in their own terms" (2014, 31). While the freewheeling semiotic spirit that Gerasimov identifies as key to this Ukrainian postcolonial revolutionary moment is evident in the humorous ripostes that marked critical moments in the Maidan ("I am a Jewish Banderite"), a friction exists when corollary values to the central notion of "dignity"—such as, I propose, the value of artistic autonomy rooted in European notions of art—are made to accommodate the revolutionary moment. This is evident in the Dakh Daughters' pivot toward the political: as their stance of artistic apoliticism was made untenable by the Maidan itself, which forced prominent artists and musicians to take on the political, artists found it necessary to instrumentalize the ethical potential of their aesthetic projects. Ultimately, for musicians of the urban cosmopolitan scene, this resulted in a shift from a privileged stance of political ambivalence to a position of ambivalence *as* political conviction.

Ambivalence is core to the hybrid gestures that comprise the wild music of "Hannusya"—but this ambivalent wild music also links to a discursive Wildness that animates the revolutionary sovereign imaginary by which binary choices for the future of Ukrainian sovereignty are refused. In the context of a revolution that suspends the activities of a government, the Dakh Daughters advocate neither for a return to a prerevolutionary condition, nor for a turn toward Russia, nor for the unfettered embrace of Europe. Instead, they are unresolved but maintain a posture of resilience, defiance, and a commitment to transformation. Homi K. Bhabha's influential idea of the "third space" (1990) as a zone of interactivity, hybridity, and ambiguity resonates with these wild sovereign imaginaries. Predictably, the ways in which this future-oriented sovereign imaginary becomes "enunciated" (to borrow Bhabha's term) is not altogether coherent. Laura Junka refines Bhabha's notion of hybridity as a feature of subaltern empowerment by recognizing the emergent qualities of third space hybridities: "instead of being an end in itself, the condition of hybridity . . . becomes a starting point that enables a movement beyond dominating representations of . . . conflict" (2006, 351). It is productive to think of this performance of wild music as embodying a politics of ambivalence that must be emergent as it hopes to guide Ukraine toward the hopeful future that Maidan revolutionaries envisioned.

No longer able to wink away any suggestion that their artistic practices were apolitical, the Dakh Daughters chose to inject their absurdist pastiche into the midst of revolution, recontextualizing their composition as a protest song. In the world of cosmopolitan Ukrainian popular music that is largely defined by semiotic hybridity, the Dakh Daughters directed the polysemic nature of pastiche toward a politicized aesthetic that embodied the ambivalence that they felt about the available binary modes of affiliation between Russia and the "West." In turn, online publics received the semiotic mash-up of this experimental popular music, and derived meanings that validated their particular political orientations. The Dakh Daughters' sonic representation of Hutsul female biography on the Euromaidan stage was charged with the politics of both the pacific *Berehynia* and the bellicose *Banderivka*, though only the latter archetype was seized upon by anti-Maidan critics. These critics focused on the symbolic connection to the *Banderivka* and remediated the video by re-titling it (otherwise unchanged) with the Russian-language title "Banderite group Dakh Daughters" (Бендеровская группа Dakh Daughters).

Despite the fact that the Dakh Daughters are not Western Ukrainian, nor do they mention Bandera (or any specific political orientation) in the performance, this association of their performance with the *Banderivka* functioned as evidence to indict the Maidan as a hostile, fascist takeover. On the original video posted of their performance, pro-Maidan commenters flooded the page with enthusiastic appraisals of the performance, seizing on the piece as a statement of survival and resilience. Both pro- and anti-revolutionary factions understood "Hannusya" as a political text, albeit one that generated different meanings as it circulated through online zones of combat. The Wildness and ambivalence that links the Dakh Daughters' aesthetic practices to their politics yields unanticipated results as publics resignify available symbols and tropes of exoticism, ultimately reinscribing the binary views on Ukrainian politics that continue to fuel opposing sides of the ongoing conflict in Ukraine.

Far from the radical Right or Left of the Maidan, the Dakh Daughters mark a middle direction without charting the course. Through the contested political history of the Banderite and the contemporary iteration of the *Banderivka*, through feminist critique and stereotypes of Hutsul authenticity, aesthetic-cum-political ambivalence became reordered as the emergent sovereign imaginary predicated on Wildness that refused binary geopolitical choices. For online publics, musical and semiotic hybridity could be interpreted to accommodate a range of political ideologies—from progressive liberals to xenophobic nationalists to anti-Russian fascists. No longer able to abstain from politics, the Dakh Daughters have shed the privileged stance of political ambivalence in favor of a sovereign imaginary premised on the Wildness of ambivalence. In this wild sovereign imaginary, the Afghan-born Kyiv-based journalist, the young internet-savvy activists, musicians of the freak cabaret, urbanites and indigenes, and the singers who compete in televised singing competitions refashion ambivalence into a position of conviction as a means to creatively reimagine the world.

THREE

Ungovernable Timbres

The Failures of the Rural Voice

on Reality TV

The camera frames Oleksij Zajets, a young man who stands in front of a microphone. He wears a white tunic with a blaze of red embroidery down the middle and a woven belt cinched around his waist. The drummer of the house band sits quietly, slightly out of focus, in the background. The young man begins to sing loudly and with a slight rasp. His voice threatens to overpower the microphone. The camera cuts to one of the four "coaches" (тренери) on this reality TV singing program called *Holos Kraïny* (Voice of the Nation), part of the global "Voice" franchise that has aired in Ukraine since 2011.[1] The coach—who is not yet able to see the singer; he can only hear him—jolts forward in his seat, mouth agape. He settles into an astonished smile as he listens to the searing voice amplified through the arena's speakers, and relaxes into his cushioned seat with his face upturned in what looks like wonder. Other coaches blink or stroke their chins theatrically, telegraphing their surprise or deep thoughtfulness for the cameras. The camera swoops around the stage to show the singer's body in full. We see his white pants and the straw slippers with laces snaking up his calves. The camera returns to the rapt judge. He is now furrowing his brow.

Cut to the reality TV host, Andrii Domanskyi, backstage with the singer's parents, who shakes his head in disbelief and says, "He wasn't just born two hundred years too late, but two thousand years." The singer's father grunts his assent. The camera languidly pans across four bulging white buttons. The television and arena audiences understand that, unless a coach hits a button before Zajets's song ends, he will not advance in the competition. Close up on one of the coaches' hands, fiddling with a pen within reach of the button. As the song progresses, the coaches glance at each other with growing alarm. The singer's face falls as he continues to sing, exhaling with force at the end of each phrase. Two of the coaches glare expectantly at another judge—Ruslana, the prominent Ukrainian *etno*-pop star—who grimaces as the singer releases his last note. She has not hit the button. The audience and house band applaud as the four coaches' chairs automatically swivel around to face the stage.

Ruslana is the first coach to speak. "Oho!" she exclaims as the singer comes into her view. She asks his name, where he is from, how old he is. She asks if he is nervous, and he admits that "there is something here." She tells him that his obvious anxiety has infected her. The camera pans over the length of the singer's body from slippers to head. Ruslana praises the singer's strong "ethnic foundation" (етнічна основа) and, in a rambling monologue, explains to the young man that she didn't press the button for him because—despite the fact that "he obviously has a right to claim (претендувати) the label of 'voice of the nation'"—she "doesn't know how to utilize him in this competition." The implication is that his exceedingly rural style, which to her indexes some authentic voice of nationhood, does not fit into the format of the show. She recommends that he "continue working in this genre." The other coaches chime in with flattery, calling him a "diamond of Ukraine" and a "hero" for practicing this style. Diana Arbenina, a Russian rocker, explains that she did not press the button for him because she would not know what to do with "all the richness" (багатство) that his voice conveys. Down the line, each coach encourages him to continue doing the vital work that he does, singing in this traditional way. Russian soft-rock singer Stas' Piekha, the coach who most theatrically expressed his awe during the performance, remarks that he even "thought it might be a woman's voice" because of the "depth and wisdom" he heard in it. The singer is stone-faced as he takes in the critique, and then exits the stage.

As the coaches' chairs swivel back in preparation for the next contestant, Ruslana comments to the other coaches that she "feels like a murderer" for not hitting the button, for not bringing him onto her team. Piekha agrees that "we should have taken him" and asserts that what they had just heard was "not just folklore, it was true and specific *etnos* (етнос конкретний) . . . it was 'Deep Forest'"—making a somewhat mismatched reference to the French "world music" group of the 1990s that synthesized Indigenous musical samples with electronic music, but nonetheless making the point that he heard something real and exotic, Ukrainian Wildness, contained in this voice. The judges decide to call an emergency time-out from the competition to consult with the creative directors of the television program. A dramatic voiceover suggests that they "may go against the rules of the program" to reverse their decision. The scene is underscored with ominous thumping music. The judges debate: How should they delimit "the voice of the nation"? Would admitting that they had made a mistake humanize them or undermine their authority in the eyes of the audience of this reality TV singing competition? Why shouldn't this "most authentic Ukrainian vocal style" be considered emblematic of the nation? Ultimately, the coaches conclude that they will not break the rules to let this singer into the competition. The show's executive producer talks at length about how difficult it would be to integrate such a singer into the program, but how vital and important it was nonetheless for the competition to showcase such voices.[2] He calls the singer a "hero."

The crisis set in motion by the presence of this disruptive voice on the reality TV singing program *Holos Kraïny* encompasses the two themes that this chapter will explore: the contradictory "epistemologies of purification" (Ochoa Gautier 2006) that mark practices of what is often called *avtentyka* (authentica) in post-Soviet Ukraine, and the politics of refusal that these *avtentyka* voices enact through their aesthetics and vocal techniques as they enter the mediatized public sphere, where they are perceived as embodying real rural Wildness. Beyond the clashes of style and genre that occur when *avtentyka* singers perform on the pop-oriented *Holos Kraïny*, I attend to a more general politics of vocal timbre and technique to examine how the *avtentyka* voice, which sits within a historical trajectory of resistance to state power, challenges the conventional wisdom about how "folklore" must point backward, toward an essentialized national past. Rather, I consider *avtentyka* as a form of expressive culture cultivated in the late Soviet period as a reaction to Soviet hegemony that also has the somewhat paradoxical potential to operate in today's Ukrainian mediasphere as an expression of Wildness that, by contesting the premises of the present, points toward an inchoate future.

By examining these sounds within the context of an extremely popular televised competition that at once purports to anoint the "Voice of the Nation" while exclusively producing victors who are fluent in generic global pop styles, the incursion of the *avtentyka* voice into the world of *Holos Kraïny*—and the failures of *avtentyka* singers to win the competition—affords the opportunity to examine how this vocal timbre enacts a particular politics in the mainstream post-Soviet

Ukrainian mediasphere. Through their vocal timbres, *avtentyka* singers disrupt the rules of the game. Through their failure to win, they call into question the game's very premise. J. Jack Halberstam's guidebook for "failing well" is instructive here, especially in so far as failure has the potential to operate as a "refusal of mastery and a critique of the intuitive connections within capitalism between success and profit" (2011, 12). *Avtentyka* singers enter *Holos Kraïny* knowing almost certainly that they will lose this reality TV competition, yet they assert that they are the truest "voices of the nation" because their voices evoke an idea of "real Ukraine" more than any indie-pop warble, R&B melisma, sentimental croon, or hard-rock rasp. In asserting this, they refuse the narrow definitions of legitimate vocality, popularity, and marketability advanced by the show. From the show's first season, when the young man's voice so unsettled the judges that they called an emergency meeting, the elimination of *avtentyka* singers from the competition is presented not only as a crisis for the coaches and producers, but also as a drama staged for the television audience, who are forced to confront the question of how these "authentic" Ukrainian voices can be eliminated and silenced in good conscience.

DEFINING *AVTENTYKA*

A note on terminology: I will refer to the two singer-competitors examined in this chapter as practitioners of *avtentyka*, despite the fact that this term is contested among many practitioners of *avtentyka* in contemporary Ukraine and often elides, in usage, with the term "folklore."[3] I resist "genrefying" the set of practices embraced by *avtentyka* singers, especially since these singers studiously toe the line of disciplined/undisciplined vocality and often premise their practices on the ability to make spontaneous (though highly specific) decisions while interpreting a song. These core values are antithetical to the codification and subsequent homogenization association with genrefication, which is why I prefer to refer to *avtentyka* as a practice (see Taylor 2014). The relationship of many Ukrainian ethnomusicologists to the terms of *avtentyka* are also somewhat vexed: as one Ukrainian ethnomusicologist told me in 2015, "We don't use this term *avtentyka* because 'authenticity' is so subjective." Yet this same ethnomusicologist has led a group that was often billed as *avtentyka* when they performed in festivals and concerts, and has published on *avtentyka* recordings, using the term itself. While *avtentyka* may have originally been used to refer to ethnomusicological field recordings that documented villagers' performances, it also became widely used to describe the urban revival ensembles devoted to replicating these rural styles in performance with maximum fidelity.

So I apply the term *avtentyka* here to define two different but related groups. First, the urban practitioners and scholars (folklorists, ethnomusicologists) dedicated to preserving and singing village materials thought to be uncontaminated by colonial encounter and Soviet cultural policy. Second, the village-based singers and ensembles who are considered to be the surviving link to this precolonial "uncontaminated" vocality. For reasons I will explain later in this chapter, the vast majority of these are elderly women. The term *avtentyka* also helps to differentiate this type of singing from the practices associated with "folk music" in contemporary Ukraine.

As a musical practice that emerged in the last Soviet period, *avtentyka* was counterposed to the culture of state-sanctioned institutionalized Soviet folklore—often pejoratively called *fol'kloryzm* ("fakelore") or *sharovarshchyna* (which specifically refers to the mixing of regional styles in order to produce a "national folklore," as described in Chapter 1).[4] Born of the dual impulses of preservationism and defiance of Soviet norms of institutionalized folklore, *avtentyka* mounted a challenge to the stranglehold that Soviet cultural policy attempted to exert on diverse regional cultural expressions. *Avtentyka* traffics in discourses of local, primordialized, and territorialized *etnos*, thereby decentering the forms of regional-cum-national identity performed by the majority of contemporary Ukrainian folk groups (who derive their "folk style" from Soviet-era folk ensembles). Broadly, then, *avtentyka* refers to particular post-Soviet musical practices in which sound—especially vocal timbre and specific vocal techniques—are used to index a rural archaic past that is marked by local—rather than by national or regional—characteristics.

In using the term *avtentyka*, I am weary of resurrecting the mostly dormant discourse of authenticity that marked early scholarship in music studies. In the early disciplinary framings of comparative musicologists, questions of authenticity were presented as problems of archaism, origin, or "evolution"; in ethnomusicological scholarship since the mid-twentieth century, the problem of authenticity has more often been treated critically, where it is acknowledged to be the "monkey on our back" (Nettl 2010, 66–68), a "floating ideology" (Taylor 2014, 164), or an empty spiral. In other words, authenticity has become a term to be sidestepped entirely, or one consigned to the realm of interpretation—where "authenticity [i]s experiential, rather than static and lasting" (Bendix 1997, 198; cf. Moore 2002).[5] Yet, to many musicians, audiences, critics, and teachers the world over, "authenticity" endures as a perpetual signifier of music that is competently performed or perceived to be aesthetically pure. In the case of the *avtentyka* voice in Ukraine, then, the central question that interests me is not to adjudicate the argument of whether *avtentyka* as a cultural practice is in some ways "more authentic" than other forms of contemporary folklore or cultural expression in Ukraine, but rather to investigate how and why this ideological construct of authenticity intervenes in debates about contemporary Ukrainian identity—especially as it maps onto notions of citizenship and statehood—at this particular time and place.

In the following section, I reflect on the techniques and aesthetics of *avtentyka* based on the pedagogical techniques of Yevhen Yefremov, a senior professor of ethnomusicology at the National Music Academy of Ukraine in Kyiv, who also influenced the two *avtentyka* singers whose performances on the reality TV singing program I write about in this chapter. Through an embodied and ethnographic understanding of vocal timbre and technique—as a participant-observer, student, and occasional teacher in the style—I examine a key paradox of contemporary *avtentyka*, one that I call the discipline of vocal abandon, as practitioners are taught to "sing on the border of yelling," to use the locution of Yevhen Yefremov when describing how Polissian ritual songs should sound. Summarizing the anthropological studies of voice, Daniel Fisher writes that the voice is "at once an index of sedimented relations, a feelingful and charged expressive medium, an 'affecting presence,' and the means and ends of difficult political labor" (2016, 8). As *avtentyka* singers' voices aspire to stand in (to borrow Fisher's term) as "avatars" of an idealized primordial, Indigenous rurality that is indexed first and foremost through their vocal timbres and technical flourishes, they assert multiple political claims. First, they reject the history of Soviet cultural policies that were directed toward engineering an "elevated" folkloric voice. Second, they exercise bodily control over the border of singing and yelling, heightening the expressive thrill of the singing voice and calling into question the limits of singing as a rational practice. Third, they assert the importance of the marginal singing practice of *avtentyka* into a fraught conversation of imperiled statehood within the global media format (and blunted discursive realm) of the reality TV singing competition. In this context, the *avtentyka* voice becomes a fully mediatized spectacle that puts the Wildness of the village into prominent circulation. Therefore, the discursive authenticity of *avtentyka* operates as a dimension of what Amanda Weidman calls the "politics of voice," or "a set of vocal practices as well as a set of ideas *about* the voice and its significance" (Weidman

2006, 5; cf. Kunreuther 2014). Through the politics of the *avtentyka* voice, singers propose a radical redefinition of the meanings and uses of a tradition ostensibly rooted in the distant past. Further, through an aesthetic practice that asserts a heterogeneous, territorialized, primordialized rurality, they present an agentive and affective model of identity that refuses national logics of state-making. The *avtentyka* voice, thus, performs a recuperative Wildness through its investments in particularized local aesthetics, mimicry of rural and animal sounds, and the acoustically resonant and agentive voice of the singer.

In this context, discursive Wildness takes form through tropes of rurality: Wildness understood as the raw, uncultivated, or "natural" singing voice of the village singer; Wildness thriving in the zone of a remote, unknowable, and marginal elsewhere; Wildness that defies "genrefication" due to its core values of spontaneity and bodily release. Singers harness the power of such associations with rural Wildness as it is embedded in the practice of sung *avtentyka* to different ends: to establish their credentials as authentic villagers with authentic voices, or—as urban scholars of *avtentyka*—to assert their mastery over rural forms of knowledge. In this way, the Wildness of *avtentyka* muddies binaries of disciplined/undisciplined vocality as they map onto the rational citizen-subject. The body of the *avtentyka* singer, resonating with and amplifying this Wildness, asserts a body sovereignty linked to cultural ways of life that undermine logics of the "voice of the nation" as they circulate in the public Ukrainian mediasphere through the reality TV singing competition.

LEARNING *AVTENTYKA*

I—along with an eclectic group of twelve singers—was learning to sing *avtentyka* from a leading practitioner and teacher in Ukraine, Professor Yevhen Yefremov. Gathered in a room in the heart of the vanishing Ukrainian neighborhood in the East Village of Manhattan, our group of singers was embarking on our second day of work, learning an archaic spring calling song from Kyivan Polissia. Yefremov told us, "Your *huk* is still too formal."[6] He was referring to the cry that punctuates the end of the refrain in the song we were learning: *Oi lele vada kalie horoda*. The *huk* is the Ukrainian term for a characteristic sound of some Eastern European singing traditions, which has been associated in the West especially with the Bulgarian women's choirs that became darlings of the "world music" boom in the 1980s, though the nuances of the sounds vary based on locality and according to repertoire. In a *huk*, the voice typically leaps up an octave or more and then swoops down before decaying to silence. The effect is one of ecstatic bodily release. Unlike a yodel, it does not emphasize the vocal break, but rather seems like a spontaneous exclamation, an eruption, usually following a drawn-out vowel sound. Over the course of weeks, as we deepened our repertoire under his guidance, Yefremov employed a range of similes to describe the sound of the *huk*. "It should sound like a kettle giving off its steam." "It should be as though you sat on a needle." "It should be like a goat bleating." The *huk* can be animalistic.

We sang the refrain of the song again, a melodic line of competing micro-variations leading to the final vowel, a dark and closed "ah," where the ensemble lingered on a strident unison before the lead singer cued the group to *huk*. Yefremov told us, "No. It should only be *roughly* together . . . it's still too formal, too . . . proper." It should be less disciplined, more spontaneous, more wild. The *huk*, Yefremov explained, is an art in itself. The sound should be maximally high and piercing, so much that "ancient peoples believed it would break through the heavens and be heard by the gods." But a *huk* should not only be cutting, it should have a particular contour. Like "comets in the sky," a *huk* may have a short tail or a long tail, the tail may go up or down, the exhalation of breath might sound especially forceful, or less so. There is a different *huk* for every region of Ukraine, he told us, and a different *huk* depending on the song itself. There is a logic to this sound of spontaneous bodily release. He went on to describe the desired sound of the refrain as "singing that borders yelling"—where the *huk* really approximates the explosive force of yelling—thus emphasizing that learning to sing *avtentyka* is to embody a paradoxical vocal Wildness—it is to master the discipline of vocal abandon (rehearsal recordings, 2011).

This discipline of vocal abandon is made audible through the particular graininess and heft of *avtentyka* vocal timbres, through a convention of melismatic embellishment of melodies, and through the stylistic flourishes—such as the precise quality of a *huk*—that sounded, in the late Soviet era, like a refusal of the "elevated" Soviet folk choir. In those professionalized contexts, where folk songs were usually arranged by trained composers, vocal grit or audible exertion were eliminated from singers' voices. Take, for example, the professionalized vocal aesthetics heard in the 1967 recording of the popular Ukrainian folk song "Blackthorn Blossom" (Цвіте Терен) as recorded by the most prominent Soviet-era Ukrainian folk choir, which still exists today: the State Honored Ukrainian Folk Choir, named after Gregory Veriovka (Державний заслужений Український народний хор ім. Григорія Верьовки), known simply as "Veriovka." The song was arranged by the celebrated choir's conductor Anatolij Avdiyevskyj, and featured Nina Matvienko and Valentyna Khytsenko as soloists.

Avdiyevskyj's arrangement begins with a chorus of low voices in chordal harmony who reverently intone the first words of the song (Цвіте Терен); the sound seems a deliberate invocation of the rich and blended sound of men's choirs in the Slavic church tradition. The voices of the two soloists—who sing the text together, in close harmony—enter soon after. Their voices, in contrast to the lush and muted background of the choir, retain some of the bright quality associated with a Ukrainian "folk voice." Nina Matvienko, whose ethereal voice made her an icon of Soviet Ukrainian state-sanctioned folklore in her youth, embellishes the soprano melody with mordant-like vocal ornaments that she repeats in each stanza. (Her daughter Tonia Matvienko, an aspiring singer, will enter this story shortly as a competitor on the first season of *Holos Kraïny*.) Unlike the *avtentyka* voice, the Veriovka soloists' voices are lighter, with more open vowel sounds, smoother phrasing, and inaudible breathing that creates the impression of effortless singing. The Veriovka arrangement of "Blackthorn Blossom" contains dramatic dynamic shifts, most likely as directed in the written score of the arrangement—another clear difference from *avtentyka* performances that are typically rendered at a consistently loud volume. Though this particular arrangement does not contain the *huk*, in other folk choir arrangements even the *huk* became domesticated and predictable, a feature of the song that *avtentyka* practitioners worked to remake as a spontaneous act of sounding.

It is important to note that the bodily posture assumed by many contemporary *avtentyka* singers is firm and grounded, but typically motionless. I interpret this as another form of refusal of the stylized gestures that marked Soviet folkloric performance. Soviet folk choirs such as Veriovka choreographed their arranged folk songs on the stage. Soloists were trained to make broad emphatic gestures with their arms as they sang, and women singers usually stood with their feet positioned in formations reminiscent of the basic positions of classical ballet. In the post-Soviet era, institutions carried over from the Soviet period—such as Veriovka—have experimented with other forms of choreography, but the performances remain highly stylized.[7] Rejecting such aesthetics of stylized Soviet folklore through the discipline of vocal abandon that is expressed solely through the voice, the aesthetics of *avtentyka* represented a discursive return to diverse Indigenous musical practices associated with archaic ways of life.

This Ukrainian phenomenon was part of a bigger trend taking shape in the Soviet 1970s, when a constellation of cultural practices emerged to expand the constrictive norms of Soviet state-sanctioned folklore and musical ethnography. Throughout the fifteen republics of the Soviet Union, official national and regional folklore ensembles performed repertoires that had been largely scrubbed of references perceived to be incompatible with Marxist-Leninist ideology or the progress of Soviet internationalism. But in villages, ethnomusicologists had been documenting rural repertoires that defied the ideology of the Soviet "civilizing mission," such as the wealth of calendrical ritual songs (which often contained sacred or religious themes), or songs about controversial historical figures or events (see Ivanytskyi 2008). Amateur village singers sang in arrangements that seemed spontaneous and sometimes imperfect. Further, they performed rural repertoires using vocal techniques that emphasized effortful singing, which made the listener acutely aware of the singer's presence, her body and breath. As one prominent ethnomusicologist told me, these voices were "unlike the smoothed-out and 'improved' voices of the Soviet professionalized folk choir" (personal communication, 2012).

In Moscow, Kyiv, and other urban centers, underground vocal ensembles began to emerge. As Theodor Levin documents in his discussion with Dmitri Pokrovsky, such ensembles often existed in a kind of tug-of-war with the shifting politics of Soviet rule, at times supported by the state, at times even permitted to perform taboo repertoires in public, and at other times heavily censored and banned from performing in public (Levin 1996). The nascent *avtentyka* movement in Ukraine, then, should be understood as one of many late Soviet cultural movements that sought to re-indigenize and diversify cultural expressions that had been flattened or homogenized to conform to Soviet ideological imperatives.[8]

Professor Yefremov's own story generally coincides with the history I have just sketched. He told me that he began singing in this style in the 1970s because he wanted to sing in the manner of the villagers he was studying, whose voices hardly resembled the "sweetened up" voices of Soviet state-sanctioned folklore. He and his graduate student cohort learned, initially, by simply singing with the villagers they recorded. They studied ritual repertoires, in particular, that were largely absent from Soviet folklore collections, deemed taboo for expressing superstition, religiosity, or "backwards" thinking (cf. Slezkine 1992). They learned to imitate the particular timbres of specific village singers through acts of disciplining of the vocal tract to reinforce the naturally occurring resonant frequencies at the fifth and the octave. They noted the diverse kinds of *huks* village singers used to punctuate the ends of lines or key textual moments. They analyzed the kinds of variations and intensive micro-improvisations utilized by singers in the field, and rehabilitated dense heterophonous moments not as errors, but as core elements of the style. (Principles of variation in village singing was the subject of Yefremov's doctoral dissertation in ethnomusicology; for an overview, see Yefremov 1985, 1997, and 2004.)

Yefremov and his cohort—who formed the first urban *avtentyka* group, called Drevo, in 1979—were motivated in part by the anxiety that these stylistic techniques and repertoires were dying away in rural areas, and in part as a remedy against the overly saccharine arranged folklore presented by state-sanctioned "national choirs" (personal communication, 2011).[9] (Notably, the name Drevo was already being used by the celebrated rural singers from the village of Kriachkivka in Poltava, who formed as a collective in 1958.) Originally, as Yefremov told me, the oblique politics of musical refusal contained within *avtentyka* were not explicitly anti-Soviet, though Yefremov recalled how one prominent folklorist reprimanded his group for singing "pagan repertoire" "like babas" in an "uncultured, unappealing, unmusical, street" way (personal communication, 2019). But as the style and ethos of *avtentyka* spread to other Ukrainian cities in the 1980s (which also motivated urban revivalists to conduct their own ethnographic salvage expeditions), the politics of *avtentyka* aesthetics developed alongside other late Soviet cultural trends that destabilized the foundations of Sovietized culture.

In the post-Soviet era, *avtentyka* became a musical revival tradition associated with independent Ukraine and the recovery of its archaic history. A primary concern of post-Soviet ethnomusicology was to document and reconstruct the regional ritual repertoires that had been avoided during the Soviet era. In the 1990s and 2000s, *avtentyka* groups were sometimes hired to perform at campaign events by post-Soviet politicians who wished to demonstrate their commitments to independent Ukraine's political and cultural sovereignty. Yefremov's Drevo, for example, performed during the Orange Revolution in support of the pro-Western reformer Viktor Yushchenko.

As already mentioned, an *avtentyka* voice is most easily identified through its characteristic timbre, though considerable variation exists among different regional and local styles. (Therefore, the mandate to "sing on the border of yelling" need not apply to all *avtentyka* styles, as Yefremov would be careful to clarify.) But broadly, some general common features exist. For example, in contrast to the bel canto operatic voice, in which singers learn to mold the vocal tract so as to suppress some of the treble overtones (Feld et al. 2004), the *avtentyka* voice reinforces certain upper partials through a balance of nasality and chest

FIGURE 3.1 An archival image of the village singers of Drevo from the village of Kriachkivka in the Poltava region of Ukraine. Used with permission by the webmaster of drevo.co.ua.

resonance. The desired effect is strident, with a pronounced fundamental pitch and a reinforced ghostly octave and fifth. Thus, the *avtentyka* voice exists on the spectrum between two extremes of global vocal tradition: the Western operatic bel canto voice, and the Tuvan throat singers who reinforce harmonic peaks through larynx, palate, and tongue positioning (and the activation of the "false vocal folds") to an even greater degree than these Ukrainian *avtentyka* singers (Levin and Süzükei 2006).

In Yefremov's pedagogical approach, vocal timbre is privileged above all other musical parameters. The quality of the vocal sound and the faithful pronunciation of words in dialect (which in turn inform the quality of vocal sound) are, to Yefremov, the most salient markers of how he evaluates the relative "authenticity" of a performance. To achieve the correct vocal sound, both Yefremov and another prominent teacher (with whom I have studied on occasion) encourage students to mimic various pastoral sounds—goats bleating, cows lowing—as they learn to produce the *avtentyka* timbre. Yet another practitioner, whose methods and artistry draw from performance art, has advised her female students to sing wearing long skirts and, optimally, no underwear in order to better absorb the earth's vibrations through the body and, in turn, produce a more grounded vocal sound.

Among contemporary *avtentyka* practitioners, Yefremov's pedagogical style is known to be strict, because he wields his authority both as a founder of the late Soviet urban revival and as a senior professor at Ukraine's foremost conservatory. When he teaches, Yefremov polices the line of "authenticity" based on his decades of field expeditions, academic publications, and the generations of singers he has trained. Though other practitioners with whom I have studied bring greater or lesser degrees of authority to the practice of interpreting *avtentyka* materials (and, in many cases, place much greater emphasis on the spiritual or mystical potential of these repertoires), a performance of *avtentyka* is always evaluated by how successfully a singer conveys "authentic" rurality, which is sonically rendered through the unmistakable timbral quality of a voice that, at moments, is defined by its seeming lack of control. The effortful laboring body, however, is made audible through performative strain and volume, but this bodily labor is expressed solely through the voice. To summarize: as the singer's voice teeters "on the border of yelling," her voice is expected to signify her own agency and simultaneously work as an avatar for primordial rural identity through the embodiment of a near-animalistic, ecstatic, full-bodied yet disciplined vocality.

Following the studied production of vocal timbre, the second emphasis of Yefremov's pedagogy are the stylistic conventions that govern variation—variation that is confined to intensive micro-improvisations. In a song sung by multiple people, such variations are generally restricted to pitch-based improvisations and small melismatic gestures. Many ritual songs from Kyivan Polissia (the ethnographic region in which Professor Yefremov specialized as a graduate student) thought to be the most archaic have a narrow melodic range, usually limited to an interval smaller than a fifth. But within this circumscribed range, selected melodies and pitches are somewhat unstable. Yefremov conveys this to his students by offering a range of possible variations for a given line of text in a song. As an example, he might sing a drone (бурдон) in three ways. First, as a straight, unwavering single pitch. Then, with small micro-deviations (usually mordant-type ornaments that are smaller than a half-step in the equal tempered system) from the root pitch that emphasize the rhythm of the text. Finally, as a slightly more elaborated improvisation that wanders farther from—but always returns to—the drone pitch. The drone pitch is often the same pitch on which a line of sung text will conclude, on which a group of singers will converge on a strident unison or octave. These moments of unison allow no flexibility on pitch; Yefremov trains his students to match timbres and pitches on unisons or octaves with razor-sharp focus, to emphasize how this unified sound stands in stark tension to the heterophonous musical sounds that precede it.

With the exception of these ending unisons, Yefremov's pedagogical emphasis on constant variation means that students do not learn an ür-version of a song. Though field recordings are a kind of wellspring for *avtentyka* singers—many of whom were trained as ethnomusicologists in the late and post-Soviet eras— contemporary *avtentyka* practitioners do not seek to simply recreate those field recordings. In fact, multiple field recordings of the same song are referenced when possible to inform an interpretation, and Yefremov at times corrected the re- corded performances of village singers on field recordings, explaining that—due to their advanced age or perhaps another impairment (nerves at being recorded, drunkenness, or even the position and quality of the microphone)—there was an error on the recording. *Avtentyka* practitioners also typically attribute their interpretations of songs to specific singers or villages (and the unstated rule of who gets to sing what usually depends on who had the face-to-face interaction with a village singer that produced a particular field recording). A field recording, then, cannot be fully trusted without the authority of the ethnomusicologist- expert.

So instead of perfecting the art of imitation, students are taught how to cre- atively utilize the conventions that govern these traditional songs in order to replicate them in as "authentic" a manner as possible, in part by exerting their own agency as singers.[10] The notion that the successful transmission of *avtentyka* depends to a large degree on singers' abilities to make spontaneous decisions within the rigid conventions of the tradition means that the ways in which an authentic performance is evaluated have little to do with how accurately a field recording is imitated. Instead, an authentic delivery merges a measure of spontaneity with a disciplined use of the voice that strategically indexes bodily abandon. To the listener, the *avtentyka* voice insists that a listener note the in- dividual body of the singer through the effortful exhalation of breath as well as through audible grit and tension, yet *avtentyka* practitioners inhabit multiple bodies as they sing, drawing together multiple previous iterations of a song to agentively fuse a new iteration within the convention's rather rigid limits.

The gendered representations on twentieth-century field recordings also deter- mine how the line of authenticity is policed and conveyed in teaching contexts. Due to wars, famines (such as the 1932–1933 famine known as the Holodomor), and various Soviet social engineering projects that decimated the male population of Ukrainian citizens during the mid-twentieth century, women have been the primary subjects of post–World War II Ukrainian ethnomusicological inquiry since they tend to constitute the vast majority of surviving village elders. Also, with the exception of the winter *koliada* songs performed by men, the remaining ritual calendar-based repertoire was traditionally sung by women, as timekeepers of the village, whose high-pitched voices were thought to be able to better pierce the barrier between the earthly and the celestial. Therefore, the ritual repertoires most prized by post-Soviet ethnomusicologists have been dominated by women's voices. For this reason, even contemporary male practitioners and teachers of the *avtentyka* style, such as Professor Yefremov, aspire to recreate the vocal timbre and range associated typically with female voices in order to transmit them to students.

In post-Soviet Ukraine, the timbral and stylistic differences of *avtentyka* singing mapped onto social differences, as the "sweet" folkloric voice became more associated with institutions carried over from the Soviet era, and the "earthy" *avtentyka* voice with a brand of late and post-Soviet revival rooted in scholarly investigations of rural practices. (The *avtentyka* voice also, especially after the 1986 Chornobyl nuclear disaster, became entangled with the politics of various environmental activist, Native Faith, and neo-Orthodox religious movements [see Ivakhiv and Sonevytsky 2016].) For its decades-long resistance to the Soviet nationalities policies that reduced Soviet republics to a caricatured version of their titular nationality in the guise of a national folk tradition, *avtentyka* singing asserted its territorialized (regional, local) particularity, what many *avtentyka* singers conversant in Polissian repertoires will refer to as *tuteshnist'*, meaning "here-ness."

Through timbral and technique-based specificity, the *avtentyka* voice aspires to be heard as the precolonial voiced authenticity of a particularized here-ness. It aims to restore the link to a past ruptured through Soviet and imperial regimes, while repurposing those pasts toward the future. In its insistence on specificity, the *avtentyka* voice embodies a paradox: even as its core aesthetic values shun codification, canonization, and genrefication, it has flourished on a small scale in the ethnomusicology classrooms of the contemporary Ukrainian academy and in a growing network of international workshops and summer camps. When it emerges from these cloistered contexts to participate in the mediatized spectacle of the reality TV singing competition, however, the *avtentyka* voice is disruptive, introducing a heterogenous notion of *etnos* into the constrained sovereign imaginaries available as coaches and television audiences deliberate over who should be crowned that season's singular "voice of the nation."

AUTHENTICATING *AVTENTYKA*

In the Ukrainian "Voice," just as in all versions of the franchise worldwide, contestants are judged and later coached by the musical luminaries of the local musical economy. In the Ukrainian version, the four coaches have been drawn from a pool of both Ukrainian and Russian musicians who are famous for their careers in Euro-American and Soviet-derived popular music genres such as rock, R&B, *etno*-pop, and *estrada* (the light entertainment music that came to prominence as Soviet state-sanctioned popular music). In its first season, there were two Ukrainian coaches (Ruslana and Oleksandr Ponomaryov) and two Russian coaches (Stas' Piekha and Diana Arbenina).[11] The program, which began its eighth season in 2018, has exclusively produced winners who are fluent in global popular styles.[12]

The first round of *Holos Kraïny*—as described in the opening vignette to this chapter—is "blind," meaning that contestants are invisible to the four judges, who sit ensconced in red boxing-glove-like chairs that are turned away from the stage. (The contestants *are* visible to the audience, however, which surrounds them in the arena-like theater and roars as they enter the stage.) The premise, then, is that all the coaches can use to evaluate a competitor in the initial round is the sound of the performer's voice—the conceit of the acousmatic voice, and nothing more.[13] If coaches choose the contestant to be on their team, they hit a big white button and swivel around in their chairs, at which point it is quite common to mime surprise at the physical appearance of the singer. ("Wow!" the judge might mime to the camera, "this person looks *nothing* like her voice!") Once a coach has pressed the button during a contestant's performance, this automatically invites the singer onto the coach's team for the competition. (If more than one coach presses the button, the singer gets to choose her preferred coach.) If none of the coaches hit their buttons for a given singer, then that singer will not move forward in the competition. Still, the singer is offered critique from the judges, whose chairs automatically turn to face the stage at the completion of the song.

Following the blind round, the show progresses through three additional stages that advance the pugilistic themes of the show: the "Fight" (Бої), in which contestants of the same team sing a duet *while* competing against each other in a boxing ring; a post-fight round in which two victors of the "Fight" go head-to-head in an elimination battle; and the "Live Streaming" final round (Прямий ефір), during which finalists from all teams compete against each other and voting rights are shared between the coach and the television audience, who submit their preferences via sms and elect the "choice of Ukraine." Beginning with Season 3 in 2013, the program added a "Superbattle" or "Knockout" (Нокаут) round, in which the remaining competitors of the same team were again paired off (but could now choose the compositions they wished to sing), in place of the post-fight elimination. The winners of *Holos Kraïny* for the first six seasons were rewarded with recording contracts from the global corporate record label Universal Music, but—beginning in 2017—winners receive an apartment in Kyiv instead.

Since it began airing on the 1+1 network in Ukraine in 2011, two competitors in particular have amplified the metaphorical resonance of the *avtentyka* voice in the Ukrainian public sphere through their participation in *Holos Kraïny*: Oleksij Zajets, the young man in traditional village garb described in the introduction to this chapter, who did not advance past the blind round in the first season of the show; and Suzanna Karpenko, a prominent *avtentyka* singer known for her work with the Kyiv-based *avtentyka* groups Drevo and Bozhychi, who made it as far as the "Knockout" round in the second season of the program (which aired in 2012). Both Zajets and Karpenko have studied with and worked alongside Yevhen Yefremov in Drevo, and both were working toward or had completed advanced degrees in ethnomusicology in Kyiv. Both came to Kyiv from small villages in Central Ukraine. Both had toured within and outside of Ukraine as part of various *avtentyka* groups.

Yet, though Zajets and Karpenko shared these biographical details, their "stories of authentication"—what Matt Stahl identifies as one of two dominant narrative styles present in the reality TV singing competition, in which a "biographical and autobiographical vignette . . . construct[s the] contestant as [a] moral being" (2013, 38)—were vastly different. If Zajets was depicted as a quintessential rural bumpkin with a "natural voice" that is simply "too rich" to include in the competition, then Karpenko was portrayed as a scholar, whose intellectual investments in "real folklore" (that is, *avtentyka*) were rewarded when she was chosen to advance in the competition *despite* the melismatic gestures, *huks*, and timbral quality that made her voice and style largely incompatible with the pop songs she was asked to sing in later rounds. Tellingly, though they circulate in the same milieu of urban *avtentyka* singers in Kyiv, Karpenko was assimilated into the program as an urban folklorist (where "folklore" became the operative term appended to her vocal style), whereas Zajets was depicted as either an idiot savant or a shaman; in either case, he was the unknowable, somewhat comic, rural other. Karpenko's less fraught integration into the program demonstrated, in part, that the show had improved at accounting for non-pop voices by the second season, but it also demonstrated the degree to which the contestant who is portrayed as and embodies "real authenticity" is destined to failure, while the singer who is depicted as an urban expert—someone who has domesticated the village style—is at least permitted to compete.[14]

In Karpenko's "story of authentication," which precedes her performance in the "blind" audition before the coaches and arena audience, she is introduced with the sound of the *trembita*, as someone who will bring "the energy of the Carpathians" to the program. Though she is depicted as an enthusiast of Western Ukrainian traditional culture, those familiar with Karpenko's work know that this is a one-dimensional portrayal of her interests, which have been equally if not more focused on traditional musical practices of Central Ukraine. Karpenko introduces herself as originally from the village of Krasilivka (Bakhmatskyi region, Chernihiv oblast'), but presently residing in Kyiv. She explains that she is a member of the group Bozhychi, which advertises itself on its website as an "ensemble of Ukrainian authentic music" (bozhychi.com.ua), though here she glosses it simply as a "folklore ensemble" (she actually is one of the leaders of the group, which she joined after leaving Drevo).

Against a sonic backdrop of multiple *trembitas*, a male voiceover enters to contextualize what Karpenko has just said for the television audience: "Susanna has one passion. To some, it may seem strange and not modern, but for Susanna, it is her life's work. She spends all of her weekends traveling to remote villages to collect Ukrainian folklore." Scenes of Karpenko in Hutsul villages flash across the screen, and then Karpenko explains all of the knowledge (woodcraft, pysanka [batiked Easter egg] designs, and music) that she pursues on her expeditions. The vignette cuts to the backstage of the *Holos Kraïny* set, and Karpenko reflects on her participation in the competition, stating that she "could not have imagined where [she] would fit" until she heard that Oleh Skrypka—the leader of Ukraine's first Soviet-era punk band, V.V., and a post-Soviet champion of *etno-muzyka* as curator of the biggest annual "ethno-music" festival in Ukraine (Kraïna Mrij)—would be a coach in that season.[15] Karpenko enters the stage to sing wearing full traditional garb. Following her performance, Skrypka is indeed the only coach to press the white button and invite her onto his team.

Zajets's authentication vignette, in contrast, advances a narrative of rurality that swings between two themes that Zajets is made to embody as a representative of "the village": the village as a wellspring of authenticity, and the village as a comically "backwards" site. The tightly edited vignette begins with the sound of his singing voice superimposed over the scenes and rural sounds of his remote village: an elderly woman on a bicycle, a white horse nosing into the camera, a noisy gaggle of geese, an elderly man leaving his dilapidated home, and then a woman (who we learn is Zajets's mother) riding her moped up to their house, where Zajets is singing as he performs a domestic chore. His mother—clearly self-conscious in front of the cameras—meets her husband outside of the house, and they call their son out. They show him the large white envelope from *Holos Kraïny* and congratulate him on being invited to audition. Zajets responds, in thick dialect, "Well, I don't know what to do." They encourage him to accept the invitation, as an arpeggiated piano underscores the scene in an attempt to sentimentalize the otherwise deadpan—and likely rehearsed—scene.

The camera rapidly cuts to Zajets singing on a village street with a group of elderly *babas*. His voiceover enters over the song, and he introduces himself: "I am Zajets Oleksij Valentynovych, born in 1990. I come from the Kyiv oblast', Makarivskij region, village [село] Fasova."[16] The song ends, and the voiceover is interrupted momentarily as one of the *babas* with whom he was singing points to him and exuberantly proclaims, "Look, the voice of the nation!" (The other *baba* on the bench looks on, amused, in a perfectly staged comedic bit of reality television.) The vignette cuts to Zajets, with parents in tow, climbing the stairs to the *Holos Kraïny* arena in his embroidered costume and straw slippers. There is a new musical underscore now, of rather clownish accordion music, as if to further accentuate the program's narrative about just how hopelessly rural this individual is. His voiceover continues, "I sing in a folkloric genre . . . from early childhood I heard these songs, and so I got used to them, so the family says." He goes on to describe how he fills his time in the village with a variety of domestic and farm chores, and tells the audience that he sings "day and night, from when I wake up to when I fall asleep." He guesses that he knows over a thousand songs.

In the next scene, in the green room crammed with eager contestants, Domanskyi, the host, asks if Zajets would be so kind as to sing—"in full voice, of course!"—for them. He silences the room, and Zajets sings a line of the song that he will soon sing for the judges (although once he is onstage, he pitches it higher, likely an effect of nerves). His voice is loud and strong yet seems to be on the edge of breaking as he fluently embellishes the melody with rapid melismatic figures. He ends the line with the characteristic forceful exhalation of village singers. It is hard for me to view this as anything but an exotic display, because other competitors are not asked to perform in the green room. After he sings, the room erupts in applause. Domanskyi exclaims, "Rammstein, just simply Rammstein!"—marveling at the force of Zajets's voice through reference to the German industrial metal band of that name. The host wishes him well, saying that "such a Zajets will not disgrace his country."[17] As suspenseful music plays—Zajets is now backstage in the moments before his performance—he explains that he hopes the program will support more singers like him, because "this is really the voice of the nation, as it was, as it is, and now it is coming together." As the logo of the program sweeps across the screen, Zajets enters the stage and begins to sing.

As described earlier, Zajets fails to advance past the initial blind round of the contest in the first season, though his exclusion becomes a major dramatic episode in the construed reality of the singing competition. In the pilot episode of the program, however, the coaches also did not press the button for a singer who they learn, after her performance, is Antonina (Tonia) Matvienko, the daughter of the legendary Soviet-era folk singer Nina Matvienko. In her story of authentication, Tonia Matvienko is introduced as part of a "Ukrainian vocal dynasty." Domanskyi fawns over her and her famous mother while they wait in the green room. At one moment, a voiceover notes that "the timbre of her voice is extraordinarily similar to her mother's." Tonia is shown reflecting on her own path as an aspiring pop singer, praising her mother (and her mother's voice) and explaining that she cannot distance herself from that sound. (Domanskyi jokes with Tonia and Nina Matvienko about whether Tonia is, in fact, simply the ventriloquist's puppet—if her mother is actually singing backstage while she lipsynchs on stage. They all laugh and say that this conspiracy theory has been floated before.) Tonia Matvienko competently performs in the blind audition, singing one of the songs popularized by her mother during the Soviet period, but none of the coaches hit their buttons. Once their chairs swivel around, the coaches explain that they did not select her because her voice sounds "too folk" and too derivative of the iconic sound of Nina Matvienko.[18] She then reveals that she is, in fact, Nina's daughter. Dismayed, Ruslana says to the other Ukrainian coach, Oleksandr Ponomaryov, "Oh Sasha, I think we really messed up this time." Ruslana then tells Tonia, "I sincerely regret that I did not press the button for you." A voiceover enters to explain that "the coaches have made the first serious mistake of the program, but according to the rules, there is nothing they can do to return Tonia to the stage."

But, in the fourth episode of the first season, following three rounds of blind auditions during which the coaches' teams have not been entirely filled (due to the exclusion of Zajets, among others), the program modifies its rules to allow a "second chance" for the top fourteen competitors who were not chosen during the first round. Konstantin Meladze, the show's executive producer—the same figure who ultimately explained why they did not allow Zajets another opportunity to compete before calling him a "hero"—talks at length about how much he wanted to include Tonia Matvienko in the competition because "this is a person who really can move our Ukrainian music forward, so I think we are obligated to take such people because this is a real Ukrainian voice." She is given a "second chance" at the blind audition and is chosen by Ruslana. Tonia Matvienko goes on to win second place in the first season of the competition.

While Zajets's heroic voice, then, is too unruly to fit into the competition and be awarded a second chance, Matvienko's cultivated "folk voice" is given this special treatment, and not only because of its association with celebrity. Matvienko's "real Ukrainian voice"—despite the fact that it represents continuity with the scrambled *folkloryzm* of the Soviet era—is also a *predictable* voice. She sings with standard pitch, rhythm, and a familiar timbre—stylistic and sonic parameters that can ultimately be molded to conform to the rules of the game. In contrast, the perceived impossibility of disciplining Zajets's (also, albeit differently, cultivated) voice poses a threat to the format of the program, so he is excluded from competing, even as he is showered with praise by all of the coaches and the executive producer.

In 2011, I sat in the ethnomusicology classroom at the Kyiv Academy of Music watching the men's group of Drevo rehearse for their upcoming performance in Poland. Zajets was absent that day, but his recent televised appearance was a recurring subject of conversation during lulls in the rehearsal. The men expressed a range of reactions to his performance. A consensus formed on two points: Zajets was visibly and audibly nervous, and he sang "like a woman," picking a key that was too high and a timbre that was, as a result, not suitably masculine. One of the singers commented on the futility of pursuing such a competition, which was clearly meant for smoother pop voices. Another singer responded by praising Zajets for his courage in trying, "because the Ukrainian public needs to know that this music is still alive in our country." Though Zajets failed tactically (by not advancing in the competition) and, in the view of his musical collaborators, aesthetically (by not adequately performing masculinity through his voice), he nonetheless introduced a sound world that cowed the judges into obsequious flattery and apology, and challenged the flimsy fantasy of the "reality" TV competition.

While the stylistic and timbral chasm between Zajets's and Matvienko's voices is evident, the voice of Suzanna Karpenko, who advanced past the "Fight" round in the second season of the program, shares in Zajets's aesthetic values of *avtentyka*, even as she is depicted as an intellectual—one of the urban scholars charged with "preserving" *avtentyka*. Karpenko is allowed to compete in part because, in the framing of the television program, her authenticating credentials are her scholarship, and not her inherent rurality, her Wildness. Yet, as Karpenko progresses in the game, her non-pop timbre and rural stylistic flourishes disrupt the competition and ultimately lead to her elimination by the audience.

DISRUPTIVE TIMBRES

Following Karpenko's successful blind audition, she is shown embracing her family as Domanskyi looks on and approvingly says, "Academic, scholar of the folkloric voice." He then goes on to express some concern at her ability to sing pop songs with her timbral quality and style. Karpenko assures him that "it will turn out" (получится). Yet ultimately, it is these qualities of the *avtentyka* voice that grate against the norms of the competition, and lead to Karpenko's elimination, again staging the inevitable failure of the *avtentyka* voice on this reality TV competition.

The dissonance of Karpenko's *avtentyka* style within the rules of the reality TV competition is dramatized in the one-on-one "Fight" round, in which Karpenko is assigned to sing a duet with—while simultaneously competing against—Ruslan Brovko, described by Skrypka as having an "*estrada* voice—in the good sense of *estrada*." (This kind of duet-as-duel format is a typical feature of the "Voice" global franchise.) The song Skrypka chooses for them is "Відрада" (Disappointment), a rock song with lyrics by Skrypka himself and originally recorded in 2000 by his band V.V. Leading up to their confrontation, the program shows clips of the duo in rehearsal with their coach. Skrypka tells Karpenko to back off from some of the technical flourishes—specifically, the *huk*-like glottal stops that she inserts between words—because it grinds against the "delicate voice" (ніжний голос) of the other singer.[19] Karpenko speaks then about how she will attempt to modify her sound, and a voiceover enters describing how "Susanna has done a lot to curb her style for rock" (приборкати стиль у рок), but that "Ruslan nonetheless proceeds to the competition more confidently." Karpenko is thus depicted as the underdog precisely because of her timbre and technique.

The "Fight" round proceeds with the theatrics of the boxing ring fully realized, as the program host barks into a microphone suspended from the rafters to introduce each singer. Karpenko, he says, is a singer for whom "the past is more important than the future." As the stage doors fly open, she enters the arena wearing a traditional vest and necklace over a modest black dress as Ruslana's Eurovision-winning *etno*-pop hit "Wild Dances" blares in the background (see Chapter 1). Domanksyi then introduces Ruslan Brovko, who "is here competing for his daughter" and who enters the arena with fists pumping to the sound of Queen's stadium anthem "We Will Rock You." The duo meets in the ring, and the ding of a boxing bell cues the song's instrumental introduction. Brovko takes the first verse. His voice is light and tender as it swoops between notes, with vibrato strategically deployed to give contour and dynamic to the melodic phrase. Karpenko joins him with a low harmony on the last word of the verse—мого, meaning "mine." She embellishes the word with small melismatic gestures; Brovko sings it straight. The sharp timbre of her voice cuts against his smooth tone. The timbral disparity is so stark that it creates an effect of out-of-tuneness, though neither singer appears to be, strictly speaking, out of tune with the instrumental track.[20] Karpenko leads on the next verse and, at the first opportunity, inserts a small yodel-like *huk* in the middle of the second word, indicated here with an apostrophe: Ya nehay'no // Я негай'но.

Karpenko sings the rest of the lyric with limited embellishment, but remains faithful to the characteristically coarse timbre of the *avtentyka* voice. She inserts another small *huk* at the end of the next line of text, and places small glottal stops and *huks* throughout the remainder of the song. In the middle of her solo verse, her face registers the struggle she is making to conform to the song's aesthetics. She grips the microphone tightly. Strobe lights flash in the arena, and each singer takes a turn at melismatic embellishment over the song's instrumental break. Brovko opts for a high, belting warble characteristic of rock vocalists, while Karpenko—who seems most at ease during this moment—vocalizes a rapid downward melismatic figure that resembles, to my ears, the conventions of Hutsul women's singing. The two singers end the song on a close harmony during which Karpenko's voice softens noticeably, a sudden surrender of the aesthetic norms of her vocal style (where, typically, the end of a line of text is sung with the most volume and expressivity) at the very conclusion of the song.

Domanskyi enters the stage, lifting the arms of the competitors (as if they had both won the boxing match), and the other coaches are invited to comment before Skrypka adjudicates the winner of the round. Oleksandr Ponomaryov tells the duo that, despite Brovko's accurate delivery, he favors Karpenko because he was surprised at how "super" (супер) it was to hear the merging of this rock song with such a "real" folk (народний) timbre. The other two judges praise Karpenko and offer criticism to Brovko, and Domanksyi then turns the decision over to Skrypka. In an extended monologue, Skrypka explains that he chose this song because "he always dreamed of having a voice like Ruslan's," which "perfectly matches this song," whereas he invited Susanna along on "the adventure" and trusted her to find a suitable approach. He tells the audience that "she sang here, for the first time, not *avtentyka* but rock 'n' roll . . . because she is a professor of folklore." He further explains that "Susanna doesn't often sing into a microphone; it's just a totally different technique." It happens to be Karpenko's birthday (something mentioned earlier in the scene), so Skrypka brings her a bouquet of flowers onstage, the house band plays the "Happy Birthday" melody, and Skrypka and Domanksyi sing (simultaneously in Ukrainian and Russian) along to the tune. Skrypka returns to his seat, apologizes to Brovko, and announces that he chooses Karpenko as the winner of the round.[21]

Despite Skrypka's performance of deference to Karpenko, he and his "consultant" (the pop singer Ani Lorak) must nominate two of his seven remaining teammates to "sing for their life" following the "Fight" round, and they nominate Karpenko for this. As the remaining seven team members of Skrypka's team stand on the boxing-ring stage, Skrypka speaks to each of them, extolling the unique merits of each singer's voice. About Karpenko, he says, "And if we are speaking about the most pure tone, the most pure energy, unquestionably the person who knows best of all the wellspring, how to properly sing, the real voice of the nation, I want this real voice of the nation to sound again today in the performance of Susanna Karpenko." The logic here is, admittedly, a bit convoluted: "singing for your life" puts Karpenko at risk of elimination, but Skrypka depicts it merely as an opportunity for the television audience to again hear the "real voice of the nation." He pits her against a pop-folk balladeer named Olesia Kyrychuk. They are asked to sing the same songs prepared for the blind audition, taking turns in the center of the boxing-ring stage.

Karpenko goes first. Skrypka wipes tears as she sings, and, as she finishes, the camera zooms in on his welling eyes. Olesia Kyrychuk enters the ring and sings a pop arrangement of a famous Ukrainian-composed folk song with lyrics by the Romantic poet-hero Ivan Franko. Kyrychuk renders the song as a power ballad, her voice reminiscent at times of Mariah Carey and—at dramatic moments—of Broadway belters. At the conclusion of Kyrychuk's song, Skrypka makes a dramatic shrugging gesture to the other coaches, as if to say, "Well, what do I do now?" Skrypka praises both contestants, stating that they both sang "better than at the blind auditions." He criticizes Olesia's bejeweled micro-dress, which "didn't fit the song," but tells her she performed it ideally. Unable to decide, Skrypka asks the audience to vote by a show of hands, saying that he is "weak" and will bow to the will of the audience. [22] They roar for Olesia in the glittering dress. Karpenko exits the competition graciously. Backstage, she coolly evaluates her elimination, stating that she will move forward independently, and continue to develop her work.

Notably, in both her blind audition and this final elimination round, Karpenko sang a Serbian—not a rural Ukrainian—song. The viewing audience knows this because it is subtitled as such, and multiple coaches comment on this following both performances. (Skrypka initially praises Karpenko for her "experiment" in Serbian song.) Yet, to Skrypka, the coach who weeps performatively, the choice of repertoire does not inhibit his conviction that Karpenko represents the "real voice of the nation," since it is her vocal timbre and technique that most indexes the "wellspring" of national authenticity, as Skrypka himself puts it. During her head-to-head duet with Brovko, when Karpenko performs Skrypka's pop song, her vocal color is disruptive through the use of a distinctly non-pop vocal timbre complete with non-pop stylistic flourishes (such as the *huk*), yet the coaches evaluate this positively. When she sings a traditional Serbian song, her vocal timbre manages to index a kind of "national authenticity" for the coach who is eager to hear it as such, but this goes unrewarded outside of patriotic platitudes, since it is the audience members who ultimately determine that her voice is not fit for the competition. In his gesture of exasperation following her last solo performance, Skrypka accedes to the arena crowd as if he knows that Karpenko is destined to fail in the competition, despite—as he repeatedly asserts—that she is the "true voice of the nation."

THE WILD, UNGOVERNABLE VOICE

In the contrived drama of this reality TV singing competition called "Voice of the Nation," it appears that the question of how to include, and when to exclude, *avtentyka* singers in a popular music competition is emotionally fraught. To the patriotically minded judges, like Ruslana and Skrypka, the *avtentyka* voice resonates powerfully not only by virtue of the body's capacities to give shape to and amplify a particular charged timbre—but also because it culls together contested modes of social belonging in post-Soviet Ukraine, drawing together a notion of village Wildness, *Völkisch* narratives of purity, and critical stances toward Soviet (and now post-Soviet) logics of citizenly belonging. On multiple seasons, with different performers, the coaches ask: Why shouldn't this "authentic voice" be considered popular and emblematic of the nation? Is the failure of these singers to win merely an example of the triumph of cosmopolitan pop in the marketplace—and are we left with a bitter Adornian culture industry critique of homogenization? Is the singers' very inclusion in the competition merely a meek gesture toward a neoliberal logic of multiculturalism that actually flattens and depoliticizes difference? Or is their participation just a cynical move on the part of television producers to add dramatic fodder by introducing these folklore revivalists as nostalgic oddities or rural buffoons? Halberstam asks: "What kinds of reward can failure offer us?" I add: What kinds of new political horizons are afforded by the inclusion of this disruptive style—and its inevitable failure, its almost ritualized exclusion—on a mainstream and global television format?

I propose that the Wildness of the *avtentyka* voice succeeds (even as it fails) in two key capacities: first, as a forward-looking form of post-Soviet qua postcolonial resistance that refuses binaries of discipline/undiscipline and civilization/barbarism; and second, as a nostalgic discourse that is at once typical of folklore and its revivals yet refuses to be elevated to signify the "nation." Because unlike the conventional theories of folkloric vocality marked by a lack of authorship and creativity (Ochoa Gautier 2014, 172), the *avtentyka* voice foregrounds individual agency through its logics of attribution, in which nuanced claims of authorship are made by *avtentyka* interpreters who are also usually ethnographers. Further, by testing the limits of rational expressivity through their manner of singing and refusing to permit their "folk style" to stand in as a "national" form, *avtentyka* practitioners negotiate a delicate balance by which the style becomes codified in its amorphousness, learned and replicated as a kind of ungovernable discipline.

In the popular reality TV singing competition, the *avtentyka* voice questions the rules of the game in ways that complicate our understanding of folklore as backward-looking through its repeated challenges to the cultural status quo: first in late Soviet times, and now, in the context of the imperiled independent Ukrainian state. The inability of these singers to win this competition is not just limited by format: in this reality TV singing competition, the *avtentyka* voice offers a rejoinder (articulated as a kind of aesthetic excess through its disciplined use of bodily abandon) to the hyper-capitalism of the post-Soviet era and a rejection of the limited, Anglo-American hegemonic forms of global pop vocal styles that are inevitably lifted up as the "voices of the nation." Within Ukraine, where the force of a program such as "Voice of the Nation" in shaping the Ukrainian public sphere is considerably greater than the marginal practice of singing *avtentyka*, the vocal style enacts a politics of refusal—a refusal to consent (Simpson 2016) to the globally mediated modes of a voiced "Ukrainian-ness" that excludes heterogeneous local and Indigenous vocalities.[23] The *avtentyka* voice, then, isn't only a reflection of a backward-looking nostalgia (though it contains nostalgia within it)—it also enacts a form of resistance that is distinctly future-oriented by circulating a politics of voice that is defiantly agentive.

In other words, the *avtentyka* voice fails in part because it does not seek to evoke the "nation," but rather, to restore a sense of heterogeneity to the very notion of "nationhood" by insisting on localized tropes of belonging, *tuteshnist'*, or here-ness. This insistence on here-ness is made audible through a vocal timbre that connotes resistance to systematization. In their insistent rootedness, the singing bodies of *avtentyka* practitioners metonymically come to stand for "the real voice of Ukraine," representatives of a local sovereignty that is pitted against globalized transnationalism (the global franchise of the reality TV singing competition). The fraught ritual by which this voice is eliminated from the competition mirrors the tensions around the erosion of Ukrainian political sovereignty by global actors. So, beyond, or below, the examples I've presented here are what anthropologist of sound Steven Feld calls "acoustemic stratigraphies" (2011): the manifestation of the body as it sings, the layers of history inscribed into this manner of singing, and the resulting symbolic excess that this sound suggests in the contemporary Ukrainian public sphere.

The symbolic excess of the politicized aesthetics of the *avtentyka* voice return us to wild music, where the resonant singing body asserts a political claim through the exercise of creative yet rationalized agency. The imperative to sing toward yelling—that is, to push the limits of the disciplined voice toward animalistic outcries of pleasure or pain—calls to mind what Mladen Dolar identifies as the "peculiar and paradoxical" position of the "the bare life of the voice," where "the voice is not some remnant of a previous precultural state, or of some happy primordial fusion when we were not yet plagued by language and its calamities; rather, it is the product of *logos* itself, sustaining and troubling it at the same time" (2006, 106). The *avtentyka* voice asks us to consider whether and how a voice might be disciplined to sound most "bare." In *Aurality*, Ana Maria Ochoa Gautier describes the colonial technology of "vocal immunity," where "to immunize the voice is to use the power of the voice to obfuscate its modes of presence in order to prevent uses that are understood as undesirable"—where undesirable uses are those heard by colonial authorities in Indigenous vocalities that are construed as savage, uncivilized, or animal (2014, 171). The *avtentyka* voice attempts to reverse such colonial technologies of "immunizing" the voice. It represents a postcolonial attempt to make the voice newly susceptible to the realm of wild and ungovernable sounds by resisting genrefication, and by existing at the knife's edge where "singing" risks being heard as "yelling." In the *avtentyka* singer's voice, the possibility of vocal breakage, collapse, noisiness, distortion, and error define an aesthetic and a practice that undermines hegemonic projects of rationalization, be they those of Soviet cultural policy or of reality TV.

A caveat remains: failure, while it holds potentiality, is still (also) failure.[24] My focus has largely been on the failure of the *avtentyka* singers to win the reality TV singing competition, though both Karpenko and Zajets reaped some benefits from their appearances on the program. (Zajets, rather unexpectedly, became a crowd favorite after his episode aired. His failure was rewarded with appearances on morning television, a concert at the Kyiv Operetta Theater, and other performance opportunities.)[25] But other failures could be enumerated here: the failure of the coaches to think beyond the restrictive format of the global TV franchise; the failure of the studio audience (the voice of the crowd) to save Karpenko when her coach could not make up his mind. These failures, perhaps, have ramifications that extend beyond the reality TV singing competition. If we take these examples as mediatized spectacles of the nation-state, what can we glean about the continuing failure of Ukraine to become a political state—despite the two revolutions that have tried to reinvent it in the twenty-first century?

As wide-ranging ethnomusicological studies have attested, the very trope of the "voice of the nation" emerged with force during the twentieth century, enabled through media technologies of sound reproduction, radio, film, and television, which lifted the voices of (usually female) singers ("divas," "queens") to become iconic of nationhood—the pantheon includes figures like Umm Kulthum of Egypt (Danielson 1997), Amalia Rodriguez of Portugal (Gray 2013, 187), Edith Piaf of France, Misora Hibari of Japan (the "queen of Japanese *enka*") (Yano 2002), Carmen Miranda of Brazil (McCann 2004), Googoosh of Iran (Hemmasi 2017), or Esma Redzepova, known as "Queen of the Gypsies" (Silverman 2012; cf. Weidman 2007). Yet, in the staged reality of the televised singing competition, the politicized timbre of *avtentyka* disrupts the link between celebrity and commodity, instead marshaling the power of twenty-first-century media to expose the inadequacy of this simplistic conflation of one voice to one nation. It subverts the logic through which the reality TV spectacle marries capitalism to democracy—what John Hartley memorably called "democratainment" (Hartley 2004; cf. Meizel 2010)—instead introducing a voice that resists commodification as it resists systematization. By being staged on mainstream television as a memorable, emotional, sensational failure, it is possible that, in the contemporary Ukrainian mediasphere, the *avtentyka* voice is destined to continue to fail. But with every interjection of its ungovernable Wildness, it fails productively, with a resounding critique of essentialized nationhood.

FOUR

Eastern Music

The Liminal Sovereign Imaginaries
of Crimea

A person who became something akin to family during my fieldwork in Simferopol told me often that she loved Radio Meydan, the local Crimean Tatar radio station. It wasn't that she loved all of the so-called Eastern music that the radio played—in fact, she thought a lot of the new Crimean Tatar artists were not that good—but she just loved that it existed. Sometimes, in the privacy of a small office that she and her husband shared across the courtyard from their apartment complex, she loved dancing to the radio, no matter what music happened to be playing at that moment. On occasion, I was invited to accompany her for these spontaneous radio dance parties. They always took place after work, after the dinner she had prepared had been consumed by her family, after she had finished cleaning the kitchen, after the evening television news or the Russian-subtitled Portuguese soap opera had been watched, after her children—and often her husband—had gone to sleep. As the radio played, she danced (and, when she knew the song, sang along) with what can only be described as uninhibited pleasure. To me, the Ukrainian American interloper, she often emphasized how good it felt to have something like the radio—*something ours*—to listen and dance to. Born in exile in Uzbekistan, inspired by the Crimean Tatar National Movement's fight for human rights and the right to return, she had fulfilled her grandparents' wish to return to Crimea, and along with some two hundred thousand Crimean Tatars in the late 1980s, she did return. Granted, it was a return to an entirely altered landscape and society from the one her grandparents had kept alive in memories (see Uehling 2004). Twenty years later, the Crimean Tatar radio's presence was a comfort, an audible token of what her community had accomplished since their return. With pride, she noted frequently that it was common to hear Radio Meydan now in the public spaces of Simferopol, too: in nightclubs, in restaurants, and on public transport.

In the mid-2000s, Radio Meydan became associated especially with urban travel on the semiautonomous public transport system of *marshrutki* (microbuses), which were often driven by Crimean Tatars but were depended upon by the majority ethnic Russian and Ukrainian population of Crimea.[1] (This was also my primary mode of transport around the city during my extended fieldwork in Crimea in 2008.) In the cramped space of the *marshrutka*, the amplification of Eastern music was perceived by many passengers as violating the norms of the Crimean public sphere, which was overwhelmingly marked as Russo-Slavic. Just as the "sonorous moral acoustics" of taped Quranic sermons in Egypt framed public spaces "discursively but also shape[d them] sensorially" in Charles Hirschkind's (2009, 124) account, the presence of "Eastern music" on the Crimean *marshrutka* motivated articulations of post-Soviet political desire through affective responses to musical sound (see also Stokes 1992, 105–8). Thus, Radio Meydan became a focal point through which opposed Crimean publics voiced their solidarity with or anxieties about the Indigenous population of the peninsula.

When, in 2005, Eastern music—an invented and capacious genre term with no coherent set of stylistic markers—began to claim time and space on the local airwaves, the radio signified as an instrument of politics. In Crimea, Radio Meydan produced a new and resonant symbolic space occupied by Eastern music, and mobilized discourses around competing and liminal forms of post-Soviet sovereignty. As many scholars have richly described, radio is a technology that fosters new political imaginaries. It can produce the "imagined community" of the nation (Hilmes 2012); it has been used, historically, to inculcate colonial subjects into hegemonic ways of being (Larkin 2008; Lovell 2015; Mrázek 2002). Yet, as many celebratory accounts of "community radio" have attested, the radio may also mobilize counterpublics, as a form of imagined community situated as knowingly subordinate to, and in many cases resistant to, dominant structures (Diatchkova 2008; Downing 2001; Fanon 2012).[2] Lucas Bessire and Daniel Fisher call attention to "the unpredictable relationships between radio technology and hegemonic or imperial formations" (2013, 368). The perception of "Eastern" sounds, in the words of Crimeans whom I interviewed, as "intrusive" or "validating" of the Crimean Tatars' rightful place within Crimea, testify to this unpredictability.

To many Crimean Tatar repatriates, such as my interlocutor described earlier, the very presence of Crimean Tatar music and language on the radio was perceived as a consequential coup toward rebuilding their community in post-Soviet Crimea. While some worried that the invention of Eastern music would only further exoticize their historically Orientalized Crimean Tatar minority, most Crimean Tatars agreed that the radio was a welcome presence in the predominantly Russophone media sphere. Broadly, then, they conceived of it as an aural assertion of the Crimean Tatars' cultural sovereignty within the dominant Russo-Slavic public sphere of Crimea. Yet the genre marker Eastern music also activated anxieties among some pro-Russian contingents in Crimea. To some, Eastern music suggested that Crimean Tatars sought to align Crimea politically with Turkey and the Middle East and, by extension, away from the Russian sphere of influence. To others, the presence of the radio on the FM airwaves was perceived as an acoustic occupation of Crimean public space.

So when "Eastern music" entered the public sphere of Crimea, it was as a semiotically generative genre term, connoting Orientalist menace to some, and a strategic exoticism to others. I identify both of these connotations as iterations of the discursive Wildness that haunts music in twenty-first-century Ukraine. Though Wildness is not a term that Crimean Tatars would likely use to describe Radio Meydan's branding of Eastern music, I extend it here to encompass the tropes of exoticism that entered public and private discourse after the arrival of this Eastern music into the Crimean mediasphere. This Wildness activated new discourses of citizenly belonging through the amplification of Eastern sounds in the public spaces of Simferopol. Conversations with Radio Meydan personnel elucidated the tensions that were felt by some Crimean Tatars about the radio's capitalization on a conceptual generic "Easternness"—which could have the effect of de-essentializing Crimean Tatars by linking their music to a broader cartography of Eastern music, and thus undermining their goals to gain political legitimacy as an Indigenous group firmly grounded in Crimea.

From when it first began broadcasting music and news at 102.7 FM in Simferopolin in 2005, Radio Meydan advertised itself as the arbiter of the station-coined genre term "Eastern music" (Восточная музыка) on the Black Sea peninsula (Kurshutov 2005). Until it set out to "promote Crimean Tatar, Turkish, Arabic, and foreign songs done in an Eastern style," Crimean radio stations mostly featured post-Soviet Russian (and, to a lesser degree, Ukrainian) dance and pop music, in addition to "nostalgia" stations that aired the hits of Soviet *estrada* (Asan 2005). Radio Meydan also introduced greater linguistic diversity into the Crimean radio fields, with programming in three languages—Crimean Tatar, Ukrainian, and Russian (which was otherwise the dominant language of the Crimean mediasphere). Radio Meydan quickly became a key institution for the Crimean Tatars, whose legacy had been "ethnically and discursively cleansed" after their mass deportation from the peninsula by Stalinist edict in 1944 (Finnin 2011, 1093).[3]

The Indigenous radio re-territorialized songs and sounds associated with the Crimean Tatars, but it did so by deferring to the sovereignty of the post-Soviet Ukrainian state. After the dissolution of the USSR in 1991, Crimean Tatars became citizens of independent Ukraine, where they grew frustrated by the state's lack of protections for their endangered language and embattled religion, while remaining overwhelmingly allied with the Ukrainian state project because it represented, as one prominent community member told me, "a lesser threat than the Russian aggressor" (personal communication, May 5, 2008).[4] Following Russia's annexation of Crimea in March 2014, tensions between the Crimean Tatars and the dominant pro-Russian Crimean public intensified.[5] The Meijlis, the Crimean Tatars' legislature, was outlawed; Indigenous activists and politicians continue to be imprisoned or exiled. Just six weeks after the tenth anniversary of Radio Meydan was celebrated in Simferopol with a black-tie gala, the Indigenous radio station was denied the renewal of a broadcasting license under the new laws of the Russian occupation.[6] April 1, 2015, was Radio Meydan's last day on the Crimean airwaves.

This chapter investigates how sovereign imaginaries were activated through Eastern music by attending to the aural sphere of Crimea, as Eastern music was produced and circulated, and as it penetrated the public spaces of microtransit. My goal is to demonstrate how this aurally mediated public sphere became politicized in part through the seemingly innocuous background of Eastern music during mundane acts of travel. I look at how the radio's sonic presence motivated Crimean passengers to affiliate with modes of political desire. I also examine how Crimean Tatars themselves made political claims through Eastern music within the fractured public sphere of Crimea before its 2014 annexation through musical production, particularly through the work of the first Crimean Tatar hip-hop DJ, whose first album and radio jingle helped to establish the Radio Meydan brand. I advance the argument that aural practices—such as the production and audition of Eastern music—could be instrumentalized to center and even contest the liminal sovereignty of the Crimean Tatars. In this chapter, I define liminal sovereignty as a form of political desire that faces in multiple directions at once and forms in the space between these directions.

Importantly, for the marginalized Crimean Tatar population, the radio centered Indigenous assertions of cultural sovereignty—but always while negotiating with the dominant juridico-political sovereignties of state actors. For the dominant Russo-Slavic public, however, the sounds of Eastern music could be perceived as an occupation; as I will describe shortly, such rhetorics of occupation conflated "acoustic occupation" with the imagined threat of future Crimean Tatar violent insurrection.[7] In pre-annexation Crimea, when tensions between the Indigenous population, the predominantly pro-Russian public, and the weak Ukrainian state simmered below the surface of everyday interactions, such divergent sovereign imaginaries catalyzed by the radio "enable[d], through making sense of, the practices of a society" (Taylor 2004, 91).

In what follows, I listen in turn as *marshrutka* passengers, radio personnel, and musicians enunciate political desires through speech around musical sound and through interpretations of musical sounds construed as "Eastern music." Though my focus is on pre-annexation Crimea, I track the presence of Crimean Tatar assertions of sovereignty through musical sounds into the post-annexation era, when "a new form of post-Soviet liminality" has come to define Crimea's suspended geopolitical status as a frozen conflict—governed by Russia, but still claimed by Ukraine (Dunn and Bobick 2014, 406). As my ethnographic examples will demonstrate, the post-annexation liminal sovereignties of Crimea had their precedents in the competing sovereign imaginaries of Crimea that were reflected and produced by Radio Meydan's aural claims on Crimean public space in 2008–2009.

MARSHRUTKA SOUNDS

One early morning in 2009, I boarded a *marshrutka* heading to Maryno, a neighborhood on the outskirts of Simferopol, and was greeted by the characteristic sounds of Radio Meydan blaring from the microbus speakers. Maryno is inhabited mostly by Crimean Tatars who, facing housing discrimination when they returned to Crimea in the late 1980s, claimed plots of land that had been collectivized under Soviet rule by building temporary four-wall structures, *vremianky*, which they often then built into proper homes. By 2008, the streets of

FIGURE 4.1 Temporary homes, or *vremianky*, on the outskirts of Simferopol.
These small structures were used to make land claims in post-Soviet Crimea.
Photo by Alison Cartwright Ketz, 2008.

Maryno were a patchwork of completed residences, homes under construction, and crumbling *vremianky*. I sat in one of the only open seats in the rear of the *marshrutka*, across the aisle from two middle-aged men with fishing rods, who, I assumed, were heading to the reservoir near Maryno for *rybalka* (fishing). A one-liter plastic bottle of unopened beer sat between them on the seat. The men initiated a conversation with me in Russian, inquiring where I was heading on that beautiful spring day. I told them that I was going to meet a musician in Maryno, to see his home recording studio and hear his latest recordings. *Ugh*, one of the men sighed theatrically, "probably another one of these Crimean Tatar 'stars' [звезды]."

His friend laughed, pointing upward, indicating the radio's presence in the *marshrutka*. We were passing by an open field stacked high with *kerpichi*, the yellow bricks that are the raw building material of Crimea. An army-style tent was pitched amid the bricks, and the sky-blue Crimean Tatar flag waved at its entrance. I had visited this site before—it was to become the central mosque (соборная мечеть) of Crimea. One of my Crimean Tatar interlocutors had told me that the Simferopol city administration had stalled and denied various plans to construct a sizable mosque in downtown Simferopol. The Crimean Tatar community interpreted this as an act of hostility against their Muslim faith, especially since numerous Christian houses of worship were erected within the city's limits.[8] After years of frustrated lobbying, activists seized land on the outskirts of central Simferopol and asked community members to contribute to the building by purchasing bricks. By 2008, there were thousands of yellow bricks stacked high on the field, a fortress of *kerpichi* protecting the men who watched over the site, day and night, from a military-style encampment. One of the *marshrutka* fishermen made an obscene gesture toward the field. Why on earth, one of them asked, would a girl (девушка) like me associate with *them*?

The condescending attitude of these fishermen turned increasingly unfriendly as I revealed that I, an American citizen of Ukrainian heritage, was in Crimea expressly for the purpose of studying Crimean Tatar music and media. It was a reaction I encountered widely from passengers on the *marshrutka*, where I often called attention to myself through markers of otherness such as my Ukrainian-inflected Russian speech. Since I was a regular *marshrutka* passenger myself, I began to take note of the various conversations into which I was enlisted, which often ended with some kind of disparaging comments about the "Eastern" sounds that dominated Simferopol's public transport. Most frequently, these conversations were with middle-aged or elderly passengers. Occasionally, the conversations became so heated that numerous passengers would get involved—some loudly defending me, others shaking their heads at the lack of civility present even in the mundane acts of local travel. Though the radio was rarely the subject that triggered these impromptu, often uncomfortable exchanges, it frequently became a focus of discussion. As the background music of the *marshrutka* became foregrounded, listeners no longer heard what had become a conventionalized Simferopol soundscape; instead, they perceived another piece of evidence in their case against what they felt was the encroaching Indigenous population.

In my morning exchange with the fishermen, for example, they equated public physical space (the open field taken over by stacked bricks) and the abstracted, virtual, or private space of listening (on the microbus saturated with "Eastern music") as analogous acts of occupation. In Susan Gal's terms, notions of the "public" are in a dynamic, "fractal" relationship to notions of "private," thus providing "fertile nodes for conflict and debate" (2002, 92). We witness here the recursions that occur when the public/private distinction normalized under socialist ideology is destabilized: as public lands are seized by desperate groups to benefit a minority counterpublic, as public transport becomes replaced by a more efficient privatized *marshrutka* network beholden to shadowy private deal-ings, and as the sole state-operated radio multiplies into a diverse mediasphere that includes stations such as Radio Meydan—which, itself, aspires to carve out space for a "Crimean public-ness" predicated on Indigenous Crimean Tatar culture within the dominant Russo-Slavic public sphere. In the view of aging Slavic populations nostalgic for a return to the order and stability of Soviet life, Radio Meydan could be interpreted as a form of reverse colonization, reclaiming Crimean public space in the name of Crimean Tatars. To the fishermen, Crimean Tatar music was perceived in both threatening and condescending terms; they conflated the post-Soviet history of squatting with the acoustic penetration of Eastern music into the semipublic spaces of transit.

Many other modes of engagement with the radio's presence on the *marshrutka* existed in less extreme forms than the example just rendered, but those with whom I spoke usually interpreted the radio's Eastern music in political terms. One Crimean Tatar teacher told me that although she herself did not enjoy the new generation of Crimean Tatar pop music, her "heart sang" when she entered a *marshrutka* playing Radio Meydan. She, too, experienced the sounds as evi-dence that the Indigenous community was "reclaiming what is ours" (personal communication, May 10, 2008). Many reported that they "felt they were in a different country" when listening to Radio Meydan; in such accounts, the sounds of the radio transported *marshrutka* passengers out of the often harsh realities of daily life in Crimea. Passengers from multiple backgrounds—Crimean Tatar, ethnic Russian, ethnic Ukrainian—testified to this experience. Yet xenophobic reactions such as those of the fishermen were also common, amounting to a belief that Crimean Tatars were overstepping their place in Crimea. Among strangers riding together in public, the radio became an aural battleground of rival sovereign imaginaries.

SOVEREIGNTY IN A LIMINAL PLACE

Crimea, a territory long coveted by regional empires and states, endowed with geopolitical import and with ancient Slavic Orthodox and Muslim holy sites, offers an exemplary case study in contested and liminal sovereignty. Take, for example, the twentieth-century history of the Crimean peninsula's relationship to neighboring state powers: designated an Autonomous Soviet Socialist Republic (ASSR) in 1921 under Leninist *korenizatsia* ("indigenization") policy (during which Crimean Tatar expressive culture, in particular, was rapidly modernized through state subsidies), the territory was redesignated as an oblast' (province) of the Russian Federative Socialist Republic (RFSR) in 1945, then transferred by Khrushchev to the jurisdiction of the Ukrainian Soviet Socialist Republic (SSR) in 1954, and finally returned to the status of "autonomous republic" within the Ukrainian SSR in the last months of Soviet rule. After 1991, Crimea became an autonomous republic within the post-Soviet Ukrainian state, until it was annexed by the Russian Federation in 2014 and became frozen in conflict.

During all of these episodes in which political status was transferred between state-like actors, the Crimean Tatars were subordinate to dominant political sovereignties. Meanwhile, the limited sovereignty of the Crimean Tatars could be characterized as perpetually liminal, albeit with different characteristics: in the period of exile after 1944, when Crimean Tatars were dispersed throughout Central Asia and the identity (and ethnonym) of Crimean Tatars was entirely suppressed; in the return to Crimea in the late 1980s and the subsequent collapse of the USSR, when they became citizens of independent Ukraine who agitated for Indigenous status (Stamatopoulou 2011); and in the period of annexation, when those who did not flee to mainland Ukraine were forced to trade their Ukrainian passports for Russian ones. During my fieldwork in Crimea in 2008–2009, I regularly observed two prominent liminal sovereign imaginaries that existed in direct opposition: one associated with Crimean Tatars and the global politics of Indigenous rights derived from the United Nations Declaration on the Rights of Indigenous Peoples; the other a neo-imperial nostalgic imaginary tied to the Soviet past and recently stoked by Russian military adventurism (as expressed by the fishermen mentioned earlier).[9]

In pre-annexation Crimea, a significant constituency of Crimeans believed that the post-Soviet Ukrainian state's inheritance of the peninsula was illegitimate; therefore, the Russian annexation of 2014 was experienced by these Crimeans as a restoration of proper juridico-political sovereignty to the Russian state. At the same time, politically active Crimean Tatars—whose liminality vis-à-vis state power is inherent in their self-proclaimed status as indigenes with desire for self-determination—usually affiliated with the post-Soviet Ukrainian state, considering it the lesser of two evils. Crimea demonstrates the degree to which "the configurations of *de facto* sovereign power, justice, and order . . . [were] partial, competing, and unsettled" (Hansen and Stepputat 2005, 4). Crimea, therefore, presents an especially hot-button example of how the political sovereignty of states overlaps with cultural sovereignties—the rights of communities (such as Indigenous or religious groups) to maintain their cultural rights, and often some measure of self-governance, within or across state borders (Bernstein 2013b, 17). These unsettled and liminal sovereignties are, in turn, used to different ends by competing sociopolitical formations, such as the dominant Russo-Slavic and minority Crimean Tatar populations. Yet all of these sovereign imaginaries long for state-like actors (that is, the Russian Federation, Ukraine, a Crimean Tatar body) to assert the practices of governance, demonstrating how the state maintains as the ultimate object of imaginaries about sovereignty.

To summarize, as the Indigenous radio made public and audible the coun-terhegemonic sovereign imaginary embraced by many Crimean Tatars, it also motivated an opposing sovereign imaginary, tied to a dominant Russo-Slavic public that could react with hostility to "Eastern" sounds and, by extension, Crimean Tatar claims on Crimean place and space. Within the liminal space of Ukrainian Crimea, sovereign imaginaries were prolific, pointing variously toward Russia, Ukraine, the United Nations, the European Union, the "East," the "West," or some combination thereof.

That such opposed sovereign imaginaries were fueled in part by the radio lies in opposition to the well-documented ways that the radio can act as a "linguistic unifier," disciplining listeners' ears and educating them in standardized modes of speech and affect (Hilmes 2012, 357; cf. Kunreuther 2014). This became audibly apparent in Crimea—where the politics of language were hotly contested in daily life—as all Crimean radio stations became disputed linguistic sites due to new Ukrainian laws that governed the proportion of language used in broadcast. Laws passed by the Ukrainian government following the pro-Ukrainian Orange Revolution of 2004 mandated that 75 percent of all broadcasts must be in the Ukrainian language, and that advertisements on various media platforms must be broadcast in the Ukrainian language in addition to any "minority languages," which include Russian as well as Crimean Tatar (see Bilaniuk 2005; Kulyk 2013).

In response, Crimean radio commercials on predominantly Russophone stations frequently accelerated the Ukrainian ad copy to such comically rapid speed that it was impossible to comprehend. A sonic cue—a guitar riff, a cymbal crash—would often then introduce the "real" commercial, which would proceed in Russian. (One commercial I heard on a pro-Russian radio station in Simferopol in 2008 even placed the sound of an explosion at the end of the incomprehensible Ukrainian text, as if to blow up the government-mandated Ukrainian speech to make way for the desirable Russian-language advertisement.) In contrast, Radio Meydan, which typically sided with the pro-Western Ukrainian government, followed these Ukrainian language laws without irony. By following the edict sent from Kyiv, such lawful compliance signaled once again the liminal sovereign desires embraced by the Crimean Tatars, formed in the space between Ukrainian state sovereignty and Crimean Tatar cultural sovereignty, but opposed to the pro-Russian sovereign imaginaries of the peninsula.

A question arises: What could liminal sovereignty feel like? Or, to rephrase this question, what affective conditions could motivate one to act on some aspect of liminal sovereignty? As I learned from the businessman who founded Radio Meydan, who narrated the radio's origin story to me in 2015, the radio's very existence was motivated by an emergent sovereign desire.[10] He wished that Crimean Tatar culture and language could be made commensurate with existing post-Soviet Russo-Slavic Crimean media outlets, so that people moving through the city could choose to affiliate with the repatriated Indigenous community: that is, to literally feel that they had reclaimed their sovereign home.

INVENTING "EASTERN MUSIC"

In the summer of 2015, I returned to Simferopol for a brief research visit, and met the founder of Radio Meydan through the kind of serendipity that ethnographic research occasionally affords: a musician whom I interviewed early in the day invited me to a posh new restaurant on the outskirts of the city, owned, coincidentally, by the same businessman who had founded Radio Meydan. Due to a taxi dispatch mix-up that left my party waiting on the curb, the musicians, who had just finished playing and stepped outside to smoke, invited us back inside for late-night sweets and coffee. The owner, seeing that we were friends of the musicians, joined us at the table, and I seized the opportunity to inquire how the radio came to be. What follows is the story he told me on that evening.

In the 1990s, shortly after returning from exile in Central Asia, the businessman was driving around Simferopol with his elderly father when their car's CD player stopped working. His father asked him to turn on the radio. All of the radio programming—music and news—was in Russian. His father, a man who had spent nearly all of his life longing to return to his childhood homeland, said that he wished to one day turn on the radio and hear Crimean Tatar music, but lamented, "I probably won't live to see that day." When AtlantSV, a telecompany, became available for purchase, the son asked the seller whether the company could broadcast in Crimean Tatar if it came under his ownership. The seller told him he could broadcast "in Chinese if [he] wanted to," so the businessman invested his resources and purchased it. It took two years to clear various bureaucratic hurdles. When the radio finally went live on February 5, 2005, it opened with a broadcast of the Crimean Tatar and Ukrainian national anthems, and then an address from Mustafa Jemilev, the Crimean Tatar human rights crusader and political leader (personal communication, June 14, 2015).

This story demonstrates, or at least personalizes, how the liminal sovereignty of Crimean Tatars spanned across different generations of Crimean Tatars and instructed them toward a particular politics around music and media. For Crimean Tatars reared under the Soviet regime of discursive cleansing, where the very notion of "Crimean Tatar music" was banned, the idea of making Crimean Tatar music public and audible was a poignant statement of resilience. To repatriates, even those born in exile, restoring their Indigenous claim on the peninsula was an obligation, one strategically pursued through the acquisition of media holdings and also through supra-state mechanisms of global governance. These liminal affiliations encompass complex positions: they appeal to past and present sovereignties, to post-Soviet nation-states as well as to bodies of global governance; and, in the realm of music, to discourses of tradition and "folk music" and to the globally commercialized and cosmopolitan realm of hip-hop. To Crimean Tatar repatriates, the insertion of Radio Meydan's "Eastern music" into the mediasphere of Crimea was a powerful assertion of their cultural sovereignty, through which they voiced their desire for recognition as political actors.

The radio was never intended, however, exclusively to amplify the political claims of Crimean Tatars. The word "Meydan" means public square or forum, and was the term for the gathering place outside of mosques that were key sites in Crimean Tatar society. "Meydan" also exists, as a Persian-Turkic loan word conventionally transliterated as "Maidan," in the Ukrainian language. The original owner of the station told me that he chose the name "Radio Meydan" because he wanted the radio to function as a virtual gathering place for the community of Crimean Tatar repatriates and beyond. In a newspaper article published shortly after its debut, the radio's first editor-in-chief introduced the station by explaining that "we plan to invite people with opposing views into the studio to debate. After all 'Meydan' in translation means a square, a plaza, and means—openness" (Asan 2005).

Yet by the end of its existence in Simferopol in 2015, the Crimean Tatar radio's name itself had fallen under suspicion because of its lexical connection to the anti-Russian Maidan Revolution. Maidan Nezalezhnosti (Independence Square) in Kyiv was the public square that became a site for two popular Ukrainian revolutions, in 2004 and 2013. It was the 2013–2014 Maidan Revolution that deposed the corrupt Ukrainian president and empowered the Western reform-minded citizenry while alienating much of the pro-Russian population. (Ultimately, the instability wrought by this revolution also made the Ukrainian state vulnerable to Russian encroachments on its sovereign borders, which led to the annexation of Crimea.) As the conflict between the Russian and Ukrainian states intensified in 2014, this shared word, Meydan/Maidan, was noted by numerous internet commenters dedicated to pro-Russian agitation.[11] For such individuals, this co-incidental lexical connection added a fresh layer to the historical stereotype of Crimean Tatar untrustworthiness, rooted in the Orientalist suspicions projected onto all Muslim subjects of the former Russian Empire, and later inflamed by wartime Soviet propaganda that legitimated the Crimean Tatars' genocidal removal from the peninsula for being "betrayers of the [Soviet] Fatherland" (Fisher 1978, 168).

The radio's marketing as a home for Eastern music on the peninsula similarly provoked complex reactions, even among Crimean Tatars. Early radio press materials struggled to position Crimean Tatar music within the new vernacular genre label while making apparent the expansiveness of this "Eastern" identification. As a form of strategic essentialism, collapsing Crimean Tatar music under the capacious umbrella of "Eastern music" provided exoticized appeal to a broad listening public. Simultaneously, however, the term "Eastern music" linked the Crimean Tatar counterpublic to a historic imperial discourse of Pan-Turkism. The elasticity of the genre term made it possible to interpret this as wild music that articulated diverse and divergent political claims. Listeners, passengers on the *marshrutka*, and musicians and radio producers could assimilate it as savvy marketing, as part of a neo-imperial nostalgic sovereign imaginary (in which Eastern music might be either enjoyed or reviled as a token of colonial conquest), or as wild music that asserted the cultural sovereignty of Crimean Tatars.

Through its invention of Eastern music, Radio Meydan also marked a new era of "sonorous capitalism" in Crimea, in that it stimulated the rapid development of new musical commodities that fueled local imaginaries oriented toward both local and supra-local markets (Moorman 2008, 85).[12] As one radio producer told me, the Indigenous radio's existence prompted an explosion of Crimean Tatar youth-oriented musical production and circulation, which, in the mid-2000s, saturated the local Crimean marketplace with aspiring pop and folk musicians. After Radio Meydan began streaming online, it had the potential to reach audiences far beyond Simferopol and its environs. Thus, many fledgling pop stars began to aspire toward international audiences, mobilizing social imaginaries that included new forms of labor, subjectivity, power, and "globally defined fields of possibility" (Appadurai 1990, 5). The shrewd marketing of Eastern music activated a sovereign imaginary that touched on a widely held perception of the popularity of "Eastern" music in the global marketplace in the 2000s. From this vantage, Eastern music signified a desirable aesthetic cosmopolitanism, one that might open avenues toward European and North American markets, where the "East" was perceived to be "hot." Further, it linked to the emergent discourse of Crimean Tatar indigeneity tied into globalized notions of Indigenous modernity.

The conceptual "East" embedded in Eastern music, then, was not an inescapable and pernicious stereotype, so much as one that exposed a certain truth of the Crimean Tatars' complex position as the tokenized "exotic" population of Crimea. Despite persistent discrimination against the Crimean Tatar community in Crimea at the level of civic, religious, and land rights, their community had begun to reap some benefits from two recent phenomena that rewarded the cultural difference that is symptomatic of postcolonial exoticism (Huggan 2001): the expansion of summertime Crimean tourism that emphasized the "oriental" cuisine and luxuries of the peninsula (though the businesses that purveyed these things were often not Crimean Tatar-owned), and the general fetish of "Easternness" that pervaded aspects of daily life when I lived in Simferopol—especially visible with the explosion of classes in belly dancing and yoga that targeted women of all ethnicities and ages, and the growing interest in Indian and New Age spiritualities in post-Soviet Ukraine. The "sonorous capitalism" enabled by the radio's existence flowed naturally into these broader domestic consumer trends.

The complex relationship of Eastern music to Crimean Tatar music emerged during a 2008 conversation with Ridvan Khalilov, who was then the general director of the radio station. We met in the broadcasting headquarters of Radio Meydan, situated in a concrete complex located in the crumbling neighborhood of old Simferopol, just up the hill from the city's only surviving mosque. Khalilov described how the radio functioned at its inception:

> We broadcast eighteen hours of the day—probably six or seven hours are [music] programs. We have Eastern music [Восточная музыка], of about which 60 percent is Crimean Tatar music. Ukrainian music is represented, and also Turkish, Arabic . . . When we first opened, we had a big problem . . . I remember when we started we had about 110 melodies. Total. When we opened, we broadcast for ten hours. And in ten hours, those songs would often be repeated two or three times. And people would listen and call in upset

that they were hearing the same things over and over [laughs]. We collected everything we could from our musicians and composers, and everything that we could find was 110 melodies . . . Back then, we would advertise that if you have any recordings of Crimean Tatar music, you should bring them here and we would immediately digitize them and make them available. Many people did this—people were interested. Many vans full of records. We found such amazing things! Records from 1933 . . . Truthfully, many of them were static more than music; our editors would try to clean them.

M.S.: And that changed so quickly in just three years?

R.K.: Yes! Of course! All of the musical activity that you've seen has emerged in the last two, three years, since the radio opened. Before, there was none of that. If I had to guess, I'd say that about thirty new young artists [have emerged]. I'm not a music critic, so I can't say if they're all professionals— perhaps some of them just think they can sing well! [Laughs] (Personal communication, November 21, 2008)

This proliferation of new acts had, according to Khalilov, activated some controversies within the Indigenous community. One effect was the exacerbation of confusion about "what Crimean Tatar music is and is not": How were radio listeners to limn the borders of Crimean Tatar music within the capaciousness of Eastern music? While Radio Meydan broadcasters contextualized non-Crimean Tatar musics during the course of programming, Khalilov told me that the station's reputation "as the Crimean Tatar radio leads people to assume that all 'Eastern music' is Crimean Tatar, or otherwise, that none of it is *really* Crimean Tatar." He explained that with the exception of the "*qaytarma* [a characteristic dance in 7/8 time], which everyone recognizes as ours," for many listeners, other "Eastern musics" lose their distinctiveness in the grab bag of popular tunes.

Khalilov attributed this genre trouble as well, however, to one success of the radio: its ability to draw in non-Crimean Tatar listeners. "I've noticed when we've traveled to villages, people—not Crimean Tatars—listen to Radio Meydan because they like 'Eastern music.'" I asked if he attributed the modishness of Eastern music in Simferopol and surrounding villages to the recent glut of young aspiring Crimean Tatar musicians. Khalilov reflected on my question and answered, "No, not entirely. I think 'Eastern music' has simply become popular all over the world, so maybe we are the ones benefiting from that . . . benefiting but also losing, to some degree." In Khalilov's view, the popularization of "Eastern music" bears on the Crimean Tatar community as both a positive effect (in increasing listenership and promoting inter-ethnic understanding) and a negative (as the specific qualities of Crimean Tatar music become absorbed into a generic and universal idea of the "East").

Khalilov's stance toward the global democratization of recording technology—which enabled the rapid production of Eastern music to be played on the radio—also embraced two opposing attitudes. In Simferopol, as everywhere, the rise of the home studio had transformed the ways in which people produced and recorded music. Khalilov explained this transformation in broad historical terms:

> When we lived in Uzbekistan, it was the state that released all the recordings that we had. There was a very strict censorship regime. It was forbidden to sing about Crimea, about your mother, about homeland, about different historical events—so basically you could sing about love, and there were about twenty-five or thirty songs in the whole repertoire, and all the artists sang the same songs and recorded them over and over. After we came back here, things were better in this regard, but there was a new problem of where to do quality recordings . . . After the return, the culture changed, everybody took to building, those years were so hard, everything was stagnated. And then around 1996–97, the festival Shelale appeared on TV . . . People started to stand on their own legs; studios began to open up. And then the Radio [Meydan] opened and everything took off, now it's flooded. You can't walk five steps before you'll bump into someone's studio. (Personal interview, November 21, 2008)

Within the Crimean Tatar community, this greater access to studio technologies had accelerated the pace at which new artists rushed to record. Khalilov explained that many elders looked at this sudden explosion of musicians critically, admonishing the younger generation for not studying their folk music sufficiently before making their own youth-oriented work: "And now many young singers have started to sing folk songs; many elders think they are doing it wrong. I don't know." Indeed, in the first years of the radio station, young artists who attempted to hybridize or montage Crimean Tatar traditional music with popular classical melodies, rock, pop, and hip-hop were especially subject to critique in the community of repatriates in Simferopol. Though such debates were often voiced as familiar anxieties policing the borders of "tradition" and "modernity," a prominent secondary theme centered on the genericizing effect of subjecting a little-known tradition to sounds associated with de-territorialized popular musics. A current of anxiety pervaded the reception of new Crimean

Tatar popular music, namely, that the undifferentiated "East" might swallow Crimean Tatar music whole and render it unrecognizable.

Yet for musical innovators invested in reconciling the tension between local Crimean Tatar sounds and those of the abstracted "East," musical success and political status became articulated together, in solidarity with an Indigenous-global liminal sovereign imaginary that aspired for access to international markets while balancing against Indigenous concerns. No individual treaded this line as publicly as DJ Bebek (Rolan Salimov), the first Crimean Tatar hip-hop DJ to emerge as the voice of Crimean Tatar youth music. His 2004 debut album, *Deportacia* (Deportation) loosely narrated the Crimean Tatar community's twentieth-century history from trauma (deportation, exile) to redemption (repatriation, rebuilding). The timing of *Deportacia's* release just before the opening of Radio Meydan meant that the album was available for broadcast in the early months of the radio station's existence, when there was a dearth of recorded Crimean Tatar material available. DJ Bebek was also hired to write the jingle for Radio Meydan. Thus, he became closely identified with the emergence of Eastern music in Crimea. Both DJ Bebek's album *Deportacia* and his Radio Meydan jingle mashed together traditional melodies and field recordings with hip-hop and electronic dance music sounds and techniques. These experiments in stylistic hybridity place contemporary Crimean Tatar music in the productive tension of being simultaneously Indigenous and international, modern and traditional, local yet aspiring to be global.

DJ Bebek's relationship to the emergent Crimean Tatar radio gave audible form to these tensions, as a critical hearing of *Deportacia*—which may be considered an early example of Eastern music—makes apparent. Throughout the album's narrative arc, a variety of sonic components index Crimea in both concrete and abstract ways. Popular folk melodies and dances played by traditional Turkic instruments, as well as Soviet-era instruments associated with institutionalized folklore (such as the accordion and trumpet) appear on all twelve tracks on the album. Rhythms are often provided by the traditional *dare* and *davul* of the Crimean Tatar percussion section in addition to electronically generated beats. Samples of birds trilling, crickets chirping, gunshots, and wolves howling are in the aural foreground on a number of tracks. The sound of crashing waves is a recurring gesture, insisting on the centrality of the Black Sea in the Crimean Tatar experience, and thus operating as a sonic rebuttal to Soviet censorship, when sonic or lyrical tropes that referenced places in Crimea or the Black Sea were banned and censored (see Uehling 2004, 39–41; Aliev 2001). Several tracks

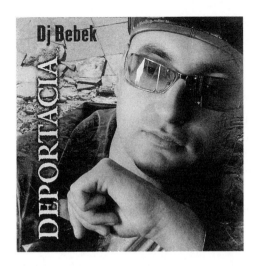

FIGURE 4.2 The cover of DJ
Bebek's 2004 debut album,
Deportacia. Used with permission
by Rolan Salimov.

feature archival and field recordings of elders singing folk songs that are widely known to Crimean Tatars for their particular symbolic resonances across historical time periods.

The third track on *Deportacia,* called "Prelude to the Deportation," blends many of these elements in an evocative way. The track opens with the sound of waves breaking, followed by the entrance of an elder woman's voice singing a traditional lullaby (*ai-ne-ne*). Soon, a low and menacing electronic sound interrupts the pastoral-nostalgic soundscape, giving way to a pulsing beat and melody that eventually buries the female's singing under a thickening electronic layer of synthetic sound. At one moment, the sounds of children playing can be heard in the background, but their laughter too is smothered by the carpet of synthesized sound. After about five minutes, these dense layers of dance-like music recede in sequence, until the woman's lullaby comes to the forefront, finally submerging again into the sound of waves. This palindromic composition is bookended by the sound of crashing waves, as a recurring soundmark of the Black Sea, which emphasizes the territorialized identity of Crimean Tatars.

The title track, "Deportacia," follows the prelude. The track opens with what could almost be a radio play: a tranquil background of crickets chirping, interrupted by the squeal of tires. Dogs begin to bark, followed by the sounds of a household awakened from sleep: doors screeching open and slamming; voices full of confusion. Then, two Russian-speaking men discuss a brutal plan to deport the Crimean Tatars, a direct reference to the deportation that took place on the night of May 18, 1944. This scene leads into a mournful leitmotif from the well-known folk song "Miskhor Kyzy." The melody continues, punctuated by gunshots, until it is overcome by a new, cinematic melody (DJ Bebek's own, but crafted to mimic a traditional Crimean Tatar folk song). As this melody swells with trumpet and k̇aval (end-blown flute), it is eventually taken over by a synthesizer figure playing in a generic dance style. For the duration of the song, these melodic fragments waft in and out, until the track diminishes to the sound of wind, the howl of wolves, and human weeping. "Deportacia" is followed by "The Return," a boisterous accordion-driven dance number, which cues the rest of the album's narrative arc toward a celebration of the Crimean Tatar repatriation to Crimea.

At the time of the album's release, DJ Bebek emerged as the voice of a new—and controversial—generation of Crimean Tatar musicians who were making music, in part, to be played on Radio Meydan. An interview in the local newspaper *Golos Kryma* (Voice of Crimea) introduced the young DJ as a savvy connoisseur of both folkloric and popular styles, the original purveyor of Crimean Tatar music "of the future":

> To achieve popularity, you must have quite a few elements—the product should be modern and its content should appeal to the deepest, oldest, 'saturated with mother's milk' qualities of human sensitivity. The novelty of the album *Deportacia* . . . succeeds in that it uses old, well-known Crimean Tatar melodies and songs . . . mixed with the contemporary rhythms of disco, techno, rap, and chaos. This gives the melodies an absolutely new, innovative sound that destroys existing stereotypes of perception. And, the fact that the tunes on the album are being played in practically all of the discotheques, all of the discs have already sold out, and the author has started working on his second album, once again confirms the reliability of the formula for success, which was derived long before us. (Yuksel' 2004)

While the album's allure is attested to by the report of its ubiquity in the dance clubs of Simferopol, the imaginary worlds that it aspired to reach stretched well beyond Crimea, toward the emerging "globally defined fields of possibility" that the media platform of the radio introduced.

DJ Bebek articulated his ambitions by positioning himself in dialogue with the pantheon of hip-hop's global superstars. His idols, he told me during a 2008 interview, were the singer Beyoncé, the rapper Jay-Z, and the producer Timbaland. In addition to the music, he said, it was the ostentatious style of hip-hop that inspired him. In Simferopol, his performances were often staged with female hip-hop dancers in revealing outfits; he had performed with a pop-lock dancer who wore a staggering amount of glittering chains (which DJ Bebek referred to in hip-hop vernacular as "bling"). None of this is exceptional in the story of global hip-hop: Thomas Solomon demonstrates an analogous example of Istanbul-based rappers who, "in their appropriations of the globalized genre of rap . . . thoroughly reterritorialized and indigenized it, embodying in their rap the sounds and discourses of other, Indigenous musical genres and creating a hybrid musical expression that serves as a vehicle for local imaginations of place" (2005b, 61; cf. Gross 1996). *Deportacia*, with its specific and iconic references to Crimea and the twentieth-century deportation of the Crimean Tatars, similarly "reterritorialized" the global sounds of hip-hop. Yet, it was through the territorializing of contested sounds, of locating them back inside a Crimea that was largely hostile to Crimean Tatars, that the productive friction of the Indigenous-global sovereign imaginary takes form. Which audience, ultimately, did DJ Bebek imagine for his debut album? Was he crafting a document that asserted the sovereignty of his own Crimean Tatar counterpublic, that addressed the mainstream Crimean public dominated by Russian state discourses, or an imagined world beyond his own experience?

In seeking this balance between the Indigenous and the global, Salimov demonstrated his commitment to using local sounds and influences in moderation—enough to retain some measure of specificity—but not so much that this specificity would inhibit the album's wide circulation and popular reception. This ambivalence is characteristic of the liminal Indigenous-sovereign imaginary: it aspires toward structures of governance that would allow work to accrue value in a lucrative marketplace (the capitalist global imaginary), while packaging it firmly in a view of Crimea-as-homeland (the Indigenous imaginary). Frustrated by the limits of the Crimean market, Salimov also looked for validation in terms that nonetheless resonated with the aspirational language of commodified music. He told me that his goal, beyond financial reward, is universal "respect"—a term that he uttered in our interview as *respekt*. As a direct transliteration from English, appropriated from the vernacular of African American hip-hop, *respekt* justifies and authenticates the hip-hop artist's mission. Uttered this way, *respekt* demonstrates how Salimov's personal musical goals were mediated by the argot and values of global hip-hop culture. Further, his self-positioning as musician speaks to the delicate way that Crimean Tatar indigenes self-define within the liminal space between "Europe" and the "East."

Yet even more than the music of *Deportacia*, DJ Bebek's most widely circulated contribution to Radio Meydan was his radio jingle, which became an iconic marker of Eastern music. The studio version of the jingle runs over four and a half minutes and was occasionally broadcast on Radio Meydan in its entirety as if it were a typical song. More commonly, however, a brief version of the jingle aired as transitional "bumper" material between blocks of news, music, advertisements, and call-in programs. The brief jingle features the sounds of accordion, trumpet, electronic dance beats, and the *daré* and *davul* drums associated with Crimean Tatar (and many other Turkic) traditional musics. The jingle concludes with the station ID: the word "Meydan," sung on one pitch by a chorus of voices in unison.[13] By 2008, through its ubiquity on public transport, the Radio Meydan jingle had become entrenched as the preeminent sonic marker of Eastern music in Simferopol. As Radio Meydan quickly became the preferred radio station for many *marshrutka* drivers in Simferopol, the jingle and the music that it introduced constructed an emergent notion of "Crimean publicness" rooted in the liminal Indigenous-global sovereign imaginary.

In post-annexation Crimea, where Radio Meydan and its brand of Eastern music is no longer available on the FM dial, the acoustic profile of the *marshrutka* has changed. Much Crimean Tatar music has migrated to new, mostly online spaces (including Canli Radio, the streaming radio station that started broadcasting from Bakhchysarai, Crimea, in 2017). Meanwhile, since 2017, Russian government-backed Radio Vatan Sedası (Voice of the Motherland) has reimagined Eastern music for Crimean listening publics on the FM dial. Notably, this post-annexation radio bolsters Russian state projects to foster affective links between Crimean Tatars and other Tatar communities in the Russian Federation; the newer pro-Russian radio, accordingly, defines its Eastern music with this agenda at heart. Since mid-2016, Radio Meydan has been broadcasting from Kyiv, Ukraine, where a large number of internally displaced persons (IDPs) have started to rebuild Crimean Tatar institutions of language, culture, and politics. The shift from Simferopol to Kyiv as a cultural capital for independent Crimean Tatar music has been articulated forcefully through music and media in recent years, emphasizing a renewed political solidarity between Crimean Tatars and Ukrainians.

AN EMERGENT POSTCOLONIAL SOVEREIGN IMAGINARY?

In Kyiv, Radio Meydan started to stream its programs online, with programming now limited to the Ukrainian and Crimean Tatar languages. Earlier, ATR television had resumed operations in mainland Ukraine, posting news clips (*roliki*) to YouTube, partly so that Crimea-based populations could also access them through the internet. When I visited Simferopol in the summer of 2015, I was repeatedly told about how these internet *roliki* were a small lifeline for the Crimean Tatar community in Crimea who were desperate for media not controlled by the Russian state.

In mainland Ukraine, pro-Ukrainian Crimean Tatar activists have established NGOs (such as CrimeaSOS) to fight the war of Russian "disinformation" and to help manage the crisis of IDPs fleeing Crimea (personal communication, June 25, 2015). Though some Crimean Tatar politicians and entrepreneurs have sided with Russia since the annexation, the majority of Crimean Tatars remain pro-Ukrainian. In late 2015, Crimean Tatar activists downed the electric pylons that powered the Crimean peninsula, resulting in a multi-week blackout in Simferopol and other locations; this action was intended both to trigger Ukrainian state action on the Crimean crisis and to stage the ongoing solidarity between Crimean Tatars and Ukrainians.

This shared history of Ukrainian and Crimean Tatar oppression under Soviet and Russian rule has given rise to an emergent sovereign imaginary, a postcolonial formation that invests in the imperiled and inadequate Ukrainian state despite its history of post-Soviet failures and ongoing losses against Russian state power. This emergent postcolonial solidarity is premised on registers of liminality: of the Ukrainian state, positioned at the border of the expanded European Union and the expansionist Russian Federation; and Crimean Tatars, split between their goals of Indigenous sovereignty and collaboration with the state power that they would prefer to govern Crimea. Such an inclusive civic space—one that legitimizes the Sunni Muslim, Turkic-language Crimean Tatars through Indigenous rights discourse within the dominant Ukrainian public sphere—suggests a sovereign imaginary that runs counter to Ukrainian ethnonationalism. Though it is grounded in fragile optimism, given Ukraine's systemic ongoing corruption, border violence, and post-Maidan political disappointments, the postcolonial sovereign imaginary is being rehearsed daily through efforts to support Crimean Tatar music, traditional arts, and language in mainland Ukraine through the activities of artist collectives (such as ArtPóle) and community organizations (such as Crimean House, Кримський Дім).

This emergent postcolonial sovereign imaginary was powerfully articulated through music and media in 2016, when a Crimean Tatar singer named Jamala, who is fluent in R&B and traditional Crimean Tatar styles, was chosen to rep-

FIGURE 4.3 Ukraine's Jamala holds the Eurovision Song Contest trophy after winning the final with the song "1944" in Stockholm, Sweden, in May 2016. AP Photo/Martin Meissner.

resent Ukraine and beat long odds to win the Eurovision Song Contest (ESC). Jamala represented Ukraine with an original ballad entitled "1944"—the year of the Stalinist Crimean Tatar deportation—with lyrics drawn from a well-known Soviet-era Crimean Tatar protest song called "Ey, Güzel Qirim!" (Oh, Beautiful Crimea!). (That song had also been a staple of Eastern music on Radio Meydan, and, during her adolescence in Crimea, Jamala's first public platform was Radio Meydan; in this way, this nascent postcolonial sovereign imaginary also links back to the work of the original Crimean Tatar radio.) The song effectively layers the generational and liminal history of Crimean Tatars, at once using the techniques of oblique political reference that were a survival strategy of Crimean Tatar self-identification during the period of exile, while simultaneously linking the specific struggle of Crimean Tatar liminality to the context of cultural genocide against Indigenous populations globally. Her song was widely understood and reported as a nakedly political jab at Russia's ongoing occupation of Crimea and its abuses of the Crimean Tatar community through suppression of the Indigenous media, disappearances and murders of activists, and the stoking of Russian neo-imperialism that encourages hostility to the local Muslim "others" (Uehling 2016).[14]

Jamala's performance further politicized this Eastern music, identifying it with Ukrainian civic belonging. Her victory sparked a furious response from the Russian mediasphere, which condemned the song as violating ESC rules that songs be "apolitical." As the representative of Ukraine at the ESC, singing a song of Crimean Tatar trauma, Jamala's presence on the global stage signified how this emergent postcolonial sovereign imaginary has come to be supported both within the Ukrainian state and by the international Eurovision audiences, who voted the song to victory despite Russian protestations of the song's political overtones. (I will return to this Eurovision performance in the conclusion of this book.)

Meanwhile, since the 2014 annexation of Crimea by the Russian Federation, the Russian state has poured immense resources into propaganda that frames the annexation of Crimea as a "return" of the peninsula to its (imperial) home. One Crimean Tatar friend told me that her family has stopped going into public on weekends, to avoid the new holidays introduced to celebrate Russia's imperial legacy on the peninsula—a weekly staging of the "gift of empire" (Grant 2009, xv). The Russian state depicts the peninsula variously: as the cradle of Slavic Orthodoxy, as the zone of nostalgic (Soviet) childhood summer vacation, and as symbolic of Russian state power—manifest especially in historical commemorations of Catherine II's conquest over the Crimean Tatar Khanate in 1783, and in celebrations of the Black Sea Fleet based in the monumental Catherinian city of Sevastopol.[15] The Crimean Tatar Indigenous radio asserted a claim on space that was untenable in Putin's restored Black Sea "jewel," despite the other favorable gestures that the Russian state has recently made toward the Crimean Tatar minority who have embraced Russian state power.[16]

The decade-long rise and fall of the Indigenous radio station located in the contested territory of Crimea is not a straightforward example of how Indigenous media "emancipates" a population or constructs the imagined community of a nation. Rather, it is a story of how the brief existence of the radio worked to repair and bolster the newly repatriated Indigenous community, while simultaneously fueling a reaction that reinforced entrenched Russian imperial discourses of Crimea as a dominated zone of exoticism. Through the dissemination of "Eastern music" on the Crimean peninsula, Radio Meydan generated a new virtual space in which the competing sovereign imaginaries of Crimea, situated within the upheavals of Ukrainian instability and Russian aggression, could be produced and negotiated.

The conditions of liminality that mark the present had precedents in the unsettled sovereignties of pre-annexation Crimea, and they structured public life through aural practices in spaces such as the *marshrutka*. For Crimean Tatars, the public amplification of the sounds of Radio Meydan's "Eastern music" asserted their cultural sovereignty within the Crimean public sphere. Now, such aural assertions of cultural sovereignty in an international forum such as Eurovision act as a generative refusal to consent to the annexation (McGranahan 2016; Simpson 2016). Through musical sounds coded as Eastern music, Crimean Tatars continue to contest their liminality, harnessing the representational force of such wild music to circulate and amplify their political claims within the shifting terrain of post-Soviet geopolitics.

FIVE

Ethno-Chaos

Provincializing Russia Through Ukrainian World Music

In the twenty-first century, DakhaBrakha has ascended to unprecedented heights of international celebrity for Ukrainian artists (*Rolling Stone* named the group the "Best Breakout from Bonnaroo 2014"), and its members have used their growing popularity to position themselves as political, as well as musical, emissaries to the world.[1] DakhaBrakha is a Kyiv-based quartet of musicians, and the sister group of the Dakh Daughters. Since DakhaBrakha's 2011 performance at the World of Music, Arts and Dance Festival (WOMAD)—co-founded by international pop star Peter Gabriel—its members became the first Ukrainian musicians to achieve the level of industry support needed to sustain a career as touring musicians and recording artists in the lucrative North American and Western European "world music" markets. During the Maidan Revolution, they designated themselves "Ambassadors of the Maidan" as they played nightly on European and American stages. In the chaotic aftermath of the Maidan Revolution—when the Crimean peninsula was annexed by the Russian Federation, and regions of Eastern Ukraine succumbed to a sub-rosa invasion by Russian forces—they continued their acts of staged protest. As the immediacy of the Maidan Revolution faded, they shifted their rhetoric; instead of Ambassadors of the Maidan, they began referring to themselves as musicians from "Free Ukraine."[2]

Media representations of the group often explain that DakhaBrakha means "give-take in old Ukrainian" (Pareles 2014). The trope of exchange has been breath-

FIGURE 5.1 DakhaBrakha displays the Ukrainian flag and
signs with slogans referring to the ongoing conflict with Russia, 2018.

lessly interpreted by North American and European critics through well-worn
tropes of world music, such as music's capacity to bridge divides, or through the
transporting mystery of voices and the "otherworldly" sounds of an intoxicating
elsewhere.[3] (The band's name also metonymically connects it to the transactionalism of capitalism, something I will address in the conclusion to this chapter.) The
well-known North American music promotion firm Rock Paper Scissors, which
promotes DakhaBrakha in the United States, features on its website a lengthy
press release that describes the band's sound and influences. It is interspersed
with quotes from band member Marko Halanevych, who often acts as the group's
spokesperson. The press materials conclude with the following passage:

> This mix of contemporary, cosmopolitan savvy and intimacy with local tra-
> ditions and meanings cuts to the heart of DakhaBrakha's bigger mission: To
> make the world aware of the new country but ancient nation that is Ukraine.
> "It's important to show the world Ukraine, and to show Ukrainians that we
> don't need to have an inferiority complex. That we're not backward hicks, but
> progressive artists. There are a lot of wonderful, creative people here, people
> who are now striving for freedom, for a more civilized way of life, and are
> ready to stand up for it." (www.rockpaperscissors.biz, accessed April 2, 2016)

The quartet's mission, in other words, is to center the perpetually marginalized place that is Ukraine and to assert its worthiness. The members of DakhaBrakha are conscious of the responsibility that they accept when they self-appoint themselves "cultural ambassadors" of Ukraine. In a 2015 interview with Hromadske. tv, the musicians commented on the urgency they felt, as they watched the Maidan Revolution unfold while they were on tour, to align themselves with a pro-revolution politics.[4] Halanevych began his comment, though, by offering a disclaimer: "We are musicians who do not make social songs and public [громадської] . . . appeals." He went on to say, "But, of course, we were worried, and we were on the Maidan and what was occurring then, and is occurring now . . . For us, it was important to carry some, even some very small, message that would be precise and easy to understand." To make their message easily intelligible to international audiences (who were likely unfamiliar with the complex unfolding political events in Ukraine), the musicians selected three slogans that they uttered and displayed, along with a Ukrainian flag, at the ends of concerts: "Stop Putin," "No War," and "Peace and Love."[5]

"Ethno-chaos" is the playful genre term that DakhaBrakha uses to describe its eclectic, often riotous style. In this chapter, it is a term I interrogate primarily through the group's recorded music and public-facing self-presentation. Through ethno-chaos—a play on the term *etno-muzyka*—these musicians direct their aesthetic projects outward from Ukraine, exporting their wild music and harnessing its powers to make statements about their desires for the future of the Ukrainian state. Michael Taussig, writing in a very different context from the one I describe here, nonetheless offers a useful interpretation of the point I intend to make: "The wildness here at stake tears through the tired dichotomies of good and evil, order and chaos, the sanctity of order, and so forth. It does *not* mediate these oppositions. Instead, it comes down on the side of chaos and its healing creativity is inseparable from that taking of sides" (1987, 220, italics in original). In this particular Ukrainian instance, the "wildness here at stake" further dismantles the impossible geopolitical "choice" that has dogged post-Soviet Ukraine, positioned as it is between Russia and Europe. As I will argue, the Wildness of DakhaBrakha's ethno-chaos also attempts to rehabilitate the fractured pasts of Ukrainian history as a way to move beyond its post-Soviet "memory wars" (Portnov 2013).

The analysis I offer here investigates the creative tactics employed by the musicians of DakhaBrakha as they alchemize diverse ethnic sounds into the contemporary popular music of ethno-chaos, while skillfully leveraging the tools of the world music market to their advantage. Here, I wish to revisit an argument that I first made in the introduction to this book, but now with special emphasis on the period since the Maidan Revolution: that, for Ukraine, the project of provincializing "Western Europe" is arguably of secondary importance to that of challenging Russia's near-monopolistic control over narratives of Ukrainian past and present. In its historic relationship to Russia, Ukraine's "special status" lies in that it "was not just a colony (if it was one!), it was a contested border-lands" (Hrytsak 2015, 734).[6] In contrast to, for example, Poland or the Baltic states, Ukraine has inhabited a historic condition of liminality, as a perpetual borderland amid the ever-shifting terrain of imperial and state formations that morphed—often quite rapidly—at its edges. Decentering the Russian master narratives from which Ukrainian history has so often been spun can elucidate aspects of both the "ethnos" and the "chaos" of contemporary Ukrainian society, particularly as they are merged in the politicized aesthetics of Ukraine's most visible contemporary international cultural export: DakhaBrakha.

DakhaBrakha's ethno-chaos attempts to provincialize Russia (and, arguably, also Europe) by centering Ukraine as both object and subject of its territorial-ized history. Ethno-chaos accomplishes this through the somewhat paradoxical process of re-provincializing sounds.[7] The primary aesthetic techniques used to achieve this are sonic juxtaposition and layering, but the effects are alchemical, generating something new (a song, an album, a music video) out of an acoustic assemblage that chaotically merges times and places. In this chapter, I refer to the discrete soundmarks that are fused in ethno-chaos as *soundmarks of sovereignty* for the ways they index various ways of life that are enabled through different regimes of power and governance. Through the bricolage of diverse soundmarks associated with diverse Ukrainian *etnosy*, ethno-chaos thrives on the kinetic po-tentiality of its "healing creativity." With its international critical and commercial success in the arena of "world music," DakhaBrakha represents an emergent form of Ukrainian cosmopolitanism. This success has been accompanied by the attendant privileges of cosmopolitanism, with which the members are able to use their wild music to amplify political messages and hope for the future of Ukrainian statehood. Through the creative process of melding sounds that index discrete, specific, and deep histories that have occurred within the territory of the Ukrainian state and beyond, DakhaBrakha deploys these soundmarks of sovereignty as a way to attempt to bring future sovereignties into being.

In this chapter, the interpretive moves that I make are grounded in my long-term ethnographic research, but they are not rooted in any systematic investigation of how audiences interpret the music of DakhaBrakha. This is mainly because I have attended DakhaBrakha concerts mostly in North America, where a large number of audience members know very little about Ukraine or the political crisis unfolding there. Therefore, I admit that my methods of interpretation might appear to make some interpretive leaps, and that these leaps risk foreclosing other modes of listening, especially those rooted in affective or somatic responses to the sounds of DakhaBrakha's compositions. I insist that such modes of engagement are valid and important, and I subscribe to Steven Feld's idea that musical "meaning is emergent and changeable in relation to the ways the moves are unraveled within situated constraints on the speakers" (1984, 13). My goal in this chapter, however, is to center an analysis of how a listener immersed in internal Ukrainian discourses *could* apprehend DakhaBrakha as wild music, as music that remediates discourses of exoticism in order to make political claims. If we read the layered tropes of Wildness that are remixed and refigured in DakhaBrakha's compositions, how might we hear them as voicing political claims about the future of Ukrainian statehood, as voiced by self-appointed Ambassadors of the Revolution? For this experimental interpretative mode to succeed, I introduce the analytic of soundmarks of sovereignty.

My argument here hinges on the ability of a soundmark to evoke temporality, a dimension that has been conventionally under-theorized in discussions of soundmarks. The term "soundmark" itself, which I borrow and adapt from the Canadian composer and environmentalist R. Murray Schafer, deserves some explanation. In *The Soundscape*, he proposed the term as an alternate to the "ocularcentric" term landmark: "The term soundmark is derived from landmark and refers to a community sound which is unique or possesses qualities which make it specially regarded or noticed by the people in that community. Once a soundmark has been identified, it deserves to be protected, for soundmarks make the acoustic life of the community unique" (1994 [1977], 10).

For Schafer and his cohort of soundscape composers, the soundmark contained a particular political valence. It was tied to preservationist environmentalist concerns of the 1970s, or perhaps even, as Jonathan Sterne has it, a "nostalgic elitism" (2003, 344). I wish to jettison these senses of the soundmark here, but to call attention to the implied historicity of the soundmark in its original figuration: to "protect" the soundmark is to acknowledge that the temporality it marks is at risk of erasure.[8] To return to Schafer's original analogy, a landmark, as is well understood, demarcates a location but also a time—a monument marks a battle, or a birthday, or some other occasion; a mountain marks geological time.

In Ukraine, monuments and mountains both evoke contested pasts (as demonstrated by the recent toppling of Lenin statues known as the "Leninopad," or the debate over what toponyms should be used to refer to Crimean mountains), just as sounds evoke contested pasts (even if the pasts they evoke are mythical). In this chapter, it is the temporal dimension that I aim to elevate in our understanding of the soundmark. Within the territory of Ukraine, which contains many rival pasts, I want to examine how the juxtaposition of soundmarks in musical ethno-chaos not only brings discrete local sounds into productive fusion, but also constructively disorders the temporal disjunctures that those soundmarks evoke, thus remaking the fragmented past into a survivable present.

Do the aesthetic techniques of ethno-chaos mount a postcolonial rebuttal to the "imperial phenomenon of temporal annexation" that Jairo Moreno calls "schizochronia" (2016, 143)? How might Ukrainian musicians restore a sense of heterogeneity not only to the spatially diffused multiethnic character of Ukraine, but also to its varied pasts (many of which present problems for coherent narratives of Ukrainian statehood)? For these Ukrainian musicians, the past is a ludic resource, but one that ultimately legitimizes Ukrainian statehood in its most basic sense: its right to exist. This bolsters Appadurai's well-known argument about how the past operates as a "plastic symbolic resource" that can be harnessed to make claims in the present and about the future, but within constraints. In the music of ethno-chaos, the "interdependence" of contested "pasts" is left unresolved (1981, 203), but instead is redirected toward the present. This present acknowledges the irreconcilable pasts of Ukraine, but nonetheless invests in the future of Ukrainian statehood, despite the existential threats it faces today.

Within the context of what is branded as "world music," the wide-ranging and sometimes indiscriminate incorporation of what Juniper Hill (2007, 69) calls "disembodied sonic markers" is standard practice. Yet the explicit politics of DakhaBrakha's mission as performers and cultural ambassadors pushes back against the conventionally anodyne politics of contemporary "world music." The members' overt commitment to the Ukrainian state project suggests that readings of such soundmarks in terms of their indexical relationship to the Ukrainian state is not amiss. Andrii Portnov describes how political elites of the 1990s used strategies of "[c]ynicism and pluralism . . . in order to deprive history of its mobilizing force," resulting in a "chaotic pluralism" that characterizes the post-Soviet Ukrainian "memory wars" (2013, 239). In this chapter, I see different uses for this "chaotic pluralism" in the twenty-first century, as musicians fuse heterogeneous regional and temporal markers along with the "disembodied sonic markers" of world music to generate new sovereign imaginaries, in which chaos becomes a kind of productive and generative collision of influence and experience. In this way, also, the "chaos" of ethno-chaos is distinct from the mish-mash of regional styles known as *sharovarshchyna* (see Chapter 1).

This chapter proceeds from here to a close listening of two DakhaBrakha songs—"Carpathian Rap" from the 2010 album *Light*, and "Salgir Boyu" from the 2016 album *Shliakh* or *The Road*—and assesses the different creative strategies the performers take in these two songs. I locate the soundmarks of sovereignty present in these songs to argue that the music of DakhaBrakha—which often fuses sounds associated with regional Ukrainian rural repertoires, along with Afrobeat, Communist "fakelore," minimalism, "world music" tropes, and more—advocates for a particular vision of Ukraine that is fundamentally diverse, but that also "tears through the tired dichotomies" of the archaic and modern, the traditional and experimental, the Indigenous and cosmopolitan, the crassly commercial and the uncommodifiable. Through ethno-chaos, DakhaBrakha conjures a Ukraine that is neither fully "Western" nor "Russo-Slavic," but rather unified in Wildness.

I move from this discussion to a brief meditation on the temporal soundmark and offer concluding thoughts on what forms of political desire are centered in DakhaBrakha's "world music" exports.

CARPATHIAN RAP: BRICOLAGING THE STATE

Light, DakhaBrakha's third full-length album, released in 2010, features six tracks based on different Ukrainian regional styles and three tracks in English. *Light* was recorded at the DAKH Center of Contemporary Art, which is the headquarters for the small but influential urban cosmopolitan cohort of artists brought together by Vlad Troitsky. Under Troitsky's aegis, the members of DakhaBrakha were brought together to experiment with fusions of archaic Ukrainian and avant-garde sounds for a theater production. Most of the quartet had some training as singers, but little formal training as instrumentalists. Still, they eventually formed a band. The three women singers of DakhaBrakha—Olena Tsybulska, Iryna Kovalenko, and Nina Haranetska—were all trained as ethnomusicologist-folklorists, which included experience on field expeditions to collect traditional Ukrainian songs. Using village songs as raw material, the quartet invented a new Ukrainian *etno-muzyka* that culled from diverse local and global influences: hip-hop, jazz, experimental theater, regional forms, and cutting-edge studio techniques. Their aesthetic process might be most aptly described as *bricolage*, a strategy of "structured improvisation" through which conventionalized meanings ascribed to sounds are repurposed, subverted, or expanded (Hebdige 1979, 104).[9] As bricoleurs, the members of DakhaBrakha creatively crash Ukrainian soundmarks together and, doing so, refuse national mythologies of continuity and coherence. From the rubble of these collisions, they begin to imagine the future of Ukrainian statehood and citizenship.

This analysis focuses on a song from the album *Light*, which formed the core repertoire for the band's North American tour in 2013. North American audiences and reviewers responded especially to the song "Carpathian Rap" (Карпатський Реп), reveling in the amalgamation of the global language of hip-hop with rural Ukrainian text and song. The song draws specifically on a Hutsul song form known as the *spivanka*, merging it with a "hook" drawn from Central Ukrainian vocal practices, rap, and attributes of other acoustic and popular music, including mid-tempo electronic dance music. In my analysis, I will focus on four categories of soundmarks of sovereignty. The first is tied to Hutsul identity located in the Carpathian Mountains (the *spivanka* [співанка] and the jaw harp [дримба]); the second, to Central Ukrainian village life (through the timbral and technical qualities of the melodic hook); the third, to Soviet history (the accordion); and the fourth, to global soundmarks (other acoustic instruments, hip-hop genre markers). Before I delve into each of these categories, I will give an overview of the song.[10]

The studio version of DakhaBrakha's "Carpathian Rap" opens by immersing the listener in the pulsating, overtone-dense sound of multiple jaw harps moving dynamically through the stereo field. More than twelve seconds pass before cellist Nina Haranetska's voice enters singing the formulaic lyrical opening of a Hutsul *spivanka*: "Listen up, good people, to what I want to say / about the boys I want to sing a *spivanka* today" (my translation). Haranetska sings using a vocal timbre that indexes rurality through its distinctive cutting twang. After Haranetska completes the first stanza of the *spivanka* against the jaw harp background, the cello enters with a bass line, followed by repeated melodic figures played on accordion and piano. The harmonic motion of the track is limited to alternation between the minor tonic and the minor seventh chord (a typical progression of much klezmer music). About fifty seconds into the five-minute recording, the feel of the song transforms into a groove suggestive of ambient dance music. When this new feel is established, the text of the song returns, doubled in speed and delivered in a spoken monotone. The rapped text elaborates a story of the various inadequate love matches available to the female narrator. I am grateful to Virlana Tkacz and Wanda Phipps for this poetic adaptation of the lyrics.

Listen good people
Listen to what I have to say
Here's a song about all the boys
A song I can sing today
Mom if you knew
It was Dmitry
Each Sunday
You'd let me dress up slyly
Mom if you knew
It was Mike
Each Sunday
I'd be a beautiful sight
Mom if you knew
It was John
Each Sunday
I'd be at the dance to have fun
Mom if you knew
It was Vasyl
"God help you,
what a pill."

For the remainder of the song, the rapid spoken text of the traditional *spivanka* is refigured as rap. On the studio recording of "Carpathian Rap," the rapper's voice is doubled, a common technique in rap production. Another verse of rapped *spivanka* precedes the melodic hook of the song. The remaining two and a half minutes of the recording alternate between the verses of rapped *spivanka*, sung chorus, and the instrumental background groove, which occasionally moves to the sonic foreground with soloistic flourishes. In "Carpathian Rap," two identifiable regional Ukrainian influences—Hutsul and Central Ukrainian soundmarks—are set against instrumental elements from the worlds of Soviet institutionalized folk, hip-hop, minimalism, and jazz.

Hutsul Soundmarks and Sovereignties

As I have described previously in this book, Hutsuls have been fetishized (by ethnographers, literary luminaries, and—more recently—urban popular musicians) as a quintessential Herderian peasant "folk" of Western Ukraine. Celebrated for their subsistence lifestyle (often glossed as their "independent spirit"), their resistance of Soviet occupation during World War II and into the 1950s, and their unique dialect, vibrant traditional dress, and energetic traditional music, the image of the Hutsuls has been frequently used to convey a vision of Western Ukrainian authenticity that was (especially in the immediate post-Soviet era) closely tethered to a politics of Ukrainian ethno-nationalism. (This is especially ironic because of the Hutsuls' own hybrid identities as a borderland people whose culture is fused from Hungarian, Romanian, Ukrainian, Roma, and other elements.) During the Maidan Revolution, when Russian propaganda drew on a deep well of stereotype based on Soviet propaganda about the threat of Western Ukrainian fascism, the image of the Hutsuls was circulated with renewed vigor, both as a symbol of Ukrainian defiance and as an ironic subversion of Russian propaganda.

The radiating sounds of the *drymba* (jaw harp) and the sung *spivanka* text situate the opening of "Carpathian Rap" within the sound world of the Hutsuls. The *drymba* circulates widely in Hutsul musical practice and is associated both with women's musicianship and with the healing practices of Hutsul shamans known as *mol'far*s. Mykhailo Nechai, who touted himself as "the last Carpathian shaman" before his tragic and untimely death in 2011, told me on repeated visits about the power of the *drymba* (which he learned to make by hand as a child) to heal. He believed that the *drymba* possessed a potent magic, but one that could be unlocked only by the rare specialist. He attested to this in *The Wisdom of the Carpathian Mol'far*, a 2007 documentary about him: "The *drymba* has such nuances that a simple person will not comprehend it; a musicologist or artist-scholar cannot understand all of the nuances of the tones of the *drymba* at its performance . . . If a regular musician plays the *drymba*, he doesn't have the same 'energy' [енергетика] that the *mol'far* has when we play it . . . These sounds can heal mental defects or a shattered nervous system. This sonic vibration cannot be reproduced with other musical instruments. These are natural sounds of sonic purity" (quoted in Yakovlev 2007).

On a visit to his home office, where a stream of visitors seeking to be cured always crammed the small waiting room, Nechai told me about the connection of *drymba* to trance:

The *drymba* can carry you into another sphere, into a trance. If I were to play for you for a long time, you would emerge in another realm and see a different world. It's very simple. There are people who specialize in trance, they can put themselves and others into a trance. And there are others who can only go into a trance with narcotics—they smoke cigarettes, or they drink [alcohol], or a special tea, or take some drugs . . . you can find another realm; it's been shown in scholarship. The *drymba* has much strength. I treat people with psychological problems by playing them various special melodies, and after this the person will understand that their psychological state is abnormal. (personal communication, February 2, 2009)

According to Nechai, the resonance of the *drymba* holds an almost supernatural potential to repair human sickness and mental frailty. For many Hutsuls, its characteristic buzz is heard as both musical sound and, potentially, Indigenous therapy. The *drymba* indexes a Hutsul cosmology that is held up with pride by many Hutsuls for its unique syncretism.

The other Hutsul musical feature in "Carpathian Rap" is the *spivanka* (співанка)—the word is just a diminutive form of the word for "song." *Spivanka*

FIGURE 5.2 Mykhailo Nechai, the self-described "last Carpathian shaman," demonstrates the resonant power of the *drymba*.
Photo by Maria Sonevytsky, 2009.

is a genre that regularly engages with satire, topics from daily life, or historical events. During my fieldwork in 2008–2009, I encountered Hutsuls who composed or improvised *spivanky* on a wide range of topics including the corruption of then-president Viktor Yushchenko, marital infidelity, drunkenness, religious morality stories (that often fused indigenous beliefs with Christian scripture), and the post-Soviet Ukrainian culture of sending remittances home from low-paying jobs in Central and Western Europe. The *spivanka* text of "Carpathian Rap" comes from a woman the band members refer to as "Baba Maria." Nina Haranetska recorded her during a field expedition to the village of Babyn in the Kosiv region of Ukraine, and now performs her text set in DakhaBrakha's arrangement (personal communication, October 29, 2018). Because the *spivanka* is such a well-known form, it is core to the musical life of Hutsuls, and is believed to be—as one interlocutor told me—accessible even to those without any musical "gifts" (personal communication, February 9, 2009). Due to the conversational nature of many *spivanka* texts, it is easy to make the imaginative linkage to vernacular forms of declamatory musicking such as rap—as DakhaBrakha does in "Carpathian Rap."

Both the *spivanka* and the *drymba* index "folkloric" Hutsul musical practices that have contributed to their objectification as an "ethnographic group" par excellence (Hirsch 2005). Remediated through ethno-chaos as mythical archaic artifacts of a culture that endures into the present, such musical practices coexist with tropes of essentialized Hutsul-ness as they circulate in the Ukrainian imaginary: independence, autonomy, subsistence, resilience, and a refusal to fully assimilate into dominant regimes are core features of this imaginary. They play into a discourse of Ukrainian-ness in which ways of life are not contaminated through state policies, in which the local expressive forms of the Carpathian Mountains form the basis for a cultural sovereignty that is ambivalent about broader sovereignties. The *drymba* and the *spivanka*, then, are soundmarks of a Hutsul sovereignty that is nested within the broader juridico-political sovereignty of the state, but refuses to fully submit to it.

Central Ukrainian Vocality and Sovereignty

The melodic hook of "Carpathian Rap," as DakhaBrakha member Marko Halanevych explained to me, was invented to sound like an amalgam of "folk songs of a similar character." The text uses the familiar tropes of many Central Ukrainian village songs. The chorus lyrics are "Kalyna moja, malyna moja" (Калина моя, малина моя), likely a term of endearment (My guelder rose, my raspberry). In either rendering, the line is semantically ambiguous in the larger context of the song. In contrast to the explicitly Hutsul/Carpathian elements of the verses, the hook is less specific in its regional referentiality, yet is clearly derived from the celebrated village vocal traditions of Central and Northern Ukraine that inspired much of the repertoire for the state-sanctioned folk choirs formed during the period of Soviet rule, and has motivated post-Soviet *avtentyka* revivals.

As discussed in Chapter 3, the particular vocal timbre suggested by the melodic hook of "Carpathian Rap" has a long and contested history in post-Soviet Ukraine, where attempts to disentangle "authentic" rural vocalities from Soviet-approved "folk" vocalities have created a rift between singers who identify what they practice as folklore or as the subcategory of folklore referred to as *avtentyka*. Ukrainian ethnomusicologists who have contributed to the circulation of *avtentyka*, which is set in opposition to the aesthetics of Soviet institutionalized folklore, are often skeptical of any "commercially oriented" musical projects that draw on rural aesthetics. When I asked a prominent ethnomusicologist who has little appreciation for various *etno-muzyka* products of the post-Soviet era whether they enjoyed the music of DakhaBrakha, they responded with a tirade: the music was crassly commercial, exploitative of traditional music, and the singers sing with timbres "given to them by the Institute of Culture." (I take this last point to mean that their vocal timbres are not specific enough in differentiating between regional and local styles.) Explaining that the female singers of DakhaBrakha had formal training in folk styles derived from Soviet legacy-style folk choirs, this ethnomusicologist voiced an especially harsh version of a criticism that I have heard echoed by others in authoritative scholarly positions. Such critiques, voiced by ethnomusicologists and folklorists who are invested in a notion of Ukrainian *avtentyka*, offer one critical perspective on DakhaBrakha, a group that is widely lauded in the North American media precisely for the searing vocal quality that its members use in moments such as the melodic hook of "Carpathian Rap," which is often rapturously interpreted as an "authentic" Ukrainian vocality. Many commentators have noted that this vocal quality is reminiscent of the "mysterious" Bulgarian Women's Voices that gripped American fans of "world music" in the 1990s, which also links DakhaBrakha to the world music industry that has enthusiastically embraced them since 2011 (on media tropes of Bulgarian women's voices, see Buchanan 2006, 361–68).

DakhaBrakha's invented melodic hook draws upon a vocal tradition associated with rural corners of the Russian Empire that were considered a "no place" to imperial historians, according to Kate Brown (2004), while at the same time invoking a brand of chart-topping "world music" that is very much a "some place," even if an imaginary and exoticized (Bulgarian women's) place. By centering a mythical Ukrainian village in the song, DakhaBrakha subverts this status as "no place," and instead redeems its Wildness as a historic and Ukrainian place. The pre-Soviet Central Ukrainian village is rehabilitated in charged opposition to the imperial narratives that constructed it is as a "no place," and is given weight as a temporal marker that pre-dates colonial encounter. This imaginary Ukrainian village is voiced as a form of wild music that asserts local sovereignty and thus rebuts the imperial powers of erasure that persistently cast it as a backwater without valuable ways of life, and devoid of a past.

The Accordion and Soviet Power

The accordion is a global instrument, but my interest here lies in how it was construed as an archetypal socialist—and Soviet—musical instrument.[11] Neil Edmunds describes the accordion in the Soviet Union as a "proletarian instrument" (2000, 135). The accordion—a mobile, inexpensive instrument ideally suited for the usually limited harmonic motion of vernacular musics—was popularized by the Soviet regime. In the USSR, the chromatic button accordion, or *bayan*, developed in Russia in the early twentieth century, became associated more with elite performing practices (Harrington 2001). The piano accordion, however, retained associations with urban Russian and Ukrainian vernacular music throughout the twentieth century (see Gronow 1975, 97).[12] Helmi Harrington and Gerhard Kubik offer the following short history of the accordion and *bayan*'s institutionalization in Soviet vernacular and elite musical practice:

> Although the accordion was well known and popular in the Baltic countries and Russia shortly after its invention—disseminated through trade and travellers as in the rest of the world—during the Soviet period its evolution was largely independent of and different from that of the Western world. The instruments were redesigned to fit the needs of the different cultures; some diatonic instruments became very different from those found in western Europe . . . The principle concert accordion is, however, the chromatic button accordion or bayan; piano accordions and diatonic models are regarded as folk instruments . . . The Communist Party's support for folk music paved the way for the establishment of

a bayan conservatory programme at Kiev Conservatory in 1927; other courses are at the Gnesin Academy of Music, Moscow, at St. Petersburg Conservatory and at the Vladivostok Accordionists Association. (2001)

Harrington and Kubik also describe how the accordion's "slightly later association with the proletarian touring performance ensembles of the former Soviet Union made the accordion acceptable in contexts where other Western instruments were banned." The piano accordion's relationship with Soviet "folk music" practices (in both formal institutionalized contexts and vernacular practice) has resonated into the post-Soviet era.

In DakhaBrakha, Marko Halanevych plays a small piano accordion that would reference—to the knowing listener—the folk accordion of the Soviet past. Halanevych, who has spoken publicly about his limited skills as an accordion player, uses the instrument primarily for short melodic gestures and to add chordal textures to various DakhaBrakha songs. The instrument is incorporated into the sonic texture of DakhaBrakha in a limited, but nonetheless essential way. I interpret the accordion's visual and sonic role within DakhaBrakha as an index of "folk music" of a particular Soviet variety—in contrast to the professionalized accordion culture of the *bayan*, which was meant to "elevate" folk music in accord with Marxist-Leninist ideology, and where elevated playing typically meant virtuosity according to Western art music standards. As a result, this particular performer's public distancing from anything more than basic competence on this instrument takes on a political possibility. Rather than mastery, Halanevych deploys the accordion as a somewhat crude, but effective tool. Rather than prolonging an older ideological mission to "elevate" vernacular musical practice, the unskilled actor-cum-accordionist reinvents an instrument invested with Soviet symbolic power into a post-Soviet object of utility. As part of DakhaBrakha's bricolage-based process, I read the accordion's presence in DakhaBrakha as a gentle subversion of Soviet organological legacies that brought the accordion into prominence as a signifier of improved proletarian culture: instead of showcasing the proletarian instrument's versatility, Halanevych reduces it to a purely auxiliary function, just one soundmark among many.

In "Carpathian Rap," the accordion plays a simple melodic ostinato that bolsters the dance music feel of the track (after the more traditional sound of its opening minute). The accordion's unremarkable, but persistent, presence on the song relegates the icon of Soviet folk music (and, by extension, Soviet sovereign power) to a supporting role. As a soundmark of sovereignty, I read the accordion as representative of a form of latent sovereign power that is incorporated as an essential background element, yet never permitted to dominate.

Global Sounds

The most obvious global soundmark in "Carpathian Rap" is the invocation of rap and the utilization of hip-hop studio production techniques, especially the doubling of rapped vocals. I will not dwell on the many studies of what hip-hop means and how it manifests in various global contexts, but I wish to restate the argument made by many others that global hip-hop exists in a tension. First, it localizes a commercially dominant popular music that traffics in discourses of "realness" but must be molded to reflect local discourses' "authenticity." Second, it retains some of the subaltern oppositional charge of its origins in communities of disenfranchised black Americans; in other words, hip-hop around the world is often used for social critique.[13] It is precisely this tension that I believe the members of DakhaBrakha mean to exploit in their utilization of "Rap" in the song's title and vocal style. Since the song refigures a *spivanka* text from the rural and often exoticized Hutsuls as rap, it ventriloquizes the Hutsul voice through the charged body of hip-hop music, leading to the question of whether this Hutsul *spivanka* narrative has something counterhegemonic about it. I propose that one might hear the rapped narrative—a woman's litany of complaint about the undeserving suitors in her life—re-voiced as twenty-first-century feminist critique. As the ethno-chaos rapper flatly intones the *spivanka*, we might hear her "flipping the script" on this classic *spivanka* subject. Instead of sentimentality, an essential trope of North American "women's culture" (Berlant 2008), the bricolaged *spivanka* suggests an unsentimental distancing from, but simultaneous critique of, failed masculine archetypes in traditional Ukrainian society. In other terms, by remaking the *spivanka* as rap, DakhaBrakha politicizes the traditional gendered dynamics of Hutsul courtship.

The song's other primary globally mediated sonic markers are the piano and cello that are two of DakhaBrakha's core instruments. The genres indexed by these instruments are just as globally dispersed as the sonic-aesthetic markers of hip-hop, but they occupy a very different place in conventional musical hierarchies of value. Though Nina Haranetska's cello is decorated with colorful geometric patterns, her technique is drawn from Western art music. In the band, the cello often provides the bass line, and that is its primary role in "Carpathian Rap."

But Haranetska also frequently takes atmospheric solos on other DakhaBrakha tracks, more often playing with the colors of the instrument than displaying Western art music–style "virtuosity." The piano (or keyboard) in "Carpathian Rap" adds moody, gestural texture—with occasional parlor-jazz flourishes—to the densely layered song. The presence of the piano and the cello literally emplaces the group that could otherwise, given in its instrumentation, be mobile.

Fused in the music of DakhaBrakha, soundmarks from two very differently coded globally mediated genres—hip-hop and Western art music—nonetheless occupy a similar place vis-à-vis the sovereign imaginary produced in "Carpathian Rap." Both genres index forms of cosmopolitanism as well as aspirational values: of commercial success (hip-hop) or perhaps conventional ideas of the musical sublime (Western art music). As soundmarks of sovereignty, they make apparent the aspirational political desires of DakhaBrakha, whose members seek validation through the recognition and consumption of their cosmopolitan Ukrainian iteration of "world music." With the incorporation of such global genres and soundmarks, DakhaBrakha invokes the contemporary cosmopolitan sovereign imaginaries supported by systems of capital.

My interpretation of the soundmarks just described is, admittedly, subjective and perhaps idiosyncratic. I cannot predict how listeners situated in different locations would interpret the semiotically dense layers of sonic gestures, and I think it is safe to assume that the average North American world music fan, for whom DakhaBrakha is likely to be the first encounter with Ukrainian cultural products, would not grok any of these meanings. For Ukrainian listeners, however, the diverse set of soundmarks in a composition like "Carpathian Rap" is likely to trigger a constellation of associations with diverse Ukrainian experiences of statehood. And for the musicians themselves, this aesthetic bricolage—the chaotic mash-up of soundmarks from different times and places—is in line with their stance as reluctant but committed political activists on behalf of Ukrainian statehood. The Hutsul elements of the song recall a particular form of (Western) Ukrainian identity that includes a history of resistance to European, Russian, and Soviet imperial powers, and offers a model of existing resilient Indigenous modernity within the Ukrainian state. The mythical Ukrainian village voice at once indexes the "no place" of imperial Russia as well as the ground zero of iconic Eastern European world music vocality associated with post-socialist Bulgarian women's voices. The accordion indexes Soviet folk culture and, by extension, the homogenizing effects of Soviet cultural policy on the cultural sovereignty of Ukrainians. Rap and the decorative instrumental aspects added by European instruments point toward global markets and cosmopolitan sovereign imaginaries.

Though none of these soundmarks designate specific places or times, they invoke spaces and temporal regimes that evoke various unsettled pasts of Ukrainian history. Through the bricolage of diverse regional and global soundmarks, DakhaBrakha creates a capacious space to accommodate multiple rival histories of regional and global social belonging, crashed together to overcome their irreconcilability and to produce new meanings. In sum, the soundmarks of sovereignty present in "Carpathian Rap" bring into being an aural imaginary of sovereignty that is formed from chaos and, instead of taking sides, is oriented to the future.

"SALGIR BOYU": SOLIDARITY, INCORPORATED

In *The Road* (Шлях), released in December 2016, DakhaBrakha also amplifies stories of Ukrainian sovereignty through soundmarks, albeit using different techniques from those described in "Carpathian Rap." Unlike 2010's *Light*, which preceded the Maidan Revolution (and was therefore created before the band started using its stage to voice political messages), DakhaBrakha's post-Maidan album is wild music with an explicit political project attached. *The Road* circulated with the following message from the band: "This album was created at a very difficult time for our Motherland. We want to dedicate it to those who gave their lives for our freedom, who continue to stand over its guard, and who go the challenging way of a free person without losing their hope."[14] In a 2015 interview, Halanevych added that "the album should be healing for the country." In order to achieve this, the band members incorporated "materials from various corners of Ukraine," especially "those regions currently under occupation." They conceptualized the album as an imagined narrative, focused on the journey of an archetypal merchant (чумак) who travels with his wares (either "salt or fish from Crimea") through various Ukrainian territories. As Halanevych put it, "As the merchant traveled, he might happen upon a wedding in one village, or a funeral in another village, and that's how we envisioned it in our album" (personal communication, March 31, 2017). Merchant songs form a substantial part of the corpus of traditional rural repertoires that DakhaBrakha draws on over the course of the album. The fourth track is a cover of a Crimean Tatar wedding song called "Salgir Boyu," and will be the focus of my analysis here.[15]

As discussed earlier in this book, the Crimean Tatars suffered a traumatic Stalinist deportation on May 18, 1944, as the cataclysm of World War II began to subside. The Crimean Tatars were granted the right to return and resettle Crimea in the last years of Soviet rule (starting in 1987); and they have been, traditionally, the most supportive pro-Ukrainian constituents within the dominant Russophone and militarized context of the Crimean Autonomous Republic of Ukraine, which was, in 2014, illegally annexed by the Russian Federation and remains a disputed territory, though it is currently governed on a day-to-day basis by the Russian Federation. As I argued in the preceding chapter, many Crimean Tatars and ethnic Ukrainians share a "postcolonial solidarity" that is rooted in a long-standing mistrust of Russian state power and the threat it poses. This postcolonial solidarity has endured even despite the repeated failures of the Ukrainian state to govern responsibly—or to defend its sovereign borders—since the dissolution of the USSR in 1991. In a chat exchange with Marko Halanevych, I asked him if the decision to include a Crimean Tatar song on the group's recent album had political overtones. "Certainly," he responded. "This was our act of support and solidarity with the Crimean Tatar people" (personal communication, March 31, 2017). He explained that Nina Haranetska, the cellist and singer, recalled the song from her days as a student-ethnomusicologist, and they decided to create an arrangement while they were in the studio recording *The Road*.

In this analysis, I eschew the taxonomic approach that I applied to "Carpathian Rap" since "Salgir Boyu" does not attempt to chaotically bricolage disparate soundmarks in the same way. In contrast to the hybrid aesthetic of "Carpathian Rap" (produced six years earlier), in which diverse soundmarks collide, the arrangement of "Salgir Boyu" is restrained: cello, playing pizzicato and sul ponticello; accordion; *daré* (Turkic frame drum used in Crimean Tatar traditional music); a vocal timbre aesthetically far from the ringing Central Ukrainian village style; and the insistent repetition of the word "Aman" (which is perhaps the most frequently used lyrical trope of Crimean Tatar and many other Arabic-, Turkic- and Persian-language songs, often used as an exclamation akin to "Oh" or "Ah, my soul"). A hint of "chaos" enters only toward the end of DakhaBrakha's arrangement, as the song accelerates manically toward its conclusion, and as its texture becomes more dense. Rather than invent a new hybrid language that merges global with local soundmarks, here DakhaBrakha reworks a Crimean Tatar song *in the style of DakhaBrakha*—a style that, it merits mention, had become somewhat more coherent and recognizable during the years of frequent touring between the release of the 2010 and 2016 albums. So as DakhaBrakha's signature sound—an ensemble featuring three female vocalists, Halanevych's pliant voice, cello, accordion, piano, and a variety of percussion instruments—became indexical for "ethno-chaos," the musicians deployed their signature sound to pay homage to Crimean Tatars. By incorporating "Salgir Boyu" into *their* existing aesthetic, I hear DakhaBrakha making a potent claim about the rightful place of Crimean Tatar indigenes within the space of Ukrainian civic identity.

I arrive at this interpretation by taking seriously Halanevych's statement that the choice to include a Crimean Tatar song on *The Road* was intended as a statement of "support and solidarity." In their postrevolutionary political awakening, DakhaBrakha's choice to pay homage to Crimean Tatars was made out of respect.

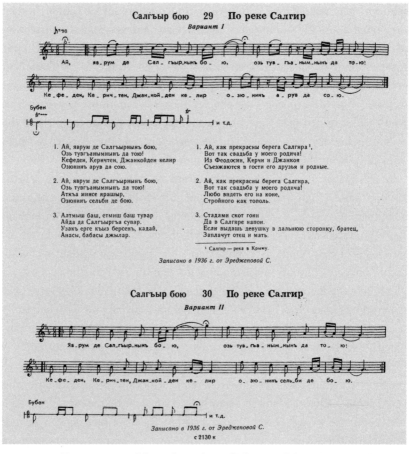

FIGURE 5.3 Two variations of the traditional song "Salgir Boyu" from the 1978 anthology published in Tashkent, Uzbekistan, as *Zvuchyt Khaitarma*, compiled by Y. Sherfedinov.

The group's conscious decision to include the entire song, without the collage-like effects of many of their arrangements, also seems to be a strategy to avoid tokenizing the Indigenous community that has historically been constructed as Ukraine's Orientalized internal other. In other words, creating an ethno-chaos cover of a Crimean Tatar song, DakhaBrakha incorporates a Crimean Tatar song as the dominant soundmark of sovereignty within an emergent sovereign imaginary of postcolonial solidarity. In this sense, the inclusion of a Crimean Tatar wedding song might still be read as a kind of bricolage in the way that it subverts the marginality of Crimean Tatars within the space of the contested Ukrainian state.

"Salgir Boyu," the fourth track of *The Road*, is a well-known traditional song among Crimean Tatars. It compares the beauty of the shores of the Salgir River (which runs through central Crimea, including Simferopol) to the pleasures of a family wedding that brings together guests from far-flung regions of the Crimean peninsula: Feodosia and Kerch in the east; Dzhankoi in the north.[16] Its optimistic lyrics shift in the last stanza, when the singer notes how sad the bride's parents will be when she leaves their home for that of her husband's family (a characteristic theme for a traditional wedding song in many regions of Ukraine). In DakhaBrakha's version, Nina Haranetska sings the lyrics with attention to the correct pronunciation of the words in Crimean Tatar.

FIGURE 5.4 This transcription shows the opening cello ostinato used in the DakhaBrakha rendition of "Salgir Boyu" and gives a sense of the melody as sung by Nina Haranetska. Haranetska appears to run the cello ostinato through an octave drop pedal (in addition to a looping pedal). In the recorded version, the opening also features atmospheric percussion flourishes, and the time of the melody is quite fluid. This serves only as a rough approximation of the feel of the performance.

So it is not in form so much as in style that DakhaBrakha's arrangement of "Salgir Boyu" departs from the customary mood and mode of the Crimean Tatar original. It also avoids the traditional instrumental interludes. A 1976 rendition (captured on video) by the Tashkent-based Ensemble Qaytarma—the exiled Crimean Tatars' equivalent of a Soviet "Song and Dance Folk Orchestra" during the era when they were not permitted to claim "Crimean Tatar" identity—provides a useful comparison.[17] Performed by the singer Fevzi Bilalov, one of the renowned soloists of Qaytarma during the era of exile, the video is staged by the side of a rushing river meant to represent the Salgir that runs through Simferopol. Three women in the modest traditional dress of Crimean Tatars fill jugs with water, while Bilalov proudly struts along the water's edge, gesturing expansively at the natural scene that surrounds him. He sings with an almost operatic vocal quality, as an off-screen instrumental ensemble featuring prominent trumpets, violins, and a dense layer of percussion supplies a rollicking and festive accompaniment. The trumpets punctuate the space between lines of lyrics with interjections of staccato fanfare, while the violins double and harmonize the vocal melody. Between verses, the melodic instruments play an interlude. Throughout, Bilalov sings smilingly of the pleasures of communal gatherings.

In contrast, DakhaBrakha's recording of "Salgir Boyu" sets a meditative and mournful mood for the song. The vocal soloist here, unconventionally, is a woman. Nina Haranetska pitches the song quite high and sings using a reedy and bright vocal timbre that is far from Bilalov's resonant baritone, the voice more typically associated with this (and similar) Crimean Tatar wedding songs. DakhaBrakha's arrangement begins sparely: a looping, minimalist cello ostinato with brief improvisatory interjections from the *daré*, which serves as a Crimean Tatar soundmark. Haranetska's voice enters soon after this mood is established and traces the melody as it snakes from the high "Aman" downward through the course of the lyrics. Atmospheric and meandering melodic solos from the cello and accordion, between verses, bear no resemblance to the structured instrumental interludes from the original song. The song builds incrementally over the course of five minutes, at which point there is a dramatic tonal shift. Suddenly, we hear the band deliver on the "chaos" element of their genre identification, with a new frenzied pace bolstered by intense drumming and layers of vocalizations (including, for the first time in this arrangement, Halanevych's characteristic vocal effect, which uses generic vocables delivered in a style reminiscent of Jamaican toasting).

DakhaBrakha thus remakes a joyous wedding song as a pensive and ultimately frenetic lament. Given the centrality of Crimean Tatar wedding music by Crimean Tatars as a repository of cultural memory and continuity, I interpret this stylistic choice as a conscious lament for the ongoing threats to the cultural sovereignty of the Crimean Tatars. In the preface to a chapter of songs devoted to "lyrical songs, in which different toponyms of Crimea are reflected" in his monumental *Anthology of Crimean Folk Music*, the Crimean Tatar musician and musicologist Fevzi Aliev writes that "in the years of deportation, in my deep conviction, our people were saved from assimilation, fundamentally, by wedding and professional musicians, professional and amateur ensembles, musical personalities" (2001, 141). Aliev's opinion is commonly held among Crimean Tatar repatriates to Crimea, who often told me that weddings—since they were held in domestic spaces and, thus, somewhat protected from the long arm of Soviet cultural policy and censorship—were, especially, venues that kept Crimean Tatar identity alive during the dark decades of exile from the Crimean peninsula. Wedding songs such as "Salgir Boyu," then, occupy a rich symbolic space within contemporary Crimean Tatar culture as soundmarks of Indigenous resilience. With this in mind, DakhaBrakha's inclusion of this wedding song is not only a statement of solidarity with the Crimean Tatar people, but, by the song's rendering as a mournful ballad rather than an up-tempo dance song, it might be interpreted as an expression of melancholic solidarity—because what is shared between these Ukrainians and Crimean Tatars is a common experience of domination under the Soviets and, now, the Russian Federation. It is as if the mournful end of the song's traditional narrative—the bridal lament in an otherwise joyous story—infects the entirety of DakhaBrakha's setting, acknowledging the most recent dislocation of Crimean Tatar people from their homeland in the aftermath of the Russian takeover of 2014.

The song "Salgir Boyu"—a standard in the repertoire of Ensemble Qaytarma and widespread at wedding celebrations during the period of exile—operates as a critical temporal soundmark of sovereignty in that it connotes Indigenous resilience and, by extension, the struggle for Indigenous survival against forms of Soviet and post-Soviet hegemonic power. "Salgir Boyu" is a soundmark in which the layered temporalities it evokes—of a Crimean Tatar "traditional" past, and of resistance to Soviet power—are, arguably, of even greater importance than the places it names.

THE TEMPORAL SOUNDMARK

I have argued that soundmarks of sovereignty draw on distinct temporalities as well as emplaced sounds to rectify the historical power asymmetries that position some communities as "backward," as failures in the present and likely unsustainable into the future. How might such aesthetic projects help to combat the belief that Ukraine itself is illegitimate due to its failures of nationalism, of state-building, or of historical coherence? As I have described in the preceding two examples, the aesthetics of "ethno-chaos" model how the irreconcilable ruptures of the past might be overcome through techniques of bricolage. In other words, the binary-defying principles of aestheticized Wildness enable future-oriented imaginaries that remake the unsettled chaos of the past into a productive chaos of a yet unknown future.

The layered and interdependent temporalities drawn on in ethno-chaos might be fruitfully examined through the metaphor of the palimpsest, as M. Jacqui Alexander, following Ella Shohat, proposed: "Not only is there no fixed past, but various technologies of timekeeping and various narratives of time can exist within the same temporality" (2006, 190). In thinking of time as a palimpsest, it is the "imperfect erasure" of the past that allows it to haunt the present, "conjoin[ing] practices that appear bounded by binary, materialized temporalities and spaces so that they constitute an ensemble and work in mutually paradoxical ways" (192). Alexander's notion of palimpsestic time resonates with how Svetlana Boym (following Walter Benjamin) understood the "unfinished critical project of modernity . . . not as a teleology of progress or transcendence but as a superimposition and coexistence of heterogenous times" (2001, 30). Katherine Verdery further pointed out that "the social construction of time must be seen as a political process" (1996, 40). In her study of "etatization," the term she coined to explain how the socialist Romanian state partitioned and made claims on the private time of its subjects, Verdery conceived of time as an ever-diminishing resource rooted in the present. In the palimpsestic temporal view that I embrace here, the temporality of the soundmark is at once a ludic and a political resource, as musicians experiment with temporalities and fuse them to make a political claim. Ethno-chaos offers a way to bring rival pasts together, criticize the present, and imagine the future, while binding listeners together in the shared and fleeting durational time that is a core feature of music as an expressive form.[18]

Musical practice, a temporally bound expressive form and social practice that structures and occupies time in an unfolding present, opens new ways to think of palimpsestic time scales of the past and future. The place of "traditional" music in the *etno-muzyka* that becomes ethno-chaos illuminates this. Since tradition, as Alexander writes, "is ostensibly placed in another time, one that is not contemporaneous with 'our' own," the reinvention of tradition through musical practices results in the "scrambling" of temporalities and allows the unfinished work of the pre- and para-modern to coexist with the "unfolding project of modernity" (2006, 190; see also Shohat and Stam 2014, 293). Musical sounds associated with tradition introduce ruptures into the temporality of the present and its inexorable march forward. Thus, what Walter Benjamin called "homogeneous empty time" (queer theorists have labeled this "chrononormativity")[19]—which describes a propulsive movement through calendrical time that is closely bound up in the ways that national myths are spun—can be troubled through musical temporalities that creatively reinvent tradition in an unfolding present.

Treating sonic gestures as markers of alternate temporalities raises the question of whether sound itself can be thought of as palimpsestic, an intellectual exercise undertaken by Martin Daughtry in his experiment of "transducing the concept of the palimpsest into the realm of the auditory" (2017, 48). In his essay, Daughtry submits his own writing process—as well as various literary and sonic materials—to excavation in pursuit of the "multiple acts of erasure, effacement, occupation, displacement, collaboration, and reinscription that are embedded in music composition, performance, and recording" (53). His premise is that "musical materials—scores, recordings, even live performances—[bear] the residue of complex networks of human and nonhuman actors, of untold dialectics between far-flung people and technologies, structures and agencies. The musical artifact is thus merely the uppermost layer of an acoustic palimpsest" (61). Yet, as Daughtry ultimately concedes, the acoustic palimpsest fails as a metaphorical equivalent to the textual palimpsest. He identifies four "serious limitations" of the acoustic palimpsest as heuristic, the first of which is the problem of temporality. He writes, "Textual palimpsests involve layers of writing that were put on one after another, with the most recent one always dominating. The palimpsests that inspired this metaphor thus encourage a unidirectional historical perspective: palimpsestic texts acquire their layers one after another, as time marches forward. You will have noticed by now that the audible and inaudible layers of which I speak have no such temporal unity joining them together. This lack of correspondence weakens the vitality of the metaphor" (78).[20]

Yet in Shohat's and Alexander's conception of "palimpsestic time," it is precisely the Benjaminian "flashes" of the past in the present, the "scrambling" of temporalities, that endows the metaphor of the palimpsest with its conceptual power. I submit that musical sound, unfolding as it necessarily has to along a bounded and temporary present, contains nested temporalities that can also be understood as palimpsestic. That is, musical time holds within it multiple temporalities. Or, to follow from Elizabeth Freeman by way of Halberstam, musical sound allows for the "temporal binding of past and present," for the creation of eccentric new archives, genealogies, or reinvented traditions (Freeman 2010, 85; see Halberstam 2006). Sonic gestures of Wildness embedded in ethno-chaos at once index the "archaic," the "pure," and "unrestrained" sounds of a mythical past while simultaneously grounding those sounds in the present through acts of performance and audition.

It is in considering the audible future that the limits of the acoustic palimpsestic metaphor become most apparent, since both theories of palimpsestic time and sound look backward but ultimately terminate in the present. However, following Muñoz, I assert that the aesthetics and practice of ethno-chaos have a future-oriented "vastness of potentiality" (2009, 141)—or that, by drawing together uneven temporalities, the aesthetics of ethno-chaos conjure a "future in the present" (55). DakhaBrakha resourcefully draws on, parodies, repackages, salvages, or recuperates the musical sounds of previous regimes in the quest for a new vocabulary from which a future might be patched together. The group does this, in part, by cross-pollinating various Ukrainian soundmarks of sovereignty with forms of global popular music, fusing a new formula for commercialized world music.

WORLD MUSIC REDUX

The world music market boom of the 1980s catapulted such famous, even notorious albums as Paul Simon's *Graceland* or Ry Cooder's *Buena Vista Social Club* to the top of the charts. Since then, many scholars have engaged with the often troubling dynamics of a field of cultural production that smacks of neocolonial logics of exploitation, in which famous "Western" stars collaborate with "non-Western" musicians to create consumable objects that overwhelmingly benefit their Western creators (see Taylor 1997 and 2014 for an overview of this critique). David Novak has chronicled the rise of "World Music 2.0," the circulation of digitally remediated musical commodities distributed through online networks. Novak observes that World Music 2.0's online listenership had "realigned against hegemonic frameworks of intellectual property" to justify the free trade of "rediscovered" popular musics from around the world (2011, 604). I propose that DakhaBrakha offers one example of a revamped World Music 1.0, in which the group has harnessed the language and tools of world music in its first iteration, but collapsed the expectation of "collaboration" or distance in projects of hybridity (Meintjes 1990). Instead, by knowingly wilding themselves while drawing on the sounds of distant others, the performers have gained access to a platform through which they can assert a political claim. Through their wild music, they assert that their place in the world is not peripheral. And further, that the ways of life expressed through wild sounds are valuable. They dismantle the undifferentiated "world" of "world music" by using the very tools and techniques of the world music industry to situate themselves *specifically*, as Ukrainian musicians. This strikes me as the kind of move that postcolonial theorists would find satisfying: Can the subaltern speak (from their marginalized Ukrainian position)? By mastering the tools of commodified world music, in effect, they are learning to sing.

But such a conclusion is too celebratory. First, it would be disingenuous to consider the members of DakhaBrakha as "subalterns," given their origins in the eminently literate and urbane world of Ukrainian experimental theater. (I surmise that they themselves would cringe at such a characterization.) Instead, one must imagine scales of nested subalternity. That such cosmopolitan musicians draw on and amplify the voices of regional subalterns such as Hutsuls, Ukrainian villagers, or Crimean Tatars could be interpreted as a form of urban-on-rural exploitation, as some Ukrainian ethnomusicologists argue in private. Further, DakhaBrakha's complicity with and success within a contemporary world music industry that is governed by Euro-American capitalism (including the hegemonic norms of intellectual property that can both protect and, at times, stifle artists) summons the question of whether the object of Ukraine's "postcolonial desire" aligns with the "glittering Euramerican MTV-and-Coca-Cola beast" rather than the Russian sphere of influence (Moore 2001, 118). The name DakhaBrakha does, as I hinted in the introduction, connect the performers metonymically with global capitalist transactionalism. The trajectory of their career underscores this as well: they first made their name as "experimental musicians" who were awarded a 2010 Sergey Kuryokhin Contemporary Art Prize (a prestigious award given by the St. Petersburg cultural elite), and only later did they rebrand as a "world music band." This is not only a shift of audience, but also a reorientation toward one of the surviving lucrative industries for contemporary musicians.

Does their participation in the infrastructure of the Euro-American world music industry limit or enhance the potentiality of their wild music? In other words, is there anything in DakhaBrakha's output that seeks to provincialize Europe in addition to Russia, or do the performers mean, instead, to fully embrace the commodification of their wild music *as* world music?

For ambitious artists, there is no reasonable safe harbor from the machine of globalized capitalism, yet DakhaBrakha's temporal soundmarks suggest a sovereign imaginary that rejects the binary modes of affiliation—Europe or Russia—presented to Ukraine. This animates the revolutionary heart of the group's aesthetic-cum-political mission. Soundmarks of sovereignty such as those described in "Carpathian Rap" and "Salgir Boyu" offer a window into the aesthetic techniques that DakhaBrakha uses to craft its brand of emergent cosmopolitan Ukrainian identity: by colliding times and places, the musicians revive deep and rival pasts of Ukraine in order to look to the future, while welcoming the sounds of commodified global popular music. In its brand of ethno-chaos, DakhaBrakha delivers not only aesthetic hybridity and eclecticism; it also imagines a varied *etno*-scape, and invites a "chaos" of ongoing experimentation with the political future of Ukraine, one that might *not* exist fully in the grip of unrestrained capitalism.

As I have argued, the soundmarks of sovereignty that I hear in the ethno-chaos of DakhaBrakha work as the anticipatory affective structures that Muñoz links to his idea of "concrete utopias," or the potentiality of striving for a better future, despite the (perhaps bleak) conditions of the present (2009, 3). This chapter has explored the temporal and territorial dimensions of the soundmarks fused in DakhaBrakha's ethno-chaos, and the chaotic pluralism that its aesthetic projects conjure. I interpret these aesthetic techniques as a form of rebuttal to the discourse that characterizes Ukraine's rival pasts as irreconcilable. Portnov writes persuasively of how "[h]istorical narratives are used by politicians in Ukraine as instruments of division, rather than consensus" (2013, 248). "The situational—and in many ways liberating—pluralism of memory that has formed in the country functions not so much as a space of dialogue, but rather as a collision of different, closed, and quite aggressive narratives that exist because they cannot destroy their competitors. Each of the narratives, nationalist and Soviet alike, avoids questions of responsibility: for pogroms, repressions, or punitive operations. The responsibility for all horrors and crimes is passed on to external forces: the Kremlin, the NKVD, the Polish underground, the Nazis" (248).

Rather than historical narratives, these Ukrainian ethno-chaos musicians collide fragments of competing pasts to foster a sonic dissensus, one that, in Ranciere's (2013) terms, is the very basis of politics. Through such sonic dissensus, the collision of apparently irreconcilable pasts generates an aesthetics of transformation, a product of Ukrainian modernity on its own terms—not filtered through the gaze of neighboring states and entities. This ethno-chaos, this sonic product of Ukrainian modernity, grapples with these clashing legacies as a means of imagining the future.

CONCLUSION

Dreamland

Becoming Acoustic Citizens

How selfless this unisonance feels! If we are aware that others are
singing these songs precisely when and as we are, we have no idea who
they may be, or even where, out of earshot, they are singing.
Nothing connects us all but imagined sound.

Benedict Anderson, Imagined Communities

Dreamland (Kraïna Mrij / Країна Мрій) is a summer festival that has been held on the outskirts of Kyiv since 2004. It was founded by the legendary Soviet Ukrainian punk rocker-cum-impresario Oleh Skrypka.[1] In 2015, the festival was held at a Soviet-era "architectural museum under the open sky" in Pyrohovo, a short bus or *marshrutka* ride out of the city. The festival, which draws a predominantly middle-class urban crowd due to its location and rather steep entrance fees, features musical groups in a variety of *etno-muzyka* genres. Many attendees dress in clothes that display some Ukrainian "folk elements" (such as embroidered shirts and flower crowns). Often, these are the very same folk elements that once marked a monolithic idea of Ukrainian culture and identity in the pantheon of Soviet "folk"; in Dreamland they are largely scrubbed of this history, recontextualized by cosmopolitan urbanites as icons of belonging to an independent Ukraine.

Despite the somewhat homogenous display of sartorial "Ukrainian-ness," the festival rejects a narrow ethno-nationalism as its premise. This is most visible through the festival's inclusion of a dedicated "Crimean Area" that features

Crimean Tatar music, dance, traditional crafts, and cuisine, as well as through the incorporation of Crimean Tatar and other non-ethnic Ukrainians into its programming on the main festival stage. In 2015, the festival included the Crimean Area for its fifth consecutive year. The area was advertised in the festival booklet in the following way: "Do you also long for Crimea? For many Ukrainians, summer vacation was long associated with its beautiful landscapes. And while the summer break will never be 'as it once was,' we decided to remedy this at least a little bit" (press materials).

The subtext was clear—Russian consolidation over Crimea had become entrenched by that summer—but a question resonates: *How* might those halcyon summertimes of the past be restored, even "a little bit"? Inviting the Ukrainian citizenry to return to an imaginary Crimea of the past—to indulge in a Ukrainian Dreamland—the organizers of the festival suggested that participating in musical and other creative-social practices could provide the means to temporarily thwart the temporal and spatial barriers posed by the overheated geopolitics of the present.

FIGURE C.1 The Crimean Tatar flag with its *taraq-tamğa* insignia waves as Elvira Sarakhalil performs with the Acoustic Quartet from Kharkiv at the Dreamland festival, 2015. Photograph by Maria Sonevytsky.

A year earlier, in June 2014—as the revolutionary zeal of the Maidan Revolution had subsided, and the crises in Crimea and the eastern borderlands had begun to congeal into frozen conflicts—a British journalist interviewed Oleh Skrypka, the founder of Dreamland. Skrypka was born in Soviet Tajikistan to parents who had some ethnic ties to Ukraine but had lived in other regions of the USSR. When Skrypka was still a child, his family relocated to Murmansk, where he formed his first rock band. In 1987, he commenced his studies at the Kyiv Polytechnic Institute, where the punk-rock band V.V. also came together. That band was known in its early years for *stiob*-ish songs such as the absurdist hit "Dances" (Танці) (on *stiob*, see Yurchak 2005).[2] After living in self-imposed "creative exile" in France from 1991 to 1997, Skrypka returned to Ukraine. In the 2014 conversation with the journalist, Skrypka articulated a rather unusual view of citizenship that explains in part his vision for the space that is Dreamland: "My role is as a singer, but if the Russians come I will take up arms, everyone will." He talked of the deep Ukrainian and traditional Cossack love of freedom. Skrypka was born in Tajikistan, but he, like several others I met, says that he "made an existential decision to become Ukrainian" (Culshaw 2014).

Despite the fact that his decision to "become Ukrainian" was "existential," Skrypka—a wealthy, influential, and cosmopolitan celebrity—claimed that he would fight for Ukraine as part of his citizenly duty. Skrypka outlined a volitional notion of citizenship that binds his musical identity ("a singer") to an imperiled state by pledging to defend its territorial sovereignty. His pledge, to be sure, is mediated through a national myth of the Ukrainian "love of freedom," but that national myth enables this Ukrainian-by-choice to attach himself to Ukraine as a sovereign state. Skrypka, whose status affords him greater possibilities for mobility than nearly any citizen of Ukraine, claims that he would put his bare life on the line for his adopted state. Why would any rational subject make such a choice? What technologies of the self did Skrypka undertake to bind himself to a state considered fragile, or "failing," by some metrics? Conversely, which political techniques exercised by the weak and corrupt Ukrainian state could have assuaged any hesitations he might have about allying himself with a perennial loser of global geopolitics? In the same 2014 article just quoted, the theater and musical producer Vlad Troitsky (who was born in Soviet Siberia, and who also elected to "become Ukrainian") was reported to say that Ukraine "can be the center of a new feeling, a new civilization" (echoing, by chance, the same claim articulated by Johann Gottfried Herder as Ukraine's "wild" potential in the epigraph to this book). What wild sovereign imaginaries are accessed here by those who envision a future that is "better than"—in Troitsky's words—either Europe or Russia?

This chapter offers a closing meditation on the possible linkages between wild music, future-oriented sovereign imaginaries, and the acoustically rooted practices of listening and sounding that comprise what I call *acoustic citizenship*. This idea of acoustic citizenship—especially as it is shaped by the cage-rattling possibilities of Wildness—has deep resonances for me as I write this conclusion in the autumn of 2018. We face a global crisis of liberal democracy: the rise of authoritarianism in the United States; the defection of Britain from the European Union; the emboldening of right-wing and neofascist movements throughout Western and Eastern Europe and, most recently, Brazil; and the entrenchment of illiberal regimes masked as "democratic," enabled by the rapacious neoliberal capitalism that has "swallowed the world."[3] Meanwhile, experiments in state socialism—at least on the level of the command economy—do not exist in any unmixed form that lies outside of networks of global capital. As the title of a *Guardian* op-ed by the eminent Marxist historian Eric Hobsbawm mused in 2009, "Socialism has failed. Now capitalism is bankrupt. So what comes next?"[4]

It is unrealistic to posit any definitive answers to this question. But, following the promise of wild music to its logical end, I want to examine the possibility that acoustic citizenship—as a model of citizenly affiliation premised on those subjects who constitute themselves and are constituted through their participation in listening and sounding publics—may outline the horizons of Wildness as a form of governance that reimagines the world beyond the oppositional forms of capitalism and socialism, or democracy and tyranny. This requires, as Kristen Ghodsee writes, that we allow political theories "to exist as ideal types even after they have become tainted by the histories of their applications" (2017, 185). She advocates that we move past our "red hangover" toward an honest assessment of "the pros and cons of both liberal democracy and state socialism in an effort to promote a system that gives us the best of both" (200). In other words, to paraphrase a member of the Dakh Daughters, we must look past the sanctimoniousness and hypocrisy of the West and the repressiveness and corruption of the East for other possibilities.

The various ways that musical sounds in circulation can be interpreted as signs of sovereignty (that, in turn, enable citizens to attach themselves to collectivities such as the state) has been a core subject of this book, yet my focus has rested primarily on the future-oriented sovereign imaginaries made audible through wide-ranging examples of wild *etno-muzyka*. By examining the question of citizenship in this concluding chapter, I want to address how everyday musical practices reflect the constant choice that some citizens make to remain attached to a state, even as it flounders, oppresses, excludes, disappoints, and fails. While the bald facts of post-Soviet Ukrainian demographic attrition and its myriad present-day crises—the emigration of both elite and precariat classes who seek opportunities elsewhere; the desire of some Ukrainian citizens in the eastern borderlands to become Russian subjects; rampant poverty; various medical emergencies (HIV, alcoholism, opioid abuse); the hybrid warfare conducted by Russia in the media as well as on the front—conjure a depressing reality that would make it understandable to reject Ukrainian legitimacy, my gaze remains trained on those Ukrainians who invest in the state project despite its persistent structural failures, but without resorting to a politics of xenophobia and hatred. Among these are the musicians who pledge to defend Ukraine, as well as the youth music festival audiences who come together in moments of conviviality to conjure a Dreamland.

ACOUSTIC CITIZENSHIP

I propose the idea of acoustic—rather than musical—citizenship for two primary reasons. First, despite the strenuous ethnomusicological assertion that listening is a form of musical competence (a view I fully endorse), a term such as "musical citizenship" suggests to me an exclusionary domain where only self-identified "musicians"—those with formal training, or whose livelihood is derived from musical performance—have the ability (or the duty) to be musical citizens. The idea of acoustic citizenship, I hope, expands beyond this to a more encompassing zone of inclusion: one in which subjects *elect* to participate in the "audible entanglements" that, according to Jocelyne Guilbault, "assemble social relations, cultural expressions, and political formations" (2005, 41). Rather than being coerced through the apparatus of the state, acoustic citizens volunteer to be drawn into the webs of signification spawned through the mutually constituted practices of listening and sounding.[5] I assert that wild sounds—which often encode histories of desire, in myriad forms—lend depth and meaning to the sensorium through which acoustic citizens attach themselves to the state.

But the distinction I mean to make here, between "music" and what I parse as "musical sound" is more than just pedantic. This book has treated music as a constellation of practices, techniques, and forms of knowledge: as performance, audition, gesture, art object, convention, aesthetic, commodity, mediatized spectacle, embodied knowledge, acoustic material, or circulating sound. Each of these dimensions of music is defined to some degree through the presence of sound (ephemeral, inscribed, interpreted, resonant), yet "musical sound" lays emphasis on the varieties of deliberate acts of sounding that cut across these practices, techniques, and forms of knowledge. Within the interdisciplinary "sonic turn" that attempts to restore a fuller sensorium to our understanding of the past and present, I wish to center sounds framed as "musical" within that interdisciplinary space while avoiding the object-oriented ontology that reduces music to the fallacy of "the music itself" (or, as the case may be, "the sound itself") (cf. Sakakeeny 2015; Porcello 2010). Yet, since acoustic citizens may draw on sounds that are not automatically assumed to be "musical" to make political claims—as in protest actions, with the banging of pots or strategic uses of silence (Abe 2016; Kunreuther 2018; Sterne 2012)—I wish to retain some distinction between "musical" and "extramusical" sounds, while asserting the capaciousness of what *can* be construed as "musical sound" (see also Bohlman 2016). Acoustic citizenship positions sonic materiality in relation to participatory practices of listening and sounding. Acoustic citizenship is meant to include sounds construed as both musical and extramusical. It foregrounds presence but does not depend on it (acoustic citizens, I would argue, are also formed through practices of private listening and sounding). But regardless of how sounds are produced and interpreted, acoustic citizenship is premised on the interdependence of the social with the sonic. It foregrounds "the experiential dimensions of citizenship and the *practices* that link private identity and experience to the public sphere" (Barney 2007, 39, cited in Lacey 16).

There are some important limitations to the idea of acoustic citizenship. First, I acknowledge that this idea of acoustic citizenship is susceptible to critiques of audism in that it may seem premised on an idealized ability to hear sound, though I hope that it could extend to other modes of apprehending sound through vibration or new technologies of auditory perception (see Friedner and Helmreich 2012). I want to stress that I understand acoustic citizenship as only one form of sensory citizenship that can be subsumed into or experienced alongside other modes of citizenly belonging, including those that have been defined as biological (Petryna 2002), cultural (Rosaldo 1994; Eisenberg 2012), or intimate (Stokes 2017).[6] Second, due to the premise of its volitional attachment to the state, the concept of acoustic citizenship stands in tension with transnational notions of flexible citizenship that are motivated through "cultural logics of capitalist accumulation, travel, and displacement that induce the subject to respond fluidly and opportunistically to changing political-economic conditions" (Ong 1999, 6). Instead of such "opportunism," acoustic citizens accept the risks of staying attached to a precarious state, though this does not preclude them from being cosmopolitan in their orientations. Despite remaining attached to an idea of statehood, it is possible for acoustic citizens to invest in the possibility of a world-renewing Wildness that harbors skepticism of the state; an investment in the persistent liminality of Wildness *as* sovereign imaginary.

Citizens become acoustic citizens, then, through volitional practices of listening and sounding in public. Citizenship as "a mode of belonging by choice" has been examined previously by the anthropologist Greg Urban. Urban positions volitional against ascriptive citizenship, and asserts that "the sense of belonging in communities, as experienced by individuals, depends on representations or signs" that, through their circulation, create communities (2008, 312). The relative "success" of models of communal belonging is predicated on signs that circulate and produce meaning. Urban argues that citizenship, at least as it is defined in European social contract theory derived from Thomas Hobbes and Immanuel Kant, is an especially potent vehicle for forming attachments because it involves a volitional sense of belonging. Urban's framework does not account for the structural limits to volitional citizenship (since it is obviously not true that the majority of humans today can freely choose any citizenship they desire), nor does he examine the circulation of signs at smaller scales than those of "citizenship" (he compares "clans" and "classes" as alternate models of belonging). The structural limits of the right to citizenship—embodied by the crisis of the refugee and the stateless—lies at the heart of Hannah Arendt's (1976 [1951]) attempts to grapple with precisely these limits of choice; she examines the figure of the refugee and stateless person with relation to the sovereign "exception" (see also Agamben 1998, 131–35).

In the introduction to this book, I described how an audience of festivalgoers at the 2014 ArtPóle remade an evening of *avtentyka* as a collective demonstration of border-defying solidarity, through a participatory rendition of the Ukrainian national anthem accompanied by Crimean Tatar musicians. While it is likely that the crowd's spontaneous performance of the anthem (punctuated by Turkic instrumental flourishes from the Crimean Tatar trio) alienated some festivalgoers—which also raises the question of who is excluded from "becoming Ukrainian"—it also fostered a temporary community of acoustic citizens who raised their voices in fleeting unisonance in order to imagine another world.

In a series of lectures on "The Musical Citizen" (2017), Martin Stokes elucidated the parallels between the limits of inclusion in musical communities and in communities of citizenship (which are premised on exclusion). Paraphrasing Stokes, I ask: If there are acoustic citizens, then who are acoustic noncitizens? In other words, if acoustic citizenship is purely volitional, who might be excluded from having the choice of, in Skrypka's words, "becoming Ukrainian"?

Moments of tension observed during Dreamland in 2015 are instructive here. As Elvira, a Crimean Tatar singer backed by a band from Kharkiv (a large city in Eastern Ukraine), spoke into the microphone in Russian, an audience member heckled her for speaking the "language of the occupiers." Taken aback, Elvira paused, and the frontman of her backing band seized the mic to defend her. He asked the audience member to empathize with Elvira's experience, and ended by proclaiming that "it's easier to be a hero here than in Crimea"—indicating that, if the heckler felt so strongly about language politics, he should take his battle to the front. Perhaps this is an instance of "agonistic democracy" (in Chantal Mouffe's sense) in action. But according to Mouffe, the agonism that sustains true democracy is a struggle to replace existing hegemonies with others. These new hegemonic forms may not be known yet, however, so the place of wild sovereign imaginaries can be central in determining what new hegemonies will ascend.

Beyond the struggle over language, a bigger question of exclusion lies in the genre constraints posed by a festival dedicated to the malleable, but nonetheless limited, forms of *etno-muzyka*. That is, those Ukrainian citizens who do not consume or engage in any way with *etno-muzyka*—which I would postulate is a majority of the Ukrainian population, given the dominance of non-*etno-muzyka* genres in the media and on the radio—would not be compelled by the particular politics of interiority (*etno-*) and exteriority (*-muzyka*, that is, rock, pop, punk, hip-hop, and so on) to which *etno-muzyka* gives form. Therefore, the kind of volitional acoustic citizenship that gives form to Wildness *as* sovereign imaginary is available only to those open to listening and sounding in particular ways.

This book has attempted to demonstrate the interpretive domains that open when we attend to the sonic and aesthetic dimensions of emergent sovereignties. Much of this argument rests on the premise that many citizens desire forms of sovereignty and that they volitionally attach themselves to the state. Popular music studies has established a well-worn trope of popular music as embodying desires—be they libidinal (Whiteley 2006; Waksman 2001), identity- and self-fashioning (Kheshti 2015; Frith 1996), or in dynamic tension with late capitalist consumerism and postmodern nostalgia (Fox 1992; Feld 2000). In this book I have sought to examine the work that popular music—especially the hybrid form of popular music known as *etno-muzyka* (ethno-music / етно-музика) in Ukraine, which fuses Indigenous musical styles with global pop music forms—does to express desires for the political; specifically, for the ways of life that are afforded through structures of governance. This returns us to a core contention of ethnomusicology that the political "is not merely an adjunct to the sound but embedded in it" (Meintjes 1990, 38). As listeners affix meanings to music-in-circulation, sounds may transmute into codes of sovereign desire.

DOES UKRAINE HAVE A FUTURE?

In the documentary film "Free People" (Вільні Люди), the musician Taras Kompanichenko—a practitioner of the *kobza* and a key figure in the revival of Ukrainian bard repertoires—speaks directly to the camera: "This is the third revolution of my life. The first was 1988–1991 [fall of the USSR], 2004 [Orange Revolution], and now [2013]. All of them have to do with the question of whether there should or should not be a Ukraine. Now my son is sixteen . . . We want freedom, respect for human life."

Today, Ukrainians are left with this question: What did these revolutions accomplish? Many Ukrainians would answer bitterly: very little, beyond a pervasive condition of revolutionary fatigue. Yet the question of whether there should or should not be a Ukraine persists only because a sizable number of Ukrainians believe the answer is yes. But how should that Ukraine police its inclusions and exclusions? How should state sovereignty—which remains the default norm for the international juridico-political order—be managed if the state itself (its institutions, its political class, its inability to provide resources to its citizens, or even to exercise a monopoly on the use of violence within its borders) is so fragile that it could fail? Legal scholar Rosa Ehrenreich Brooks posits that "weak, failing, and failed states are not the exception in many parts of the world. They are the norm, and have been since their inception" (2005, 1174). The anthropologist Catherine Wanner, responding to the crisis in Ukraine, asserts that the failures of state sovereignty in Ukraine reveal its fragility "everywhere" (2014). In 2018, as we witness the steady erosion of liberal democratic norms in tandem with the forceful and grasping reassertion of state sovereignty ("America First"), I feel the urgency of asking, "What comes next?"

Repeated Ukrainian attempts to conform to international ideals of state sovereignty—those drawn from European nation-states—have played out through frequent revolutions. These revolutions have failed. Perhaps this is, as Tlostanova and Mignolo argue, because the "modern idea of revolution [is] obsolete" in the era of neoliberalism and "polycentric capitalism." In other words, because it is too entangled in webs of global capital, the state can never be fully overtaken from within. But the second reason Tlostanova and Mignolo posit brings us closer to the transformative notion of Wildness-*as*-sovereign-imaginary. They assert that the idea of revolution suggests a teleology of progress and development "within the realm of sameness." When the entire globe is implicated in the "colonial matrix of power . . . the very idea of revolution (a keyword in the vocabulary of modernity) lost its historical possibilities." Instead, they propose a "decolonial option," in which local epistemologies are mined for their transformative potentiality (2012, 18–19). Following this cue, my aim in this book has been to center various local Ukrainian epistemologies through various iterations of "wild music," to witness how Ukrainian musicians and audiences strategically remediate tropes of exoticism in order to imagine the future of sovereignty in Ukraine. Discursive Wildness, the master trope of my argument, has operated in this sense as a "border epistemology" that refuses limited binary choices.

In the idiosyncratic archive I have constructed throughout this book, this master trope of Wildness has shape-shifted, from the auto-exoticizing kitsch and pragmatic patriotism of Ruslana's wild music, to the freak cabaret's creative recoding of Hutsul tropes on the Maidan stage, to the Crimean Tatar Indigenous radio's strategic branding of "Eastern music," to the ungovernable vocality of *avtentyka* singers on reality television, to the export form of "ethno-chaos" architected by DakhaBrakha. In all of these cases, Wildness rebels against the constraints—both musical and political—imposed on it, but is nonetheless articulated within these constraints, at times at the risk of reinscribing forms of essentialism, exoticism, or nationalism. Unable to break its frame, Wildness nonetheless consistently operates as a technology of escape, as a future-orientated promise that might finally release an imperiled state such as Ukraine from the "colonial matrix of power" that situates it on the perpetual limen of either the authoritarian East or the liberal democratic West.

For one final iteration of this argument about wild music, acoustic citizenship, and sovereignty, I return to the place where I began, where mass-mediated "democratainment" meets geopolitics in an annual pageant of song.

WILDNESS, REVISITED

My interest in Wildness as a Ukrainian discourse began in 2004, when Ruslana's Eurovision victory with the song "Wild Dances" piqued my interest about what she intended with her exoticizing depictions of Hutsuls. It led me to ask how Wildness was received by the Hutsuls she was ostensibly representing, but it also made me follow the resonances of Wildness in other musical expressions as musicians continued to make political claims. In 2016, the Crimean Tatar singer Jamala, representing Ukraine, won the Eurovision Song Contest through a performance of another kind of wild music.[7] Her performance destabilized the trope of "friendly competition" that the ESC has staged since 1956, when its founding mission was to soothe Europe following the abject ravages of World War II.

Jamala's song, "1944," made specific reference to the Stalinist mass deportation of the Crimean Tatars from Crimea during World War II, but played on the metanarrative of longing that has defined Crimean Tatar Indigenous modernity (Sonevytsky 2019).[8] Jamala dedicated the song to her great-grandmother, who died during the deportation. Its chorus used lyrics from a song called "Ey, Güzel Qirim!" (Oh, Beautiful Crimea!), which originated during the period of Soviet exile (1944–1987) as a protest song and serves today as an anthem of Crimean Tatar resilience.[9] Thus, fusing together various soundmarks of sovereignty drawn from Crimean Tatar experience, "1944" articulated a just ambiguous enough political claim to enrage the Russian media and political establishment. Russia sought to ban the song from the competition on the grounds that it was a "political" comment on Russia's annexation of Crimea. ("Political songs" are not allowed in the competition according to the rules of the European Broadcasting Union [EBU].[10]) Ukraine countered with the argument that the song made reference only to a distant history of trauma, and was therefore "apolitical." After the EBU determined that the song did not "contain political speech," Jamala went on to win the competition. This victory was widely interpreted as the European public's rebuke of Russian aggression toward Crimea, and, more broadly, as an affirmation of the human rights of Indigenous peoples everywhere (Uehling 2016).[11]

In the ongoing war of Russian disinformation in Ukraine, the Eurovision Song Contest remains a perennial target for fabricated Russian news stories. In fact, as students of Ukrainian politics have long been aware, many Russian internet-age techniques of hybrid war were first piloted in Ukraine, where they deepened existing social divides and—even more significantly—have called into question basic norms about what kinds of knowledge are verifiable. As our understanding of how the 2016 US presidential election (in addition to elections in other European countries) was impacted by Russian meddling, we should not dismiss the ways in which even the most seemingly banal realms of popular culture can be exploited to sow confusion or circulate "fake news."[12]

The Eurovision Song Contest, a mass-mediated spectacle of pop pageantry, appears to remain of propagandistic use to Russian online trolls and Putin-allied media. To wit: in the furor and fallout from Jamala's triumph at Eurovision, Russian-generated stories purported to expose Ukrainian corruption with respect to the competition, or put forward paranoid theories about how the "homosexual West" is eroding the traditional (heterosexual) morality of Russians.[13] The Ukrainian fact-checking operation StopFake—a reputable enterprise run through Kyiv Mohyla University's journalism program that works to rebut fabricated Russian news stories—has created and circulated a series of "bingo cards" intended to help Ukrainian audiences recognize the recurring tropes that constitute Russian-generated "fake news." One such common trope, frequently featured on the cards, is "Something about Eurovision." (Therefore, when a dubious story about Eurovision appears, viewers are one step closer to "Bingo!")[14]

Unlike the internal orientation of the Dreamland festival that opened this conclusion, where Ukrainian citizens were invited to imagine a Ukraine healed from its recent geopolitical fracture, Jamala's staging of "Ukraine" was developed for the benefit of outsiders, specifically the Eurovision-viewing public. Much post-Eurovision media analysis argues that, through their votes, the television public of the forty-two participating competitor states in 2016 forcefully rejected the politics of Russian occupation.[15] But I am reluctant to reduce Jamala's victory to such stark terms; I do not view the victory as an implicit embrace of Ukraine by the European liberal public. I hear instead an iteration of Wildness in practice, one that calls into question the very rules of the game and, while doing so, invites a broad public of television viewers to forge a temporary solidarity around one version of Ukrainian acoustic citizenship. If we agree that this is wild music, then it is wild music that attempts to reach beyond the internal discourses of Ukrainian otherness, to establish citizenly solidarities relationally among a diverse listening public that is not limited by territorial sovereignty.

Throughout this book, I have argued that Wildness informs emergent sovereign imaginaries by destabilizing the hegemonies of the present. Normative "Western" values and institutions—democracy, the nation-state, freedom, the free market, equality, human rights, dignity—are, in effect, called into question,

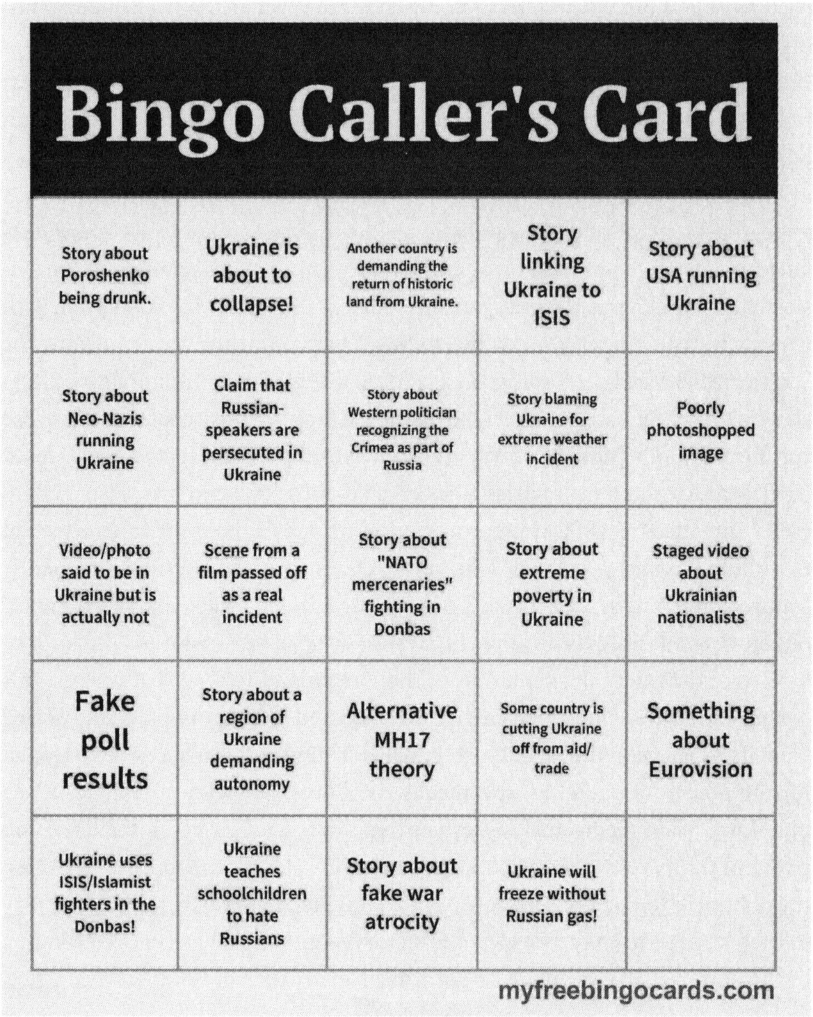

Bingo Caller's Card

Story about Poroshenko being drunk.	Ukraine is about to collapse!	Another country is demanding the return of historic land from Ukraine.	Story linking Ukraine to ISIS	Story about USA running Ukraine
Story about Neo-Nazis running Ukraine	Claim that Russian-speakers are persecuted in Ukraine	Story about Western politician recognizing the Crimea as part of Russia	Story blaming Ukraine for extreme weather incident	Poorly photoshopped image
Video/photo said to be in Ukraine but is actually not	Scene from a film passed off as a real incident	Story about "NATO mercenaries" fighting in Donbas	Story about extreme poverty in Ukraine	Staged video about Ukrainian nationalists
Fake poll results	Story about a region of Ukraine demanding autonomy	Alternative MH17 theory	Some country is cutting Ukraine off from aid/ trade	Something about Eurovision
Ukraine uses ISIS/Islamist fighters in the Donbas!	Ukraine teaches schoolchildren to hate Russians	Story about fake war atrocity	Ukraine will freeze without Russian gas!	

myfreebingocards.com

FIGURE C.2 A StopFake bingo caller's card featuring the square "Something about Eurovision." Used with permission by the StopFake.org/Media Reforms Center.

unsettled by the repeated failures of Ukraine to actualize these ideals while its citizens tenaciously hold on to the project of statehood and stage massive revolutions in the ostensible service of such values. Jamala's song, after all, spans the history of an Indigenous people dominated by empire, exiled and silenced under state socialism, neglected and oppressed under a fitful post-Soviet Ukrainian democracy, and then repressed through twenty-first-century technologies of hybrid warfare. Interpreting "1944" as a coherent representation of "Ukraine" is impossible. Instead, the song's provocation reveals the politics of the Eurovision Song Contest to itself, exposing how rhetorics of international "friendship" mask the violent unresolved histories and ongoing conflicts between competitor states. Indeed, in reminding us of the fragility of contemporary state sovereignty everywhere, the Ukrainian Eurovision-wining song demands that we consider alternate future sovereignties. Once again, wild music challenges us to make new sense of the political.

NOTES

Preface

1. It should be noted that Tlostanova and Mignolo derive this principle of "learning to unlearn in order to relearn" from the curriculum of Amawtay Wasi, the Intercultural University of the People and Nations of Ecuador (Tlostanova and Mignolo 2012, 12).

2. I was also referred to by a variety of other diminutives, which are common in Slavic languages. In Western Ukraine, I was addressed most commonly as *Marusia*, a female diminutive of Maria that rings of rurality or quaintness to many Ukrainian urbanites, and that was my family name growing up in the United States (where I had no idea of such rural connotations). Often, Western Ukrainians would also call me *Marichka*, another popular diminutive form. In Crimea, I was *Maria* or, in the Crimean Tatar community, sometimes the Turkic *Meriem*; by Russian speakers, I was sometimes addressed as *Masha*, a common Russian diminutive of my given name.

3. For general background on post–World War II displaced persons, see Wyman 1998. For a specific account of Ukrainian experiences in the DP camps, see Luciuk 2000.

4. See Khanenko-Friesen 2015 on the Canadian-Ukrainian diasporic imagination and its resonance in post-Soviet Ukraine.

5. These are translated lyrics from one anthem of the PLAST Ukrainian Scouting Organization to which I belonged until my teenage years. The anthem was sung by the young scouts (*novaky*), and remains a vivid childhood musical memory. The overt patriotism of the chorus (cited earlier) is set against verses that remind of Woody Guthrie's iconic American folk song "This Land Is Your Land." Verse 1 (my translation): "We are Ukrainian children / we are young, like flowers / Small *zhovtodziuby* [lit. Yellowbeaks, the name for the youngest scouts, like the Boy Scouts' "bear cubs"] / PLAST newcomers [*novaky*]." Verse 2: "We love our family homes / the wide steppe and groves / From the Sian to the Kuban / Lies our native land." The song reinforces the idea that children of the Ukrainian diaspora were mantle holders, preparing for the day when Ukraine would be free of "enemy" (Soviet) hands. A significant part of the campfire repertoire also rewrote

classic 1960s songs from Anglo-American folk and rock with Ukrainian lyrics. Later, I was surprised to learn that the melodies to songs such as Bob Dylan's "Blowin' in the Wind" and the Rolling Stones' "As Tears Go By" were not originally Ukrainian scouting songs.

6. The Chornobyl Songs Project brought together thirteen singers (including myself) in New York to train intensively under Yevhen Yefremov. Over the course of six weeks, we learned village repertoires on the basis of his pre-Chornobyl nuclear disaster field recordings, and recorded "a year in song." The Yara Arts Group and the Center for Traditional Music and Dance offered critical support and collaboration throughout the process. An album of these recordings was released on Smithsonian Folkways Records in 2015 (https://folkways.si.edu/ensemble-hilka/chornobyl-songs-project-living-culture -from-a-lost-world/world/music/album/smithsonian).

INTRODUCTION *On Wildness*

1. Leading up to the 2004 competition, Ruslana also helped to *construct* this narrative. For example, in a May 2004 Ukrainian-language interview for BBC Ukrainian, conducted before the Eurovision finals, Ruslana was asked about her "emotions" leading up to the contest. She replied, "I am really thinking about the image of the country, and not my own [image]. I do not exist right now. I do not worry about myself right now, I do not exist right now as a person; that is, Ruslana does not live for herself, not even for a second. Frankly, we are doing everything so that we feel like full members of Europe" (my translation).

2. Whenever I refer to wildness in lowercase, or in scare quotes as "wildness," it is to differentiate it from this discursive master trope of Wildness.

3. In line with my argument here, Kevin Karnes has recently argued that "the anthropology [Herder] imagined was a sensuous one. It was foremost an anthropology of listening, an anthropology of the ear, and it was conceived within the broader, deeply sensual project of inventing Eastern Europe" (2018, 80).

4. See, for example, Witwicki 1873 and Kaindl 1894. For a variety of depictions of Ukraine in Western European colonial travel narratives, see also Wolff 1994.

5. See Kappeler 2003 for an overview of these fraternal discourses and Sunderland 2004 for a history of the wild field.

6. The topic of wildness has been productively taken up by a number of queer theorists in recent years (see especially Nyong'o and Halberstam 2018). While I will draw on these theorists in many places in this book, this study does not examine the rather impoverished status of LGBTQ communities in Ukraine—though there are excellent studies emerging on queerness and sexuality from both Ukrainian and North American scholars (for some recent examples, see Chernetsky 2016; Martsenyuk 2014; and works by Olga Plakhotnik and Maria Mayerchyk). With reference to queer theory, though the body and sexuality are present throughout this study, they are not foregrounded in the first tier of my analysis.

However, if queer can be intended as "a political metaphor without a fixed referent" (Eng 2005, 1), as the authors of "What's Queer About Queer Studies Now" wrote more than a decade ago, I stretch the metaphor, extending the lessons of queer modes of thought to apply to the case studies that comprise this book.

7. Within Jacques Attali's well-known framework, my usage of "wild sounds" might be understood as a form of "noise" that becomes rendered intelligible as music under certain political and economic conditions (Attali 1985). My thinking on this point is also indebted to Andrea Bohlman's study of how historians of Polish Solidarity engaged with what she terms "sound documents," showing that they "did not necessarily treat all music *as music*, they responded to, described, and incorporated diverse musical materials *as sound*" (2016, 238). This framing allows her to incorporate an expanded view of how to write the cultural history of collective opposition through sound, both within and external to "music."

8. An entire tradition of scholarship in ethnomusicology could be cited to substantiate this claim, but for a brief summary of this position, I refer the reader to Matt Sakakeeny's (2015) excellent overview of music in the context of "sound studies."

9. My understanding of the "social imaginary" draws on the philosopher Charles Taylor. Taylor emphasizes that practices are what comprise the social imaginary, which he defines as "the ways people imagine their social existence, how they fit together with others, how things go on between them and their fellows, the expectations that are normally met, and the deeper normative notions and images that underlie these expectations." Taylor goes on to locate the social imaginary "in images, stories, and legends" (2004, 23). Taylor excludes sound—including music—from his list, but this book asserts that both sound and music should be included as a central sites through which social imaginaries are negotiated.

10. The sacred man (*homo sacer*) who is the protagonist of Agamben's study of sovereignty is described as possessing a "bare life" (the condition of living). But for Agamben, there is no a priori "bare life"; it coexists with "ways of life" (life in community) in which "exclusion and inclusion, outside and inside, *bios* and *zoe*, right and fact, enter into a zone of irreducible distinction" (1998, 9). "Ways of life," such as the norms and practices of a society, are further distinguished from the good or idealized Aristotelian "form-of-life." Humphrey intervenes to suggest that ethnographers might "thicken" their studies of "ways of life" (2004, 420).

11. Medić (2014) notes that the Serbian post-socialist genre term *etno muzika* was aspirational in nature, much as it is in Ukraine. See also Comaroff and Comaroff 2009 on the global commodification of ethnicity, though I note that *etno-muzyka* is so elastic as a market category, and can be deployed in such particularized ways, that it often does not ramify to the scale of the national "ethno-commodity."

12. The *etno-* of *etno-muzyka* derives from the Greek term *etnos* (or *ethnos*), and should be understood as distinct from other terms of collective affiliation such as "ethnicity," "na-

tionality," "minority," or "Indigenous group." As Francine Hirsch (2005) has documented, *etnos* emerged as an important concept in Soviet ethnography of the 1920s along with *narodnist'*, meaning nationality. For more on *etnos* in the Soviet usage, see Slezkine 1992 and Bassin 2016. Theories of *etnos* also intersect with categories of post-Soviet citizenship (Oushakine 2009, 83). See Balibar 2013 for an overview of these and other terms with respect to the problem of contemporary (supra-national) "European citizenship."

13. I am grateful to Charles L. Briggs, who originally suggested the idea of "acoustic citizenship" to me on the basis of a presentation of a chapter of this book. Trnka, Dureau, and Park define "sensory citizenship" as "the points at which sensory being mediates and is mediated by state and other forms of citizenship, thereby constituting an intricate dialectic between lived experience, ideological formations, and political forces within which normative ideologies naturalize particular forms of belonging" (2013, 1). I elaborate on acoustic citizenship as a mode of sensory citizenship—and as distinct from musical citizenship—in the conclusion to this book.

14. Wanner points out that Russia had previously infringed on the sovereignty of the post-Soviet states of Georgia and Moldova. She concludes by asserting, "Enduring forms of postimperial subjugation suggest that some states are especially vulnerable to diminished sovereignty" (2014, 437). See also Brown 2014 and Ong 2006.

15. For Muñoz, utopia "offers a critique of the present, of what is, by casting a picture of what *can and perhaps will be*" (2009, 35, italics in original). Importantly, Muñoz restores the German idealist usage of utopia, where it is not a "no place" of unachievable perfection, but rather a "not yet here." With this notion of utopia at work, I find that Muñoz's utopia can be reconciled with the musicologist Richard Taruskin's spirited "anti-utopian essays," where he decries the discourse of "perfection" implicit in utopianism, which he sees replicated in discussions of musical autonomy in Western art music (see Taruskin 2009, xii–xiii). Rather than a belief in perfection, Muñoz's utopia is much in line with Agamben's application of the Aristotelian term "potentiality," or the residue of "potential" reality within the "actual" reality of the present (Agamben 1998, 44–45).

16. A canonic text that artfully dismantles the "music as a universal language" cliché is John Blacking's *How Musical Is Man?* (1973). Feld and Fox (1994) offer a valuable analysis of the connections and differences between music and language as poetic and communicative forms.

17. Reflecting on this shift in programming three years after the Unizh festival, Myroslava Ganyushkina, one of ArtPóle's main organizers, explained that ArtPóle could not ignore the "non-festival mood in the country" (нефестивальний настрій у країні) (personal communication, June 28, 2017). Since 2014, the organizers have been programming smaller and more frequent events, often pertaining specifically to the occupation of Crimea or the war in Eastern Ukraine.

18. Writing in the *Guardian* in 2017, Sophie Pinkham notes that, by the time of the

Russian annexation of Crimea, "The Russian propaganda machine was already in overdrive, convincing the Russian populace, as well as the inhabitants of Crimea and eastern Ukraine, that post-Maidan Kiev was a 'fascist junta' led by bloodthirsty Ukrainian nationalists who planned to exterminate Russian speakers, crucify Russian children, and so on" (https://www.theguardian.com/commentisfree/2017/mar/22/annexing-crimea-putin-make-russia-great-again). This is not to say that these narratives sprang from nowhere; Russian cyberintelligence and media strategies have been directed at destabilizing Ukrainian statehood through a variety of "hybrid war" tactics that include the aggressive circulation of "disinformation" or "fake news." Ukrainian journalists have tried to counter Russian narratives with websites and TV programs such as *StopFake*, whose sole mission is to debunk Russian fabrications (see Khaldarova 2016; Carroll 2017).

19. Alexei Yurchak (2014a) called the method of annexing Crimea "a new technology of non-occupation." It was staged through the incursion of "little green men," green-clad soldiers without insignias, who suddenly became an armed presence in the already tense urban spaces of Crimea, and whose ubiquity established the space as one of domination, albeit without the usual trappings of military invasion and conquest.

20. The terms "separatists" and "rebels" have been contested in this case, since it has been well documented that Russian military personnel served as leaders of the insurgency, and Russian soldiers are known to have traveled across the Ukrainian-Russian border by their own geotags on social media. For context, the ArtPóle festival I describe here took place in the weeks before the "separatists" downed Malaysian Airlines Flight 17 over the village of Hrabove near Donetsk, an act of warfare that international courts agree was accomplished with a Russian BUK missile, which is widely believed to have been provided covertly by the Russian military, despite Russian protestations against this version of events (see, for example, https://www.theguardian.com/world/2015/oct/13/mh17-crash-report-plane-partially-reconstruced-blames-buk-missile-strike).

21. The Roma population of Eastern Europe presents an interesting point of comparison for such racialized stereotypes of otherness. On "Gypsy music" and Roma "blackness," see Trumpener 2000, O'Keeffe 2013; Silverman 2007. For yet another example of racialized internal otherness in Ukraine, Helbig (2014) offers a fascinating view of how African Ukrainians strategically engage and remediate "blackness" in Afro-Ukrainian hip-hop.

22. The press release explained that members of two groups—Bai (led by L'viv-based actor-turned-documentary-filmmaker Ostap Kostiuk) and the Hutsuls—came together to perform that evening. According to press materials, both groups were "unified in their desire to preserve the old musical forms and to extend the 'old style' (старий стиль) of the performance of authentic Hutsul music" (my translation from Ukrainian). I originally became acquainted with these musicians during my fieldwork in the Carpathians in 2008–2009.

23. The strange story of "Albinoni's Adagio in G Minor" and its salience to the Crimean

Tatar community merits a slightly extended footnote. Thought to be one of the most successful hoaxes in Western European art music, the tune was supposedly recovered from the minor baroque composer Albinoni's archives by the Italian musicologist Remo Giazotto, but it is widely believed that he authored it himself. The "Adagio" has been prominently featured in film scores (including *Flashdance* and the Oscar-nominee *Manchester by the Sea*), and became a hit in Europe in 1999 for the polyglot singer Lara Fabian, who added English lyrics to her orchestral-synth-pop setting of the tune. During my fieldwork in Crimea, I heard the melody performed with both Russian and Crimean Tatar lyrics. The first time I heard it in Simferopol, it was performed instrumentally by the all-women's violin ensemble Sel'sebil during a conference held on the 90th anniversary of the execution of Numan Çelebicihan (1885–1918), the first leader of the Crimean Tatar national government (Qurultay), who was gruesomely murdered by the Bolsheviks in 1918 (see Allworth 1998 for this history).

24. I note that the politics of inclusion that I describe here are in sharp contrast to the exclusionary nationalist myth-making that Catherine Wanner observed at the Ukrainian youth-oriented festival Chervona Ruta in the early post-Soviet era (Wanner 1996).

25. See Agamben 1998 for an exploration of the paradoxical relation between the "constituting power and constituted power" of sovereignty, which he examines through the Aristotelian concept of potentiality.

26. A number of ethnomusicological works on post-3.11 Japan offer productive comparisons to my study of nascent solidarities in crisis Ukraine. Manabe (2015, 262) describes post-Fukushima festivals as Foucauldian heterotopias; Novak (2017), following Butler (2015), treats festivals as spaces that enable new modes of political performativity, and Abe emphasizes festivals as zones where musical performance enables "a relational understanding of sociality, and an ethical orientation that prioritized not only atomized, precautionary politics that sought to prevent future catastrophe but also the desire for a better future based on the past/death being integral to the present/life" (2016, 254). Despite the different challenges facing Japanese and Ukrainian citizens, this fleeting yet palpable sense of future-oriented possibility (and even tenuous optimism) resonates closely with the evening I describe at ArtPóle.

27. Hardt and Negri define modern national identity as "a cultural, integrating identity, founded on a biological continuity of blood relations, a spatial continuity of territory, and linguistic commonality" (2000, 95). This resonates closely with Stalin's (1913) definition, which I cite here because it was so influential in the USSR. Long-standing debates over the nature of the nation as "civic" or "ethnic" complicate these definitions, however (see, for example, Ignatieff 1995; Habermas and Cronin 1998).

28. For one iteration of the debate as to whether Ukraine is postcolonial in the sense of "having been colonized" by the USSR, see Timothy Snyder 2015, and Yaroslav Hrytsak's rejoinder, where he makes the point that Ukrainians were core, not peripheral, to strate-

gies of Soviet domination throughout the fifteen republics. Hrytsak notes that "within the Russian empire and Soviet Union, [Central and Eastern] Ukraine was more core than colony. *Colony* fits the [Western] Ukrainian lands of the Habsburg monarchy better" (2015, 733). Further, he delineates "two opposite extremes in the varieties of Ukrainian colonial experiences": "as the core of the Russian and Soviet projects, on the one hand, and as the center of anti-imperial and anti-Soviet resistance, on the other" (733–34). In the same issue, Gerasimov and Mogilner (2015) respond to Snyder and further challenge his claims. Elsewhere, Gerasimov (2014) argued that the Maidan was a "postcolonial revolution." Theodore Levin (2002) offers a valuable viewpoint on this question from the perspective of musical culture in Soviet Uzbekistan, which he considers to have been colonized by the Soviets. For other perspectives on the postcoloniality of the post-Soviet, see also Spivak et al. 2006 and Moore 2003.

29. See Bilaniuk's (2005) rich study of the micropolitics of language use in Ukraine.

30. Crimean Tatars typically date their Gumilëvian "ethnogenesis" to Crimea in the twelfth or thirteenth centuries (see Williams 2001). Despite the fact that they are not legally given this status by the Russian Federation and were not given this status by the Ukrainian government until just *after* Crimea was annexed by Russia in 2014, I will refer to Crimean Tatars as "Indigenous people" throughout this book. For an anthropologist's overview of the origins of Indigenous rights discourse in legal contexts, see Niezen 2003.

31. A note on the lexicon of sovereignty: in this study, I generally avoid Foucault's terms of "governmentality" and "biopower" in favor of the resurgent language of sovereignty in three registers: political, cultural, and body. For a useful overview of modern forms and transmutations of sovereignty, see Hansen 2006 and Ben-Porath 2013. For a lucid defense of the uses of sovereignty in the modern world, see De Boever 2016. See the essays in Edmonson and Mladek on the "enormous staying power of sovereignty" (2017, 12).

32. For a contrasting example of how music intervenes in debates about citizenship, see Andrew Eisenberg's work on how music gives access to and enables forms of "cultural citizenship" among Muslims on the Swahili coast of Kenya (Eisenberg 2012 and 2013).

33. I am grateful to David Novak for pushing me to think about how self-governance may be enacted against government through institutions and bureaucracies. Examples of this have been prevalent in the post-2016 United States, where civil servants have at times successfully prevented or lessened the effects of especially harmful or careless policy proposals put forward by the presidential administration.

34. Of course, the success of the care-giving state ultimately further consolidates power in the state. Aihwa Ong offers an analysis of how such "pastoral care" operates in discourses of Asian liberalism, where the state constructs "the caring society" that "is integrated into the government itself and culturally constructs relations between the ruler and the ruled" (1999, 201). The goal of the state in these contexts is to target the middle

class as the recipients of the state's benevolent care in order to bolster the disciplinary mechanisms by which middle-class subjects are made maximally productive and, by extension, the engines of Asian "tiger economies."

35. Kristen Ghodsee (2011 and 2017) has written evocatively of the harsh everyday realities faced by ordinary people caught in the "transition" between command economies and neoliberal capitalism. She writes of her hope that her readers might "walk a hundred or so pages in someone else's postcommunist shoes," in order to demonstrate how nostalgia for the socialist past—or, as she puts it, "why people might accept more state interference in their lives after twenty years of political instability and social upheaval" (2011, xiv)—can be a rational desire.

36. Yet, as the Ukrainian historian Yaroslav Hrytsak writes, "There are two main groups that embody these values [of self-expression]: the new middle class that arose in the postindustrial (service) economy, and the younger generation that emerged in conditions of relative democracy post-2004. To a large extent, the Euromaidan was their revolution" (2015, 737).

37. See also Lila Abu-Lughod on how the "ephemerality of the postmodern" represented by mass-mediated forms presents a challenge to fundamental anthropological goals to offer "profound insights into the human condition" (2005, 30–31).

38. Those familiar with the immensely popular Ukrainian act known as Verka Serdiuchka, for example, would likely find it easy to read Wildness into the post-Soviet carnivalesque depicted in Verka's wild world.

39. Notably, Ana Maria Ochoa Gautier's *Aurality*—which not only expands our view of the aural sphere with regard to how human/nonhuman colonial taxonomies privileged certain modes of sounding and inscription—builds on Roberto Esposito's (2011) "immunitarian paradigm," which he developed to explain the crisis of sovereignty.

40. Anthropologists have paved the way for various approaches to the ethnographic study of sovereignty. See, for example, Bernstein 2013b and 2013a; Chalfin 2010; Humphrey 2004; Simpson 2014; Yurchak 2015.

41. I acknowledge that in daily usage, these two contested terms are not as clear-cut as I make them out to be, but I wish to retain this sharp conceptual distinction for the sake of my argument. These capsule definitions of nationalism versus patriotism are indebted to George Orwell, who provides a clear distinction between these two terms in an essay originally published in 1945. To Orwell, nationalism is "power-hunger tempered by self-deception" (2000 [1968], 362). Patriotism, on the other hand, is "devotion to a particular place and a particular way of life, which one believes to be the best in the world but has no wish to force on other people." Patriotism is "of its nature defensive, both militarily and culturally" (362–63). This definition overlaps with Habermas's examination of constitutional patriotism as the prospect that "democratic citizenship need not be rooted in the national identity of a people" (1998, 500). Of course, in the Ukrainian case, the gap

between the political culture that is actually existing and the political culture desired by citizens is vast.

42. Mark von Hagen pointed out that, if we look at the "political geography" of where Ukrainian history is taught, "we find virtually no recognition that Ukraine has a history" (1995, 658). This leads, as von Hagen argues, to the depiction of Ukrainian attempts to claim a history as "'searching for roots,' national advocacy or some other partisan pleading, and to deny the field [of Ukrainian history] the valorization it seeks as 'objective history'" (659). Von Hagen worries that, since an independent post-Soviet Ukraine will need to have a history, it may be reduced to dogmas of ethno-nationalism: "Federalist, regionalist and autonomist political thought in general is likely to be one of the casualties of an overly nationalist rewriting of the past that posits a sovereign, national state as the teleological outcome of history" (666). Yet, despite the discontinuities of Ukrainian national history, its amorphous and shifting borders, the legacy of occupying powers' destabilization of Ukrainian identity, and its assimilation of elites into dominant occupying powers, von Hagen lands on a hopeful prognosis for Ukrainian futurity: by rooting the search for history in cultural continuities (in both elite and non-elite musics, literatures, and other expressive forms) rather than in the unbroken history of its "state and national traditions," Ukrainian history "can serve as a wonderful vehicle to challenge the nation-state's conceptual hegemony and to explore some of the most contested issues of identity formation, cultural construction and maintenance, and colonial institutions and structures" (673).

43. The sociologist Volodymyr Ishchenko, whose repeated Cassandra-like warnings about the empowering of neo-Nazi and ultranationalist Ukrainians during the ongoing military conflict in the east of Ukraine, may be correct in predicting the damaging long-term effects that far-right militias will have on Ukrainian society.

44. Yurchak is responding here, in particular, to the binary Cold War paradigms that centered Western European master narratives in particular. Related to this point, Nicholas Tochka's essential study of Albanian socialist "light" popular music underscores how "[m]any of the analytical categories and assumptions that music scholars employ have been constructed in contexts shaped, at least in part, by the Cold War itself" (2016, 20).

45. Kyiv, now the capital of independent Ukraine, is the cradle of all Slavic Orthodoxy; the "Saint Volodymyr" claimed by Ukrainians as a unifier and Christianizer of the Slavs in the tenth century is the same "Vladimir the Great" of Russian historical narratives. Valentina Izmirlieva (2018) has spoken about how the "cult of St. Volodimer" functions today as a weapon to assert Russian supremacy over Ukraine and its history.

46. According to the widely cited "Fragile States Index" compiled by the Fund for Peace (previously known as the "Failing States Index"), in 2017 Ukraine was rated 90 out of 178 countries (where a higher number correlated to a more stable regime; in 2017, Finland was ranked number 178, and South Sudan was number 1) (http:fundforpeace .org/fsi). The Fund for Peace is a US-based nongovernmental and nonprofit organization.

47. In *Listening to War*, Martin Daughtry (2015) poignantly evaluates the limits of music to express, to heal, or to comfort, in dehumanizing contexts of violence.

ONE *Wild Dances: Ethnic Intimacy, Auto-Exoticism, and Infrastructural Activism*

1. Ruslana's releases between 2002 and 2018 recycle a few key terms that she translates between Ukrainian and English. For clarity, I provide the transliterated Cyrillic when applicable to mark these distinctions. To further clarify: *Dyki Tantsi* (in Cyrillic, Дикі Танці; in English, lit. Wild Dances) was the album originally released as part of Ruslana's Hutsulian Project and included the hit single "Znaiu Ya" (Знаю Я) described here. The song "Wild Dances" (with its original title in English, and with lyrics in both Ukrainian and English) won the 2004 Eurovision Song Contest and was included on the chart-topping album *Wild Dances*, as will be discussed at length further in this chapter.

2. Ruslana was not the first Ukrainian pop singer elected to the Verkhovna Rada: Oksana Bilozir, a half-generation older than Ruslana, served as a representative of the Our Ukraine bloc from 2002 to 2005, and again in 2006. In the interim, she was appointed by President Viktor Yushchenko to serve as the minister of culture and tourism of Ukraine in 2005. Though her party allegiances have shifted over the past decade, Bilozir also has close connections to the post-Maidan Poroshenko government.

3. Ruslana's press materials described the *trembita* as follows: "the longest [wind] instruments in the world, four meter trumpets that Hutsul craftsmen make out of pine trees that were stricken by lightning. The sound of the instrument is as mystic as the story of its creation [sic]" (accessed April 2005). According to the master instrument builder Mykhailo Tafiychuk, a *trembita* should typically be two or three meters in length and is typically made from the wood of a birch tree.

4. For a vivid anecdote of the Soviet practice of staged folkloric weddings, refer to the introductory chapter of Levin and Süzükei's *Where Rivers and Mountains Sing* (2006, 12–19).

5. Unlike the original mandate of Eurovision, in which cultural difference was emphasized and performed through linguistic diversity and musics with no recognizable Anglo-American influence, the contemporary pageant of Eurovision emphasizes ethno-national pop-rock's isomorphism, which Regev describes as the nation's "own" (Anglo-American influenced, folk-tinged) pop-rock, "believing this is the way to perform uniqueness in late modernity" (2007, 319).

6. These feminine stereotypes resurfaced in musical performances during the Maidan Revolution (see Chapter 2). In particular, the aggressive feminine archetype of the *Banderivka* was foregrounded during the Maidan Revolution (see Phillips 2014). For an exemplary ethnographic case study of how musical performance aligns with the performativity

of gender, see Sydney Hutchinson's *Tigers of a Different Stripe* (2016), which powerfully reverses the stereotypical gaze of "Northern feminism" on Dominican (and, more broadly, Caribbean) gendered discourses, particularly those of *machismo*.

7. As Thomas Solomon has pointed out, Turkey's 2003 victory was also nationally debated on the subject of representation: first, regarding the matter of language (Sertab Erener, Turkey's representative, insisted on singing in English); and second, on the "orientalist content in the video clip made to promote the song," with one critic voicing his disapproval by asking her, "[A]re you going to present us to Europe with Turkish baths and concubines?" (Solomon 2005a, 3–7). Sertab later claimed that the uniqueness of the "orientalist imagery" of the song and the use of English led to her victory.

8. Though Ruslana's wild presentation conjures only vague images of domination and violence, Anya Bernstein (2013a) makes a convincing case for how the bodies of the convicted women of Pussy Riot became lighting rods for contemporary Russian discourses of sovereignty-as-violent-spectacle.

9. I also asked Tafiychuk his perspective on the Hutsul-punk band Perkalaba, who had visited him at his home with a film crew and later featured the scene in a documentary about pilgrimaging to Hutsulshchyna for inspiration. His response: "Ah, let them have their fun, they're good kids. There's nothing Hutsul about it, but what's the harm?" (interview, January 27, 2009). Though Tafiychuk himself never elaborated on the reasons for his differing judgments of Ruslana versus Perkalaba, it may be postulated that the revenue, celebrity, and social capital that Ruslana accrued with "Wild Dances" fostered harsher appraisals of her work than that of other, less well-known groups who experimented with hybridizing Hutsul motifs in popular music forms at around the same time, but whose access to non-Ukrainian audiences was limited.

10. I heard this joke in variations as well as many other jokes about Hutsuls during my fieldwork (including a substantial repertoire of "dirty" Hutsul jokes told to me mostly by [male] Hutsuls themselves). Memorably, the particular variation cited here was told to me when I first met the violinist and teacher Ruslan Tupeliuk, the director of the children's music school in Verkhovyna. He was dressed in full Hutsul regalia and rushing to meet his band of carolers during the Christmas ritual season, but before rushing out the door, he shared the quick joke (прикол) (personal communication, January 12, 2009).

11. It is not clear which seventy countries he was referring to. Based on tour dates available through her website, I did not count seventy countries at the time, but Ruslana's performances have taken her to many European countries as well as to Canada, Brazil, and the United States.

12. I will decode this passage for those not versed in the Ukrainian language. *Oblmuzdramteatriv* is a somewhat overstuffed Soviet acronym that refers to "regional music and dramatic theater." (It is still used today.) "Prosvita" refers to a society founded in Western Ukraine in the nineteenth century that was devoted to the development and

revitalization of Ukrainian culture and ways of life (see Noll 1991). *Oseledets'* refers to the hairstyle worn by Ukrainian Kozak warriors. More commonly, this hairstyle is referred to as a "chub" (чуб), and it features one long lock emanating from the top center of an otherwise shaved head.

13. Helbig has written extensively about the symbolic capital of blackness in contemporary Ukrainian popular music. In a 2011 article, she noted that the song "Moon of Dreams" (which featured T-Pain and was included on the Ukrainian-language release *Amazonka*, as well as on the English-language release *Wild Energy*) is "as much a commentary on race as it is on gender and East/West expressions of financial mobility . . . [it] reinforces the argument that in the post-Soviet sphere, people determine their relationship to each other in terms of money and status within racialized frames" (2011a, 321).

14. Portnov also points out that Yuschenko's decision to "award Bandera the title of 'Hero of Ukraine' represented a serious blow to the president's reputation, most of all in Poland" (2013, 247), where the OUN legacy is remembered as one of genocidal attack on Polish citizens of the Western Ukrainian borderlands during World War II.

15. As is well known, the rehabilitation of Yanukovych's image, which helped him to win the 2010 Ukrainian election, was orchestrated by none other than Paul Manafort, who also worked for a time as Donald Trump's campaign manager during the 2016 election. In 2018, Manafort was convicted in US federal court on eight counts of financial fraud, many of which were connected to his shady dealings with the pro-Russian Yanukovych government.

TWO *Freak Cabaret: Politics and Aesthetics in the Time of Revolution*

1. For a detailed study of how music at protest events "bounces between cyberspace and real space" in the context of post-Fukushima protests in Japan, see Manabe (2015, 111).

2. To draw a comparison with a much more famous example, the viral video of the Dakh Daughters' performance—and its radically different interpretation by different publics—bears some analogies to the well-known controversial "Punk Prayer" video of Pussy Riot. Both videos are edited to include footage and sounds outside of the original context; they draw on genres with deep historical roots and emotional resonance for national audiences (Dakh Daughters reinvent the female lament and the stereotype of exotic Hutsul ethnic intimacy, and Pussy Riot parodies Russian Orthodox liturgical song and applies the aggressive sounds of hardcore punk); international audiences interpreted both performances differently from national audiences (see Tochka 2013); both were articulated by groups of women as performative feminist statements; and both spoke directly to the leaders of corrupt regimes. But there are important distinctions as well: though both groups originated as art collectives more than "bands"—Dakh Daughters emerged from

experimental theater, while Pussy Riot grew out of the radical Voina group—the Dakh Daughters quickly became established as musicians within Kyiv's cosmopolitan music scene, while Pussy Riot was not part of the network of punk musicians in Russia, and the members were not identified as musicians per se before their "Punk Prayer" went viral (Steinholt 2013). Most importantly, however, unlike Pussy Riot, whose prior activities as part of the Voina (War) art collective were explicitly directed against Putin's regime and Russian state power, the Dakh Daughters defined themselves as apolitical artists until their appearance at the Euromaidan.

3. Bilaniuk explains how protestors eventually came to reject "Europe" as the object of desire during the Maidan: "After receiving no actual support from the European Union during the first months of the protests, there was much disillusionment, and a realization that many political leaders in the West are more concerned with their countries' material interests rather than with the lofty ideal of democracy and human rights. As one editorial [by Oleskiy Kaftan] argued, 'We shouldn't call the Maidan European, because that idealized Europe that is being referenced—it does not exist' " (Bilaniuk 2016, 359).

4. This might be understood as a resurgence of the binary distinctions that defined Cold War politics (and, following Schmelz 2009, Cold War musicology).

5. The Dakh theater also spawned the "ethno-chaos" "avant-garde folk" band and WOMEX darlings DakhaBrakha, who, as part of a busy international touring schedule, took on the role of speaking to the world as "Ambassadors of the Maidan." DakhaBrakha's cellist, Nina Haranetska, also performs with the Dakh Daughters. Chapter 5 examines DakhaBrakha in detail.

6. In the video of the Euromaidan performance analyzed in this chapter, Nina Haranetska is absent (likely on tour elsewhere with DakhaBrakha), so the group in the video features only six members of the Dakh Daughters.

7. Just like the subjects of Deborah Wong's study of "Asian Americans making music," these musicians rejected the essentializing label of "Ukrainian musicians" in favor of being "Ukrainians making music" (Wong 2004, 15).

8. "No more be grieved at that which thou hast done: / Roses have thorns, and silver fountains mud, / Clouds and eclipses stain both moon and sun, / And loathsome canker lives in sweetest bud. / All men make faults, and even I in this, / Authorizing thy trespass with compare, / Myself corrupting salving thy amiss, / Excusing thy sins more than thy sins are; / For to thy sensual fault I bring in sense— / Thy adverse party is thy advocate— / And 'gainst myself a lawful plea commence. / Such civil war is in my love and hate, / That I an accessary needs must be / To that sweet thief which sourly robs from me" (Shakespeare 2000 [1977], Sonnet XXXV, 32).

9. By mid-2016, it had nearly a million views.

10. http://tvi.ua/program/2013/08/15/solomiya_melnyk_u_prohrami_rankovi_kurasany (accessed November 8, 2014). Author's translation.

11. The composition makes use of the phrase "fantastische Donbass" at key moments. The phrase is uttered bitterly by Ruslana Khazipova in German, making it sound to my ears like a perverse socialist-era tourist slogan used to lure East Germans to the industrial Soviet stronghold of Eastern Ukraine.

12. The Maidan-era "Leninopad" phenomenon has its historical precedents, especially in the period immediately following the fall of the USSR, when many monuments to Soviet leaders were toppled throughout the former Soviet republics. See Portnov (2013, 244–45) for a quick overview of the battle over the erection of Ukrainian anti-fascist monuments in Crimea and other parts of Ukraine in 2007–2010.

13. This chapter takes place in the early period of the Maidan, a few months before protestors ousted the corrupt (but democratically elected) president Viktor Yanukovych, who fled to Russia and remains there under President Vladimir Putin's protection, and well before Ukraine's territorial integrity was challenged by Russian-backed forces.

14. I have written about Perkalaba's relationship to Hutsulness elsewhere, and the tensions present in their mode of representing Hutsulness as a form of post-Soviet nihilistic hedonism (Sonevytsky 2012).

15. *Stiob* describes a particular manner of creating satire through overidentification with a subject, a humorous modality associated with late Soviet society (Yurchak 1999). For an analysis of *stiob*-like parody in settings such as "The Colbert Report" in the United States, see Yurchak and Boyer 2010.

16. http://www.day.kiev.ua/ru/article/kultura/iskusstvo-nezhnogo-skandala (accessed October 23, 2013). Author's translation.

17. "When I die, then bury me / Atop a mound / Amid the steppe's expanse / In my beloved Ukraine, / So I may see / The great broad fields, / The Dnipro and the cliffs, / So I may hear the river roar. / When it carries hostile blood / From Ukraine into the azure sea . . . / I will then forsake the / Fields and hills— / I'll leave it all, / Taking wing to pray / To God Himself . . . till / Then I know not God. / Bury me, rise up, / And break your chains / Then sprinkle liberty / With hostile wicked blood. / And in a great new family, / A family of the free, / Forget not to remember me / With a kind and gentle word" (Shevchenko 2013, ix). Despite the overt patriotism of this poem, however, as Portnov argues, Taras Shevchenko is one of the Ukrainian literary figures who is "accepted calmly and unanimously across the whole of Ukraine" (2013, 245). Portnov examines the symbolic politics around Shevchenko (along with Ivan Franko and Lesia Ukraïnka) and points out that "these [figures] happen to be the ones who were sanctioned by the Soviet canon" (245). This is in contrast to a trifecta of controversial figures demonized by the Soviets—Hetman Mazepa, Otaman Symon Petliura, and OUN leader Stepan Bandera—who have been used as "a negative metonym for the Ukrainian movement" (246).

18. FEMEN, like Pussy Riot and Voina, deploys sexuality in acts of extreme social

protests. For more on the similarities and differences of these Ukrainian and Russian "sextremist" activists, see Channell 2014.

19. In 1942, the Ukrainian Insurgent Army (UPA), which grew out of the Organization of Ukrainian Nationalists (OUN), began guerilla-style warfare against all of the forces that sought to occupy Ukrainian territories—be they Soviet, Polish, or German. Mass violence against Polish and Jewish populations was part of this brutal history.

20. Bandera was assassinated by the KGB in 1959 in Munich.

21. After 1945, and Stalin's re-annexation of Western Ukraine into the USSR, a massive policy of deporting Ukrainians from the West to the Gulag was enacted. Historian Timothy Snyder reports that "between 1944 and 1946 . . . 182,543 Ukrainians were deported from Soviet Ukraine to the Gulag: not for committing a particular crime, not even for being Ukrainian nationalists, but for being related to or acquainted with Ukrainian nationalists" (2010, 328).

22. Plytka-Sorokhan was featured in much regional—and some national—media. One comprehensive story about her life was published in June 2013 in the online journal *Chas i Podii* (Time and Events), which was titled "Living Legend of Hutsulshchyna" (accessed July 21, 2016, http://www.chasipodii.net/article/11868/).

23. Struve (2014) further details the effects that this propaganda campaign had on the reluctance of European and US leaders to get involved in the conflict: "A central part of the Russian government's struggle against the Euromaidan, its activities instigating a violent conflict in eastern Ukraine, and its support for the Donets'k and Luhans'k Republics is a massive, extremely distorting and manipulating campaign of Russian television and other media . . . This narrative had a strong impact in Russia and eastern Ukraine, pushed the separatist movement and contributed to the violent escalation of the conflict. It mobilized fighters from Russia and legitimized the increasingly open Russian interference. But the view of the events as driven by 'fascists' had also an impact on Western attitudes. It contributed to the fact that the public in western countries was reluctant in the support of the Euromaidan and the Ukrainian struggle with the Russian aggression."

24. The emergence of a post-Soviet "cult of motherhood" that was partially rooted in the depopulation that accompanied the social and economic collapse of the Soviet Union further blurred the roles of women-as-mothers with women-as-propagators, and stewards of, the nation (Pavlychko 1996). Anthropologist Maureen Murney describes how this elision of motherhood with nationhood exerts pressures on post-Soviet women who negotiate problems such as drug addiction, and who are perceived widely to be "women who have consciously rejected the very essence of Ukrainian womanhood" because of their inability to function as good wives and mothers (2007, 141). Sarah Phillips (2014) traces how the stereotype of the *Berehynia* operated on the Maidan to activate a feminist backlash against the conflation of female bodies with maternal-nationalist discourse.

25. For a contrasting example of how female lament is reframed in a post-Soviet space, see Ninoshvili 2012. Stokes also writes about how the "nation imagined as suffering woman" (2010, 110) manifests in a particular performance of a well-known Turkish political song, which he also identifies as contributing to the emergence of an intimate form of Turkish citizenship.

26. Freedom House reported that in 2014, Ukraine and Russia were "Partly Free" societies when it came to freedom to access online information (though Ukraine's score of 33 places it significantly closer to the "Best" end of the spectrum than Russia's score of 60, where 0 is "Best" and 100 is "Worst"). According to the report, close to 50 percent of Ukrainian adults regularly use the internet. Among users, the vast majority (82 percent) reside in urban areas, though usage in rural areas is on the rise. The report also includes data on the explosion of social media users that occurred during the Euromaidan protests, with two hundred thirty thousand new users joining Facebook in Ukraine in January and February 2014, and half a million users checking Twitter daily in January 2014. In 2014, a central controversy emerged over the management of popular Russian-owned social media sites such as VKontakte, which cracked down on Euromaidan activists and pro-Ukrainian sentiment. Russian attacks on pro-Ukrainian media, such as a January 2014 article in the German newspaper *Die Zeit*, swelled, and numerous outlets reported "insulting, combative" anti-Western and anti-Ukrainian comments "on any articles posted online related to Russia or Ukraine" ("Ukraine: Freedom on the Net 2014").

27. In early Soviet history, for example, perceived "formalism" in musical compositions or visual art—that is, overt attention to the formal structure of an artwork without an accompanying correct ideological message—was demonized as bourgeois decadence. (Perhaps the most famous story from the Soviet 1930s was the denunciation of Shostakovich and his opera *The Lady Macbeth of Mtensk* as a work of decadent bourgeois formalism in a *Pravda* editorial that many believed to be authored by Stalin himself.) For fascinating primary source documents on the contested meanings of musical "formalism" in the first fifteen years of Soviet rule, see Frolova-Walker and Walker 2012. Alexander Werth's (1949) report on the 1948 All-Soviet meeting of Soviet composers offers a dramatic interpretation of how accusations of "formalism" were used to silence, terrorize, and coerce musicians into compliance with the Soviet ideological demands of late Stalinist rule.

28. Taylor underscores the paradoxical nature of this ideology of the autonomous art object: "This belief in their separateness from society meant that many composers, like other artists, fought to keep market forces at bay even as they hoped to earn their livelihoods from the market. They proclaimed themselves to be artists while struggling to make their works autonomous from market forces in order to service their inspiration" (2016, 32).

THREE *Ungovernable Timbres: The Failures*
of the Rural Voice on Reality TV

1. The program began as *The Voice of Holland* in 2010 and quickly became a global franchise. In 2011, Ukraine was the first country to launch a version, followed shortly thereafter by the United States, where the program was initially called *The Voice of America* before being abbreviated to *The Voice*. Notably, the majority of franchises have retained the original formula for naming the program: "The Voice of China," "The Voice of Brazil," "The Voice UK," "The Voice of Indonesia." In the United States, Russia, and Australia, the program is called only *The Voice* (in Russian, *Golos*). The Ukrainian version called *Holos Kraïny* is an unusual departure from the international naming conventions for the program, since it does not name the specific place (that would be *Holos Ukraïny*) but does specify that it is the voice of the *Kraïny*—which could be translated as "country" (in the political, not rural, sense) or as "nation." To avoid confusion with the various meanings of "country," I am translating the name of the program as "Voice of the Nation."

2. Though he is not introduced during this segment, the producer featured here is the well-known composer, producer, and impresario Konstantin Meladze. As producer of the first two seasons of *Holos Kraïny*, Meladze intervenes to provide a meta-commentary on the happenings of the show and, given his background in music, shares strong opinions on the merits of certain vocalists.

3. Indeed, the two terms are sometimes used together—*Avtentychnyi fol'klor*, or "authentic folklore"—to mark the particular kind of folklore that a group or singer practices, but I mostly avoid this formulation in order to not further confuse the issue. I also conspicuously avoid the term *bilyi holos* (білий голос, meaning "white voice") to refer to this style of singing. I have been warned away from this term by influential Ukrainian ethnomusicologists, despite the fact that it remains a prominent term of art used to describe this style in the North American Ukrainian diaspora and in Poland. As it was explained to me, *bilyi holos* is a term meant to convey the utter raw and uncultivated "naturalness" of village singers who sing in the loud and effortful style of the village. One Ukrainian ethnomusicologist argued that labeling village singers as fundamentally unskilled—or, rather, as the beneficiaries of a God-given "natural" voice—undermined the creativity and agency of the singers who have cultivated their "very colorful" voices over a lifetime of singing. Finally, to fill out to this terminological thicket, I should mention that *avtentyka* is sometimes posed against "reconstruction" (реконструкція) to differentiate between "true" *avtentyka* (from villages) and urban reconstructions of "authentic" (not "folklorized") village traditions. See also Potoczniak 2011.

4. Ana Hofman's (2010, 2011) valuable work on Slovenian and Serbian socialist-era folk music challenges simplistic narratives that reduce all socialist state-sanctioned "arranged folklore" to one monolithic state project that deprived musicians of any agency. Though

it is beyond the scope of this chapter, my own research in various regions of Ukraine supports Hofman's claim that socialist official culture was "multifarious, contradictory, and creative" in the ways that localities actually integrated ideology into projects of "folklorization" (2011, 239). For the purposes of this chapter, however, I stress that practice bundled as *avtentyka* in Ukraine arose in opposition to the arranged and systematized folkloric practices implemented by the state during the Soviet period.

5. One fascinating iteration of musicological debates over authenticity took place in the 1980s among scholars of the early music "authenticity movement." A 1984 issue of the journal *Early Music* on "The Limits of Authenticity" debated the issues from various perspectives; Richard Taruskin's delightfully provocative entry, titled "The Authenticity Movement Can Become a Positivistic Purgatory, Literalistic and Dehumanizing," offered one skeptical perspective on the fetish of authenticity in early music (Taruskin 1984).

6. *Huk* (гук) is pronounced with the middle vowel resembling the "oo" in the word "boot."

7. Anthony Shay has also written on the phenomenon of institutionalized folk dance groups such as the Virsky Ensemble—another example of a national Soviet-era group that exists today. Shay observes that "the Ukrainian State Ensemble under the direction of Pavel Virsky visually represented the entire Ukrainian nation through an opening choreographed spectacle in which all of the dancers appeared in the major costume types, representing villages and regions from all over the Ukraine. The dancers paraded impressively around the stage, and, in a final gesture, symbolically presented bread and salt, the Slavic ritual of welcome and greeting, to the audience" (1999, 39). This practice continues today in the post-Soviet version of Kyiv's Virsky Ballet. The Veriovka Choir and Virsky Ensemble represent two prominent Soviet-legacy groups that some Ukrainians criticize for their *folkloryzm* or *sharovarshchyna*.

8. Many scholars of the former Soviet Union have documented the various ways that Marxist-Leninist cultural policies transformed Indigenous musical practices throughout the fifteen Soviet republics. Theodore Levin has written extensively about this in Central Asia (Levin 1980, 1996, and 2002; Levin and Süzükei 2006). For examples from other republics and former socialist contexts, see Buchanan 1995; Frolova-Walker 1998; O'Keeffe 2013; Slobin 1996; Nercessian 2000; Zemtsovsky 2002.

9. *Drevo* is an archaic Slavic term for "tree."

10. While studying Ayacuchano huayno music, Joshua Tucker describes a similar process of learning to please his teacher only by asserting his agency as a performer, albeit within the constraints of convention: "Finally, out of sheer frustration, I stopped trying to mimic him and simply played the melody as I saw fit, embellishing it with a combination of figures that I had seen him use and things that I had heard on CD. It was the first time he approved, and I soon discovered, in sharing music with other friends

from the city, that the spontaneous use of idiomatic ornaments was the surest way to elicit positive reactions" (2013, 58).

11. To clarify, what I mean is that there were two coaches who were Ukrainian citizens, and two who were Russian citizens.

12. One could quibble on this point. For example, Yulia Yurina, who won Season 6 of *Holos Kraïny*, was presented on the program as an expert of Ukrainian folklore. As the season progressed, however, Yurina—a Russian singer originally from the Kuban—demonstrated her ability to switch among various vocal styles, and competed with songs such as the Britney Spears hit "Oops, I Did It Again," which she rendered with a jazzy, sultry voice that was quite distinct from the folkloric voice that she presented at the beginning of the competition.

13. I refer here to Mladen Dolar's lively study of the acousmatic voice (2006, 60–71), and specifically where he defines the impossibility of the acousmatic voice (via Schaeffer and Chion) to overcome the "rift between an interior and exterior." He writes that "the voice embodies the very impossibility of this division, and acts as its operator" (71).

14. It is worth mentioning that the dialect—colloquially, *hovir* (ровір)—used by Zajets and his parents also fed the depiction of him as "more rural" than Karpenko, whose speech on the program conformed mostly to standard Ukrainian. In contrast, Zajets's noticeable *surzhyk* blend of Ukrainian, Russian, and possibly Belarusian, marked him as a villager who likely had limited exposure to the refined and cosmopolitan city (despite the fact that this was not entirely true).

15. Skrypka replaced Ruslana in the second season of the program; Ponomaryov and Arbenina returned for the second season; and Piekha was replaced by Valeria, another Russian *estrada* singer. That Karpenko could "not imagine" Ruslana selecting her to compete may be a comment on the previous season's failure to draft Zajets onto any team, but it may also have to do with the fact that Karpenko and Skrypka had previously collaborated on projects together under the aegis of his *etno-muzyka* initiatives, including the festival Kraïna Mrij.

16. Fasova, Zajets's home village, lies approximately seventy kilometers to the west of the capital city of Kyiv. The village population was 672, with 428 households, at the time of the last Ukrainian census (http://www.ukrcensus.gov.ua/). According to the history of the village provided on the website for the Makariv regional governmental administration, the village was founded in 1640, suffered tremendous losses during the Stalinist famine (Holodomor) of 1932–1933 and during World War II, and became a site for Kyivan Polissia villagers displaced by the Chornobyl disaster in 1986.

17. The line uttered by the host, Domanskyi, who speaks in Russian, is "Такой заяц страну не опозорить." Zajets, of course, is the surname of the singer, but it also means "rabbit" in Ukrainian and approximates the sound of the word for rabbit in Russian.

18. Ponomaryov, who is the first coach to speak to Matvienko, tells her that "her vocal quality in this style is perhaps only second to Nina Matvienko, simply divine [Божественно]," but that he felt it "was too great a risk" to select her because he simply didn't know if she would be able to sing in a "non-folk style."

19. Though it is somewhat beyond the scope of my argument here, I want to note the gendered strategy that Karpenko reveals to her television audience, when she talks about how happy she was to be paired with a male singer in the "Fight" round. As she explains, she likes singing with men because pairing something "weak" (feminine) against something "strong" (masculine) will naturally make the strong actor back off a little, which may work to her advantage. I have encountered such binary views of femininity and masculinity among other *avtentyka* singers who adhere to a patriarchal view of traditional gender.

20. In contrast to the valued out-of-tuneness that Charles Keil wrote about in his well-known essay on "participatory discrepancies," the out-of-tuneness at play here works against fostering the potential "groove" of the music (Keil 1994).

21. Backstage, Brovko is greeted by friends who tell him that Karpenko was "so much worse" than he was. Brovko tells his friends that the outcome was predetermined, and one friend responds, "Aha, so it was a falsification of the vote." Brovko nods in agreement and then, suddenly aware of the cameras, abruptly changes the topic. All manner of conspiracy theories crop up on the program, which may demonstrate something more broadly about how quickly Ukrainians jump to assume that the culture of corruption that has pervaded their post-Soviet political reality carries through to the staged reality of television as well. In the first season, as previously mentioned, the host casually jokes with the Matvienko family backstage about whether Tonia is simply the ventriloquist's puppet for her mother's voice; in the second season, the coach Ponomaryov asks Skrypka—after he has selected Karpenko for his team and acknowledges that they have collaborated on musical projects in the past—whether they conspired together (по блату) somewhere backstage to assure that Karpenko was selected. See Kuzio 2011 and Ortmann and Heathershaw 2012 for more on the pervasiveness of conspiracy theories in post-Soviet Ukraine.

22. Specifically, Skrypka frames his "weakness" and failure to choose as a failure of masculinity. He says, "I need masculinity, but I cried like a *baba* [треба маскулінність, але розплакався як баба]."

23. Bilaniuk notes an opposite effect when non-ethnic Ukrainian or immigrant contestants appear on the program and perform a version of "Ukrainian-ness" that is rewarded by the audience and coaches. She describes the performances of various African and African Ukrainian contestants on *Holos Krainy* whose inclusion in the program "reveal[s] tensions regarding construction of Ukrainianness and foreignness" (2016, 353). At the same time, as Helbig (2014) notes in her study of discourses of blackness in Ukrainian music, the acceptance of otherness as Ukrainian typically reinforces stereotypes of monolithic national Ukrainian folk culture that are directly opposed to *avtentyka*.

24. I am grateful to Larissa Babij for challenging me to take up this point.

25. In an appearance on the program *Breakfast with 1+1* about six months after his failure to advance on *Holos Kraïny*, Zajets spoke about the attention he had been getting as the television host showered him with praise, calling him a treasure of Ukraine. A caller was aired on the program who raved about Zajets's authentic "intonation"—a term derived from the Soviet-era musicological theories of Boris Asafiev (see Zemtsovsky 2002) (https://www.youtube.com/watch?v=q9bTiY2uiBk, accessed Dec. 21, 2017).

FOUR *Eastern Music: The Liminal Sovereign*
Imaginaries of Crimea

1. In March 2015, a Crimean researcher shared (via private Facebook chat) that driving the microbuses was often the only job available to post-Soviet Crimean Tatar repatriates, due to the shadowy nature of the microbus operation. He also verified that Crimean Tatar drivers, whom he believed to be the majority, preferred Radio Meydan, whereas the "Russian drivers" preferred to listen to "generic *chanson* [Russian-language urban popular music] on the radio."

2. I adapt Michael Warner's (2002) application of the "counterpublic" from queer contexts back into a more classic subaltern context, as it was first articulated by Nancy Fraser (1990). Yet I depart from Warner's abstracted notion of the "public" as a zone purely of texts-in-circulation by asserting the importance of physical public space and face-to-face interaction in mediating contested constructions of "Crimean-ness."

3. Finnin describes the specific methods of "discursive cleansing" from Soviet life, as Crimean Tatars were made "subject to a coordinated campaign of censure and slander that erased their ethnonym from the pages of print media and their toponyms from the face of the earth" (2011, 1093). Since the term "Tatar" was a generic term for any Muslim subjects of the Russian Empire, the modifier "Crimean" before Tatar is critical to Crimean Tatars for making their ethnonym specific. Under Soviet rule, they became designated by the nationality of "Tatars." During the period of exile under Soviet rule, in response to censorship regimes that banned direct political utterance, the Crimean Tatars maintained a sense of community through expressive culture, and in particular, through musical performances that sometimes coded subversive political messages (see Sonevytsky 2019). As Uehling (2004) documents, political scientists anticipated ethnic violence to erupt in post-Soviet Crimea, yet large-scale violence was kept at bay, due in large part to the Crimean Tatar political leaders' commitment to nonviolent resistance.

4. Discourses of post-Soviet Ukrainian and Crimean Tatar fraternity are rooted in a shared perception of oppression at the hands of Russian, and later Soviet, ruling powers. I benefited from such feelings of shared trauma during my fieldwork in Crimea in 2008–2009, as I—a Ukrainian American ethnographer whose speech betrayed a com-

petence in Ukrainian before Russian—was repeatedly welcomed into Crimean Tatar social environments as a "sister Ukrainian," a reversal from the hostilities I occasionally encountered among Russian speakers in public, where I was sometimes told to "speak a civilized language" when my Ukrainian speech was detected.

5. According to the State Emergency Service of Ukraine, approximately twenty thousand "internally displaced persons" (IDPS) have fled from the Crimean territory since March 2014, though the UNHCR cautions that "the real figure of IDPS remains unknown and is likely to be higher" (unhcr.org.ua/en/who-we-help/internally-displaced-people, accessed January 11, 2016).

6. Pro-Russian media depicted the non-continuation of the broadcasting license as a "choice" made by the owner of the ATR media company, though the owner publicly denied this in numerous media reports.

7. See Daughtry 2014 for how sound "occupies" space.

8. The denial of adequate worship space for Muslims was justified by Crimean politicians at the time through insinuations that Crimean Tatars were untrustworthy citizens, a stereotype linked to Stalinist projects of discrediting them as "enemies of the Soviet people." Resistance to the mosque could also be linked to the contemporary panic over mosques in the Euro-American context where an ostensibly tolerant, secular society bristles against non-Christian forms of worship, especially when they are made publically audible (cf. Weiner 2014).

9. These are, of course, only two extreme positions. As shown in the Russian state's high-profile prosecution and imprisonment of Crimean filmmaker Oleg Sentsov, some ethnic Russian Crimeans also held strong investments in Ukrainian political sovereignty.

10. At his request, I have kept the original owner's name confidential in this article.

11. This lexical connection was perceived in opposite terms by radio personnel. The original radio owner also told me that the beginning of "Yushchenko's Maidan"—the popular protest that became the Orange Revolution—took place just months after Radio Meydan came into existence and was taken as an auspicious sign by the Crimean Tatar radio employees (personal communication, June 14, 2015).

12. Moorman proposes "sonorous capitalism" as an extension of Anderson's "print capitalism."

13. I consulted with a Crimean Tatar musician as to the origin of the instrumental excerpt used in the jingle. The tune is squarely in 4/4 time, and therefore not one of the many 7/8 qaytarma touted by Crimean Tatars as their iconic dance genre. The musician reported that, to his knowledge, the jingle was a new composition in "an Eastern style, not dissimilar from the 'Balkan beat' style popular in much of Eastern Europe" (personal communication, March 26, 2011).

14. Greta Uehling (2016) notes that Jamala's Eurovision victory accompanies a worsening human rights situation for Crimean Tatars living in Russian-occupied Crimea.

Uehling worries that the universalizing discourse that has accompanied the song's victory as an anthem for "oppressed peoples everywhere" distracts from the Crimean Tatars' specific struggle.

15. For numerous perspectives on how Crimea became fetishized as a tourist destination in different centuries, see Gorsuch 2006 and Schönle 2001.

16. In 2017, for example, the Russian government finally began constructing an official *sobornaya mechet'* in Simferopol (personal communication, November 21, 2017).

FIVE *Ethno-Chaos: Provincializing Russia Through Ukrainian World Music*

1. There is a case to be made that Slava Vakarchuk, the frontman of Ukrainian rock band Okean Elzy and an emerging political figure, occupies an equally prominent place among Ukrainian musicians in the world, though his particular embodiment of the musician-intellectual celebrity falls outside the scope of this chapter, especially since his music is not branded as "world music." Also, it should be noted that DakhaBrakha's turn toward explicit politics is somewhat surprising given the milieu from which the band emerged, which is the same as that of its sister group, the Dakh Daughters, about whom I wrote in Chapter 2. Both groups emerged from the Kyivan arts scene built by the cultural impresario and experimental theater director Vlad Troitsky, who has been outspoken about his disdain for the contamination of art by the carnival of Ukrainian politics.

2. Even as the members of DakhaBrakha have refrained from calling themselves "Ambassadors of the Maidan Revolution," they continue to take their role as ambassadors of Ukrainian culture very seriously. In a 2016 interview, Halanevych spoke at length about the responsibility his group feels, given that they are usually the first and only contact that their North American, Australian, and European audiences have with anything Ukrainian; so not only is it their mission to instruct their audiences where to find Ukraine on the map, but also what a "unique and fascinating" country it is (https://www.youtube.com /watch?v=PFCofbADZZM).

3. "By the end of the set, across the language barrier, listeners were clapping and whooping along" (Pareles 2014). See Buchanan 2006 and Levin and Süzükei 2006 for two valuable analyses of the sacralization of non-Western music in the cases of Bulgarian women's choirs and Tuvan throat singing, respectively. Before DakhaBrakha, Ukraine had not usually been fetishized in such exotic terms (with perhaps the exception of the Ukrainian, German-based singer Mariana Sadovska, whose experimental interpretations of Ukrainian village songs has drawn effusive and at times exoticizing critical praise since the late 1990s).

4. https://www.youtube.com/watch?v=LOQtKMoSKec.

5. Halanevych goes on to describe how, while they were touring in France in the

summer of 2015, they pleaded, in every interview, that the French halt their plan to sell warships to Russia. When the French, indeed, backed away from the sale, the members of DakhaBrakha self-deprecatingly joked that it must have been their intervention—to which the interviewer generously responded, "Every drop adds to the ocean." Halanevych agreed, explaining that their political activism was motivated first by the difficult position Ukraine occupies with respect to its northern neighbor, but is actually "an appeal to the entire civilized world."

6. Hrytsak points out that regime changes in Ukraine between 1917 and 1920 occurred at breakneck speed: "Kyiv, which became the Ukrainian capital in 1917, witnessed eleven turnovers; L'viv—the capital of the West Ukrainian People's Republic in 1918–19—experienced seven political regime changes. And in a remote railway station in the Donbass, power changed hands twenty-seven times during just the first half of 1919" (2015, 734).

7. Unlike Ochoa Gautier's (2006) critique of re-provincialized sounds, I assert that DakhaBrakha is not provincializing sounds in the name of epistemological purity, but rather, often, the opposite. Much like the aesthetic "cannibalism" practiced by Brazilian tropicalia musicians, DakhaBrakha undertakes an exercise in fully embracing all inputs— including the ugly legacies of colonialism—and then purging those that have no utility.

8. Steven Feld (2015) devised a response to Schafer's limited conception of the soundscape in the term "acoustemology," a portmanteau of acoustics and epistemology meant to suggest the kinds of situated knowledges that sound can convey. This coinage usefully centers the ways in which sounds relationally reverberate in spaces that are also culturally informed—that are *emplaced*—and in the ways that sounds can be grounded, that is, associated with specific territories). Sakakeeny's (2010) work on the orientation of the listener to sound (in the context of a hurricane-ravaged New Orleans) also helpfully overturns Schafer's dismissive attitude toward urban soundscapes, which he considered part of the troubling "lo-fi soundscape of the contemporary megalopolis" (1994 [1977], 216).

9. Interestingly, R. Murray Schafer (1980) also draws on Levi-Strauss's idea of "bricolage" in a short essay describing his early sound sculptures. Schafer does not, however, bring his understanding of bricolage into conversation with his extensive soundscape-derived lexicon (which includes the soundmark). Hebdige also drew on Levi-Strauss's usage of the term in *The Savage Mind*.

10. The official video for this song, animated by the artist Sashko Danylenko (who provided the cover art for this book), also deserves attention for its evocative blend of folk art style motifs with absurdist and mythical elements, but that is beyond the scope of this analysis. I do recommend that the reader consult the music video, which can be viewed here: https://vimeo.com/49745103.

11. Simonett (2012) documents the circulation of the instrument well beyond the United States. Well-known albums such as *Planet Squeezebox* and *Global Accordion* present sonic histories of the globally dispersed squeezebox. I myself have written about the accordion

as an instrument that connotes "ethnic whiteness" in certain US contexts as a case study in critical organology (Sonevytsky 2008).

12. See Kwan for a fascinating parallel history of the accordion in socialist China, where ideological mandates proclaimed that "the bourgeois piano would no longer be privileged over the 'working-class' accordion" (2008, 90).

13. For recent volumes on hip-hop in various regions of Europe, see Miszczynski and Helbig 2017 and Rollefson 2017. For an earlier overview of global hip-hop, see Mitchell 2001. See Amsterdam 2013 for an exemplary study of how Native American hip-hop artists negotiate the tensions of the local and global, and harness the power of the genre to enact critiques.

14. In an interview with Hromadske.tv, DakhaBrakha introduced the genre term "steppe blues" (степовий блюз) to take the place of "ethno-chaos" (which they classified as a subgenre of "world music") for the group's then-still-forthcoming album, *The Road*. At the time of the interview, the album was still unnamed, but the musicians had narrowed their choice to two options meaning almost the same thing: Шлях ("path," though they translate it into English as "road") or Дорога ("road"). Though some critics appraised the new album as "steppe blues," DakhaBrakha remains associated primarily with ethno-chaos.

15. A Hromadske.tv interviewer asked the band if "Manakh" (a track on the new record) was a kind of sequel to "Carpathian Rap." The band said that it was not intended as such, explaining that it was drawn from the region of Kyivshchyna. Later, the interviewer asked about Jamala, saying that "she must be excited about inclusion of Crimean Tatar song on the record." They agreed that she was, and that Nina Haranetska (the singer on "Salgir Boyu") had asked Jamala to coach her on the correct Crimean Tatar pronunciation of the lyrics.

16. Based on its use of non-Crimean Tatar toponyms, which were largely erased over the course of three centuries by Russian imperial and, later, Soviet names, this particular wedding song was likely composed after the late eighteenth century since it uses Russian names for cities.

17. Ensemble Qaytarma was a key vehicle for the continuation of Crimean Tatar expressive culture during the period of exile between its establishment in 1957 and into the period of repatriation, when it relocated to Yevpatoria, Crimea. During the Soviet era, Qaytarma had a fraught relationship with Soviet censors, who preferred to scrub traditional songs of lyrical tropes or toponyms that might invoke Crimea, so it is peculiar that "Salgir Boyu" was not only allowed in the repertoire, but also presented on Uzbek television as a music video.

18. In her 2007 Dent Medal lecture, Georgina Born offers a useful overview of four "modes of temporality" that are possible to observe in music in order to construct a "non-teleological approach to time" (Born 2010, 239). Though she references (via Jona-

than Kramer's work) anthropological theories of time, she delineates categories that are resonant with but distinct from the palimpsestic temporality that I borrow from Shohat and Stam, and from Alexander.

19. Elizabeth Freeman explains this term through the following example: "The advent of wage work, for example, entailed a violent retemporalization of bodies once tuned to the seasonal rhythms of agricultural labor" (2010, 3).

20. The other key limitations Daughtry enumerates are that "2. It fails to deal with motion convincingly; 3. It presumes a privileged vantage point from which all sounds can be heard . . . [and] 4. It treats the world as a text" (2017, 78–79).

CONCLUSION *Dreamland: Becoming Acoustic Citizens*

1. The festival is named after a song by Skrypka's band Vopli Vidopliassova (colloquially known as V.V. (pronounced "Ve-Ve"). Dreamland usually takes place during the Ivana Kupala festival in Ukraine, which corresponds to the Feast of St. John the Baptist in the Christian tradition, though Ivana Kupala retains associations with pre-Christian fertility rituals (see Helbig 2011 and Kononenko 2004 for studies of the post-Soviet revival of Ivana Kupala festivals in Ukraine). Skrypka was also the coach who championed the *avtentyka* singer Suzanna Karpenko on *Holos Kraïny*, addressed in Chapter 3.

2. The delightful 1989 music video for "Tantsi" can be viewed on YouTube at https://www.youtube.com/watch?v=xXhHRswpoGU.

3. I borrow this phrase from Stephen Metcalf's overview of neoliberalism-as-idea and total system in the *Guardian* (https://www.theguardian.com/news/2017/aug/18/neoliberalism-the-idea-that-changed-the-world).

4. https://www.theguardian.com/commentisfree/2009/apr/10/financial-crisis-capitalism-socialism-alternatives.

5. My idea of acoustic citizenship builds on Kate Lacey's contention (following Arendt) that listening "is at the heart of what it means to the *in* the world, to be active, to be political. Thinking in this way about listening as a political action in and of itself is strangely counterintuitive. Listening tends to be taken for granted, a natural mode of reception that is more passive than active, but listening is . . . a critical category that ought to be right at the heart of any consideration of public life" (2013, 163). However, in addition to refiguring listening as active, I also emphasize that *being heard* through acts of sounding is key to my formulation.

6. Petryna's idea of "biological citizenship" emerged from her ethnographic research on survivors of the Chernobyl disaster that occurred in late Soviet Ukraine. She observed, "In Ukraine, where an emergent democracy is yoked to a harsh market transition, the damaged biology of a population has become the grounds for social membership and the basis for staking citizenship claims" (2002, 5). Petryna's pathbreaking study tracks

how post-Soviet "biological citizens" produced "a fundamental reconfiguration of human conditions and conditions of citizenship" by redefining how citizenly claims are voiced in "the most rudimentary life-and-death terms" (7). In lectures delivered on the subject of "The Musical Citizen," Stokes (2017) revisited his earlier work on Turkish sentimentality and popular music, which, he noted, "elucidates modes of connection that suggest an alternative history of citizenship, complex and intimate transformations, transmissions and translations as well as subtle continuities."

7. In one way, Ukraine's selection of Jamala was not entirely unsurprising, given that previous representatives to Eurovision had also challenged nationalist narratives of who deserved to represent Ukraine. Bilaniuk explains how the mixed-raced singer Gaitana's selection for Eurovision in 2012 sparked a conversation about Ukrainian belonging in racialized terms (2016, 355–57).

8. Scholars of Crimean Tatar history identify five major traumatic episodes of exile, mass migration, colonization, and dislocation that have marked the Crimean Tatar experience since the late eighteenth century (see Kozelsky 2008; Fisher 1978).

9. Fevzi Aliev, a Crimean Tatar musician and folklorist, introduces the song "Ey, Güzel Qirim!" in his anthology with the following words: "Under such conditions [of exile], neither poets nor composers could write about Crimea, because they knew that arrest was imminent. But all of this was still reflected in the songs. And so, in 1968, one of the most popular songs of exile appeared, 'Ey, Güzel Qirim'" (2001, 84). It existed with many variants. The song has no attributable author; though, as Aliev complains, many have pretended to the authorship since the risk of imprisonment vanished. In "1944," Jamala sings the first two lines of the chorus, or *baglama*, in reverse order and set to an entirely different melody. The lyrics to the first verse and chorus are as follows: Алуштадан эскен ельчик / Юзюме урды / Балалыгъым кечкен ерге / Козьяшым тюшти (The wind blows / from Alushta [a town on the southern coast of Crimea] and hits me in the face / Tears are dropping / in the place where I spent my childhood) // CHORUS Мен ву ерде яшалмадым / Чокъ ерлерни коралмадым / Ветаныма асрет олдым / Эй, гузель Къырым! (I can't live in that place / many places in Crimea I couldn't see / I miss my homeland / my beautiful Crimea!). I am grateful to Milara Settarova for assisting with the translation of these lyrics from Crimean Tatar to Russian, and to Zeyneb Temnenko and Zarema Seidametova for correcting my translation in English.

10. The controversy triggered a wide array of media reports. For one sober account, see https://www.rferl.org/a/eurovision-jamala-overly-political-controversy/27739159.html. The effects of Jamala's win spilled over into the 2017 competition, when the Russian contestant was banned because she had traveled to Crimea after its annexation, which resulted in Russia's withdrawal from the competition and boycott of the broadcast on Russian media.

11. The anthropologist Greta Uehling, it should be noted, cautioned against the soaring

and universalizing discourse of Jamala's victory as a victory for the human rights of all minority and indigenous groups.

12. By making this claim, I do not intend to paper over the well-known US histories of meddling in foreign elections, including, importantly, the post-Soviet Russian election that installed Boris Yeltsin as president and set a long-term trajectory for Russian state politics.

13. Throughout 2017, StopFake.org published a number of articles debunking Russian Eurovision stories, including "Fake: Kyiv Homeless to Be Run out of Town for Eurovision," "Fake: Ukraine Has No Money for Eurovision 2017," "Fake: Eurovision to Be Moved to Moscow," and so on. Russian legal bans against "homosexual propaganda" have been documented widely, and the question of traditional Russian morality was also tightly bound up in the Pussy Riot affair (see Bernstein 2013a; Tochka 2013).

14. For the entire bank of bingo cards, see https://www.stopfake.org/content/up loads/2017/04/StopFake-Bingo.pdf.

15. It should be noted that the Russian competitor Sergey Lazarev, who was a favorite in the competition, came in third place. Turkey did not take part in the 2016 competition, and Romania was expelled from the competition due to outstanding payments to the EBU. The roster of competing countries fluctuates year to year (it is open to any member states of the EBU), but it usually includes most states in the European Union, Israel, Turkey, Ukraine, Russia (until it boycotted the 2017 competition), and some other former socialist states (Azerbaijan, Albania, and so on).

BIBLIOGRAPHY

Abe, Marié. 2016. "Sounding Against Nuclear Power in Post-3.11 Japan: Resonances of Silence and Chindon-ya." *Ethnomusicology* 60 (2):233–62.

———. 2018. *Resonances of Chindon-ya: Sounding Space and Sociality in Contemporary Japan, Music/Culture.* Middletown, CT: Wesleyan University Press.

Abu-Lughod, Lila. 2005. *Dramas of Nationhood: The Politics of Television in Egypt.* Chicago: University of Chicago Press.

Agamben, Giorgio. 1998. *Homo Sacer: Sovereign Power and Bare Life.* Translated by Daniel Heller-Roazen. Stanford, CA: Stanford University Press.

Alexander, M. Jacqui. 2006. *Pedagogies of Crossing: Meditations on Feminism, Sexual Politics, Memory, and the Sacred.* Edited by Jack Halberstam and Lisa Lowe. Perverse Modernities series. Durham, NC: Duke University Press.

Aliev, Fevzi. 2001. *Antologia Krymskoj Narodnoj Muzyky* [Anthology of Crimean Folk Music]. Ak'mesdzhit (Simferopol): Krymuchpedgiz.

Allworth, Edward. 1998. *The Tatars of Crimea: Return to the Homeland: Studies and Documents.* 2nd ed. Central Asia book series. Durham, NC: Duke University Press.

Amsterdam, Lauren. 2013. "All the Eagles and the Ravens in the House Say Yeah: (Ab)original Hip-Hop, Heritage, and Love." *American Indian Culture and Research* 37 (2): 53–72.

Anderson, Benedict R. 1991. *Imagined Communities: Reflections on the Origin and Spread of Nationalism.* London: Verso.

Anter, Andreas. 2014. *Max Weber's Theory of the Modern State: Origins, Structure and Significance.* Translated by Keith Tribe. New York: Palgrave MacMillan.

Appadurai, Arjun. 1981. "The Past as a Scarce Resource." *Man* 16 (2):201–19.

——— 1990. "Disjuncture and Difference in the Global Cultural Economy." *Public Culture* 2 (2):1–24.

Arendt, Hannah. 1976 [1951]. *The Origins of Totalitarianism.* New York: Harcourt.

Aretxaga, Begoña. 2003. "Maddening States." *Annual Review of Anthropology* 32:393–410.

Asan, Emir. 2005. "'Meydan' otkryt dlia vsekh ['Meydan' is open to all]." *Poluostrov*, February 25–March 3.

Askew, Kelly. 2002. *Performing the Nation: Swahili Music and Cultural Politics in Tanzania*. Chicago: University of Chicago Press.

Attali, Jacques. 1985. *Noise: The Political Economy of Music*. Translated by Brian Massumi. Minneapolis: University of Minnesota Press.

Balibar, Etienne. 2013. "How Can the Aporia of the 'European People' Be Resolved?" *Radical Philosophy* 181 (1). https://www.radicalphilosophy.com/article/how-can-the -aporia-of-the-european-people-be-resolved.

Barney, Darin. 2007. "Radical Citizenship in the Republic of Technology: A Sketch." In *Radical Democracy and the Internet: Interrogating Theory and Practice*. Edited by Lincoln Dahlberg and Eugenia Siapera. New York: Palgrave, 37–54.

Bassin, Mark. 2016. *The Gumilev Mystique: Biopolitics, Eurasianism, and the Construction of Community in Modern Russia*. Culture and Society After Socialism series. Ithaca, NY: Cornell University Press.

Bendix, Regina. 1997. *In Search of Authenticity: The Formation of Folklore Studies*. Madison: University of Wisconsin Press.

Ben-Porath, Sigal R., and Rogers M. Smith, eds. 2013. *Varieties of Sovereignty and Citizenship*. Democracy, Citizenship, and Constitutionalism series. Philadelphia: University of Pennsylvania Press.

Berlant, Lauren. 1998. "Intimacy: A Special Issue." *Critical Inquiry* 24 (2):281–88.

———. 2008. *The Female Complaint: The Unfinished Business of Sentimentality in American Culture*. Durham, NC: Duke University Press.

Bernstein, Anya. 2013a. "An Inadvertent Sacrifice: Body Politics and Sovereign Power in the Pussy Riot Affair." *Critical Inquiry* 40 (1):220–41.

———. 2013b. *Religious Bodies Politic: Rituals of Sovereignty in Buryat Buddhism*. Chicago: University of Chicago Press.

Bessire, Lucas, and Daniel Fisher. 2013. "The Anthropology of Radio Fields." *Annual Review of Anthropology* 42 (1):363–78.

Bey, Hakim. 1991 [1985]. "The Temporary Autonomous Zone, Ontological Anarchy, Poetic Terrorism." https://hermetic.com/bey/taz_cont.

Bhabha, Homi K. 1990. *Nation and Narration*. London: Routledge.

Bickford, Tyler. 2017. *Schooling New Media: Music, Language, and Technology in Children's Culture*. Oxford: Oxford University Press.

Bilaniuk, Laada. 2003. "Gender, Language Attitudes, and Language Status in Ukraine." *Language in Society* 32:47–78.

———. 2005. *Contested Tongues: Language Politics and Cultural Correction in Ukraine*. Ithaca, NY: Cornell University Press.

———. 2016. "Race, Media, and Postcoloniality: Ukraine Between Nationalism and Cosmopolitanism." *City & Society* 28 (3):341–64.

Blacking, John. 1973. *How Musical Is Man?* John Danz lectures. Seattle: University of Washington Press.

Bohlman, Andrea F. 2016. "Solidarity, Song, and the Sound Document." *Journal of Musicology* 33 (2):232–69.

Bohlman, Philip V. 2004. *The Music of European Nationalism: Cultural Identity and Modern History*. Santa Barbara, CA: ABC-CLIO.

———. 2010. *Music, Nationalism, and the Making of the New Europe*. 2nd ed. London: Routledge.

Born, Georgina. 2010. "For a Relational Musicology: Music and Interdisciplinarity, Beyond the Practice Turn." *Journal of the Royal Musical Association* 135 (2):205–43.

Bourdieu, Pierre. 1984. *Distinction: A Social Critique of the Judgement of Taste*. Cambridge, MA: Harvard University Press.

———. 1996. *The Rules of Art: Genesis and Structure of the Literary Field*. Translated by Susan Emanuel. Stanford, CA: Stanford University Press.

Boyer, Dominic, and Alexei Yurchak. 2010. "American Stiob: Or, What Late-Socialist Aesthetics of Parody Reveal About Contemporary Political Culture in the West." *Cultural Anthropology* 25 (2):179–221.

Boym, Svetlana. 2000. "On Diasporic Intimacy." In *Intimacy*, edited by Lauren Berlant, 226–52. Chicago: University of Chicago Press.

———. 2001. *The Future of Nostalgia*. New York: Basic Books.

Brooks, Rosa Ehrenreich. 2005. "Failed States, or the State as Failure?" *University of Chicago Law Review* 72 (4):1159–96.

Brown, Kate. 2004. *Biography of No Place: From Ethnic Borderland to Soviet Heartland*. Cambridge, MA: Harvard University Press.

Brown, Wendy. 2014. *Walled States, Waning Sovereignty*. Cambridge, MA: Zone Books.

Buchanan, Donna A. 1995. "Metaphors of Power, Metaphors of Truth: The Politics of Music Professionalism in Bulgarian Folk Orchestras." *Ethnomusicology* 39 (3):381–416.

———. 2006. *Performing Democracy: Bulgarian Music and Musicians in Transition*. Chicago: University of Chicago Press.

Butler, Judith 2015. *Notes Toward a Performative Theory of Assembly*. Cambridge, MA: Harvard University Press.

Butler, Judith, and Gayatri Chakravorty Spivak. 2010. *Who Sings the Nation-State?* London: Seagull Books.

Carroll, Jennifer J. 2014. "Ukraine's EuroMaidan Isn't Just for the Right." *Yale Journal of International Affairs*. http://yalejournal.org/article_post/ukraines-euromaidan-isnt-just-for-the-right/.

———. 2017. "Image and Imitation: The Visual Rhetoric of Pro-Russian Propaganda." *Ideology and Politics Journal* 8 (2):36–79.

Chakrabarty, Dipesh. 2000. *Provincializing Europe: Postcolonial Thought and Historical Difference, Princeton Studies in Culture/Power/History*. Princeton, NJ: Princeton University Press.

Chalfin, Brenda. 2010. *Neoliberal Frontiers: An Ethnography of Sovereignty in West Africa*. Chicago: University of Chicago Press.

Channell, Emily. 2014. "Is Sextremism the New Feminism? Perspectives from Pussy Riot and Femen." *Nationalities Papers: The Journal of Nationalism and Ethnicity* 42 (4):611–14.

Charles, Dan. 2008. "A Ukrainian Pop Star's Would-Be Revolution." National Public Radio, *All Things Considered*, accessed April 8, 2008. http://www.npr.org/templates /story/story.php?storyId=89436819.

Charron, Austin. 2016. "Whose Is Crimea?" *Region: Regional Studies of Russia, Eastern Europe, and Central Asia* 5 (2):225–56.

Chernetsky, Vitaly. 2016. "Ukrainian Queer Culture: The Difficult Birth." In *Queer Stories of Europe*, edited by Karlis Verdins and Janis Ozolins. Newcastle upon Tyne, UK: Cambridge Scholars Publishing.

Coalson, Robert. 2014. "Petro Poroshenko, Ukraine's Shadowy Man of the Hour." Radio Free Europe/Radio Liberty, accessed July 13, 2014. http://www.rferl.org/content /poroshenko-profile-ukraine-presidential-candidate/25314782.html.

Comaroff, John L., and Jean Comaroff. 2009. *Ethnicity, Inc.* Chicago: University of Chicago Press.

Culshaw, Peter. 2013. "Rock the Barricades: The Ukrainian Musicians Soundtracking the Unrest." *Guardian*, accessed June 15, 2014. http://www.theguardian.com/music/2014 /may/29/rock-barricades-ukrainian-musicians-soundtracking-unrest.

———. 2014. " 'I Am a Singer. But if the Russians Come I Will Take Up Arms, Everyone Will.' " *Noisey Blog*, last modified June 23, 2014, accessed January 10, 2017. https://noisey .vice.com/en_uk/article/6wqwyz/kiev-sound-of-a-revolution.

Danielson, Virginia. 1997. *The Voice of Egypt: Umm Kulthum, Arabic Song, and Egyptian Society in the Twentieth Century*. Chicago: University of Chicago Press.

Daughtry, J. Martin. 2003. "Russia's New Anthem and the Negotiation of National Identity." *Ethnomusicology* 47 (1):42–67.

———. 2014. "Thanatosonics: Ontologies of Acoustic Violence." *Social Text* 32 (2):25–52.

———. 2015. *Listening to War: Sound, Music, Trauma, and Survival in Wartime Iraq*. Oxford: Oxford University Press.

———. 2017. "Acoustic Palimpsests." In *Theorizing Sound Writing*, edited by Deborah Kapchan, 46–85. Middletown, CT: Wesleyan University Press.

De Boever, Arne. 2016. *Plastic Sovereignties: Agamben and the Politics of Aesthetics*. Edinburgh: Edinburgh University Press.

DeNora, Tia. 2000. *Music in Everyday Life*. Cambridge, UK: Cambridge University Press.

Desiateryk, Dmytro. 2013. "'Rozy/Donbass'" as an Example of Correct PR." Accessed July 22, 2013. http://day.kyiv.ua/en/article/day-after-day/rozy-donbass-example-correct-pr.

Diatchkova, Galina. 2008. "Indigenous Media as Important Resource for Russia's Indigenous Peoples." In *Global Indigenous Media*, edited by Pamela Wilson and Michelle Stewart, 214–31. Durham, NC: Duke University Press.

Dolar, Mladen. 2006. *A Voice and Nothing More*. Edited by Slavoj Zizek. Short Circuits series. Cambridge, MA: MIT Press.

Downing, John D. H. 2001. *Radical Media: Rebellious Communication and Social Movements*. Thousand Oaks, CA: Sage Publications.

Dunn, Elizabeth Cullen, and Michael S. Bobick. 2014. "The Empire Strikes Back: War Without War and Occupation Without Occupation in the Russian Sphere of Influence." *American Ethnologist* 41 (3):405–13.

"*Dyka Harmoniia Voli* [Wild Harmony of the Will]." 2004. https://www.bbc.com/ukrainian/entertainment/story/2004/05/040513_ruslana_interview.shtml.

Edmonson, George, and Klaus Mladek, eds. 2017. *Sovereingty in Ruins: A Politics of Crisis*. Durham, NC: Duke University Press.

Edmunds, Neil. 2000. *The Soviet Proletarian Music Movement*. Bern: Peter Lang.

Eisenberg, Andrew J. 2012. "Hip-Hop and Cultural Citizenship on Kenya's 'Swahili Coast.'" *Africa* 84 (2):556–78.

———. 2013. "Islam, Sound and Space." In *Music, Sound and Space: Transformations of Public and Private Experience*, edited by Georgina Born, 186–202. Cambridge, UK: Cambridge University Press.

Ellingson, Ter. 2001. *The Myth of the Noble Savage*. Berkeley: University of California Press.

Eng, David L., with Jack Halberstam and José Esteban Muñoz. 2005. "What's Queer About Queer Studies Now?" *Social Text* 23 (3–4):1–17.

Erlmann, Veit. 1999. *Music, Modernity, and the Global Imagination*. Oxford: Oxford University Press.

Esposito, Roberto. 2011. *Immunitas: The Protection and Negation of Life*. Cambridge, UK: Polity Press.

Fanon, Frantz. 2012. "This Is the Voice of Algeria." In *The Sound Studies Reader*, edited by Jonathan Sterne, 329–35. London: Routledge.

Feld, Steven. 1984. "Communication, Music, and Speech About Music." *Yearbook for Traditional Music* 16:1–18.

———. 2000. "A Sweet Lullaby for World Music." *Public Culture* 12 (1):145–71.

———. 2011. "Acoustemic Stratigraphies: Recent Work in Urban Phonography." *Sensate*, last modified March 11. sensatejournal.com/steven-feld-acoustemic-stratigraphies.

———. 2015. "Acoustemology." In *Keywords in Sound*, edited by David Novak and Matt Sakakeeny, 12–21. Durham, NC: Duke University Press.

Feld, Steven, and Aaron A. Fox. 1994. "Music and Language." *Annual Review of Anthropology* 23:25–53.

Feld, Steven, Aaron A. Fox, Thomas Porcello, and David Samuels. 2004. "Vocal Anthropology: From the Music of Language to the Language of Song." In *A Companion to Linguistic Anthropology*, edited by Alessandro Duranti, 321–45. Oxford: Wiley-Blackwell.

Finnin, Rory. 2011. "Forgetting Nothing, Forgetting No One: Boris Chichibabin, Viktor Nekipelov, and the Deportation of the Crimean Tatars." *Modern Language Review* 106 (4):1091–1124. doi: 10.5699/modelangrevi.106.4.1091.

Fisher, Alan. 1978. *The Crimean Tatars*. Stanford, CA: Hoover Institution Press.

Fisher, Daniel. 2016. *The Voice and Its Doubles: Media and Music in Northern Australia*. Durham, NC: Duke University Press.

Foucault, Michel, ed. 1980. *Power/Knowledge: Selected Interviews and Other Writings, 1972–1977*. Edited by Colin Gordon. New York: Pantheon Books.

Fowler, Mayhill C. 2017. *Beau Monde on Empire's Edge: State and Stage in Soviet Ukraine*. Toronto: University of Toronto Press.

Fox, Aaron A. 1992. "The Jukebox of History: Narratives of Loss and Desire in the Discourse of Country Music." *Popular Music* 11 (1):53–72.

Fraser, Nancy. 1990. "Rethinking the Public Sphere: A Contribution to the Critique of Actually Existing Democracy." *Social Text* 25/26:56–80.

Freeman, Elizabeth. 2010. *Time Binds: Queer Temporalities, Queer Histories*. Durham, NC: Duke University Press.

Friedner, Michele Ilana, and Stefan Helmreich. 2012. "Sound Studies Meets Deaf Studies." *Senses and Society* 7 (1):72–86. doi: 10.2752/174589312X13173255802120.

Frolova-Walker, Marina. 1998. "'National in Form, Socialist in Content': Musical Nation-Building in the Soviet Republics." *Journal of the American Musicological Society* 51 (2):331–71.

Frolova-Walker, Marina, and Jonathan Walker, eds. 2012. *Music and Soviet Power, 1917–1932*. Woodbridge, UK: Boydell Press.

Gal, Susan. 2002. "A Semiotics of the Public/Private Distinction." *differences: A Journal of Feminist Cultural Studies* 13 (1):77–95.

Garland, Shannon. 2012. "'The Space, the Gear, and Two Big Cans of Beer': Fora do Eixo and the Debate Over Circulation, Renumeration, and Aesthetics in the Brazilian Alternative Market." *Journal of Popular Music Studies* 24 (4):509–31.

Gerasimov, Ilya. 2014. "Ukraine 2014: The First Postcolonial Revolution." *Ab Imperio* (3):22–43.

Gerasimov, Ilya, and Marina Mogilner. 2015. "Deconstructing Integration: Ukraine's Postcolonial Subjectivity." *Slavic Review* 74 (4):715–22.

Gessen, Keith. 2010. "The Orange and the Blue: After the Revolution, a Politics of Disenchantment." Last modified March 1. http://www.newyorker.com/magazine/2010/03/01 /the-orange-and-the-blue.

Ghodsee, Kristen R. 2011. *Lost in Transition: Ethnographies of Everyday Life After Communism.* Durham, NC: Duke University Press.

———. 2017. *Red Hangover: Legacies of Twentieth-Century Communism.* Durham, NC: Duke University Press.

Gill, Rosalind. 2009. "Supersexualize Me! Advertising and 'The Midriffs.'" In *Mainstreaming Sex: The Sexualization of Western Culture*, edited by Feona Attwood, 93–110. London: I.B. Tauris.

Gilroy, Paul. 2006. *Postcolonial Melancholia.* Wellek Library Lectures. New York: Columbia University Press.

Gorsuch, Anne E., and Diane P. Koenker, eds. 2006. *Turizm: The Russian and East European Tourist Under Capitalism and Socialism.* Ithaca, NY: Cornell University Press.

Goscilo, Helena. 1996. *Dehexing Sex: Russian Womanhood During and After Glasnost.* Ann Arbor: University of Michigan Press.

Grant, Bruce. 2009. *The Captive and the Gift: Cultural Histories of Sovereignty in Russia and the Caucasus.* Ithaca, NY: Cornell University Press.

Gray, Lila Ellen. 2013. *Fado Resounding: Affective Politics and Urban Life.* Durham, NC: Duke University Press.

———. 2016. "Registering Protest: Voice, Precarity, and Return in Crisis Portugal." *History and Anthropology* 27 (1):60–73.

Gronow, Pekka. 1975. "Ethnic Music and the Soviet Record Industry." *Ethnomusicology* 19 (1):91–99.

Gross, Joan, David McMurray, and Ted Swedenburg. 1996. "Arab Noise and Ramadan Nights: Rai, Rap, and Franco-Maghrebi Identity." In *Displacement, Diaspora, and Geographies of Identity*, edited by Smadar Lavie and Ted Swedenburg. Durham, NC: Duke University Press.

Guilbault, Jocelyne. 2005. "Audible Entanglements: Nation and Diasporas in Trinidad's Calypso Music Scene." *Small Axe* 17:40–63.

———. 2007. *Governing Sound: The Cultural Politics of Trinidad's Carnival Musics.* Chicago: University of Chicago Press.

Habermas, Jürgen. 1998. *Between Facts and Norms: Contributions to a Discourse Theory of Law and Democracy.* Translated by William Rehg. Studies in Contemporary German Social Thought series. Cambridge, MA: MIT Press.

Habermas, Jürgen, and Ciaran Cronin. 1998. "The European Nation-State: On the Past and Future of Sovereignty and Citizenship." *Public Culture* 10 (2):397–416.

Halberstam, Jack. 2006. "What's That Smell?: Queer Temporalities and Subcultural Lives." In *Queering the Popular Pitch*, edited by Sheila Whiteley and Jennifer Rycenga, 3–25. New York: Routledge.

———. 2011. *The Queer Art of Failure*. Durham and London: Duke University Press.

———. 2014. "Wildness, Loss, Death." *Social Text* 32 (4):137–48.

Halberstam, Jack, and Tavia Nyong'o, eds. 2018. "Wildness." Special issue, *South Atlantic Quarterly* 117 (3).

Hansen, Thomas Blom, and Finn Stepputat. 2005. *Sovereign Bodies: Citizens, Migrants, and States in the Postcolonial World*. Princeton, NJ: Princeton University Press.

———. 2006. "Sovereignty Revisited." *Annual Review of Anthropology* 35 (16):1–21.

Hardt, Michael, and Antonio Negri. 2000. *Empire*. Cambridge, MA: Harvard University Press.

Harrington, Helmi Strahl, and Gerhard Kubik. 2001. "Accordion." In *Grove Music Online*. http://www.oxfordmusiconline.com.

Hartley, John. 2004. "Democratainment." In *The Television Studies Reader*, edited by R. C. Allen and A. Hill, 524–33. London: Routledge.

Hebdige, Dick. 1979. *Subculture: The Meaning of Style*. London: Routledge.

Helbig, Adriana N. 2006. "The Cyberpolitics of Music in Ukraine's 2004 Orange Revolution." *Current Musicology* 82:81–101.

———. 2011a. "'Brains, Means, Lyrical Ammunition': Hip-hop and Socio-racial Agency among African Students in Kharkiv, Ukraine." *Popular Music* 30 (3):315–30.

———. 2011b. "Ivana Kupala (St. John's Eve) Revivals as Metaphors of Sexual Morality, Fertility, and Contemporary Ukrainian Femininity." In *The Oxford Handbook of Music Revivals*, edited by Caroline Bithell and Juniper Hill. Oxford: Oxford University Press.

———. 2014. *Hip Hop Ukraine: Music, Race, and African Migration, Ethnomusicology Multimedia*. Bloomington: Indiana University Press.

Heller, Dana. 2007. "t.A.T.u. You! Russia, the Global Politics of Eurovision, and Lesbian Pop." *Popular Muisc* 26:195–210.

Hemmasi, Farzaneh. 2017. "Iran's Daughter and Mother Iran: Googoosh and Diasporic Nostalgia for the Pahlavi Modern." *Popular Music* 36 (2):157–77. doi: 10.1017/S0261143017000113.

Herder, Johann Gottfried. 2011. *Journal meiner Reise im Jahr 1769*. Amazon Digital Services.

Herder, Johann Gottfried, and Philip V. Bohlman. 2017. *Song Loves the Masses: Herder on Music and Nationalism*. Translated by Philip V. Bohlman. Oakland: University of California Press.

Herodotus. 2003. *The Histories*. Translated by Aubrey de Sélincourt. Revised with introduction and notes by John Marincola, ed. London: Penguin Books.

Herzfeld, Michael. 2005. *Cultural Intimacy: Social Poetics in the Nation-State*. 2nd ed. New York: Routledge.

Hesford, Victoria, and Lisa Diedrich, eds. 2008. *Feminist Time Against Nation Time: Gender, Politics, and the Nation-State in an Age of Permanent War*. Lanham, MD: Lexington Books.

Hill, Juniper. 2007. "'Global Folk Music' Fusions: The Reification of Transnational Relationships and the Ethics of Cross-Cultural Appropriations in Finnish Contemporary Folk Music." *Yearbook for Traditional Music* 39:50–83.

Hilmes, Michelle. 2012. "Radio and the Imagined Community." In *The Sound Studies Reader*, edited by Jonathan Sterne, 351–62. New York: Routledge.

Hirsch, Francine. 2005. *Empire of Nations: Ethnographic Knowledge and the Making of the Soviet Union*. Ithaca, NY: Cornell University Press.

Hirschkind, Charles. 2009. *The Ethical Soundscape: Cassette Sermons and Islamic Counterpublics*. New York: Columbia University Press.

Hofman, Ana. 2010. *Staging Socialist Femininity: Gender Politics and Folklore Performance in Serbia*. Leiden: Brill.

———. 2011. "Questioning Soviet Folklorization: The Beltinci Folklore Festival in the Slovenian Borderland of Prekmurje." In *Audiovisual Media and Identity Issues in Southeastern Europe*, edited by Nicola Scaldaferri and Gretel Schwörer Eckehard Pistrick, 238–57. Newcastle upon Tyne, UK: Cambridge Scholars Publishing.

Holusha, John. 2006. "Bush Says Anthem Should Be in English." *New York Times*, April 28. https://www.nytimes.com/2006/04/28/us/28cnd-anthem.html.

Hounshell, Blake. 2011. "The Revolution Will Be Tweeted: Life in the Vanguard of the New Twitter Proletariat." *Foreign Policy* 187 (July–August):20–21.

Hrycak, Alexandra. 2006. "Foundation Feminism and the Articulation of Hybrid Feminisms in Post-Socialist Ukraine." *East European Politics and Societies* 20 (1): 69–100.

Hrycak, Alexandra, and Maria Rewakowicz. 2009. "Feminism, Intellectuals and the Formation of Micro-Publics in Postcommunist Ukraine." *Studies in East European Thought* 61 (4):309–33.

Hrytsak, Yaroslav. 2015. "The Postcolonial Is Not Enough." *Slavic Review* 74 (4):732–37.

Humphrey, Caroline. 2004. "Sovereignty." In *A Companion to the Anthropology of Politics*, edited by David Nugent and Joan Vincent, 418–36. Oxford: Blackwell Publishing.

Hutchinson, Sydney. 2016. *Tigers of a Different Stripe*. Chicago Studies in Ethnomusicology series. Chicago: University of Chicago Press.

Ignatieff, Michael. 1995. *Blood and Belonging: Journeys into the New Nationalism*. New York: Farrar, Straus and Giroux.

Ishchenko, Volodymyr. 2016. "Far Right Participation in the Ukrainian Maidan Protests: An Attempt of Systemic Estimation." *European Politics and Society* 17 (4):453–72.

Ivanov, Oleksandr. 2014. "O Brother, Who Art Though? [sic]." Accessed April 25, 2014. http://kyivweekly.com.ua/pulse/society/2014/04/25/145540.html.

Ivanytskyi, A. I. 2008. *Khrestomatiia z Ukrainskoho muzychnoho fol'kloru* [A Reader in Ukrainian Musical Folklore]. Kyiv: Nova Knyha.

Izmirlieva, Valentina. 2018. "The Cult of St. Volodimer and the Theft of History: Why Moscow's Competition with Kyiv Pivots on St. Volodimer and How His Cult Is Revamped Today." George Shevelov Memorial Lecture in Ukrainian Studies, April 27. New York: Columbia University.

Junka, Laura. 2006. "Camping in the Third Space: Agency, Representation, and the Politics of Gaza Beach." *Public Culture* 18 (2):348–59.

Kaindl, Raimund Friedrich. 1894. *Die Huzulen. Ihr Leben, ihre Sitten und ihre Volksüberlieferung*. Wien: Alfred Hölder.

Kappeler, Andreas. 2003. *"Great Russians" and "Little Russians": Russian-Ukrainian Relations and Perceptions in Historical Perspective*. Donald W. Treadgold Papers in Russian, East European, and Central Asian Studies. Seattle: Henry M. Jackson School of International Studies.

Karnes, Kevin C. 2018. "Inventing Eastern Europe in the Ear of the Enlightenment." *Journal of the American Musicological Society* 71 (1):75.

Keil, Charles. 1994. "Participatory Discrepancies and the Power of Music." In *Music Grooves*, edited by Charles Keil and Steven Feld, 96–108. Chicago: University of Chicago Press.

Khaldarova, Irina, and Mervi Pantti. 2016. "Fake News: The Narrative Battle Over the Ukrainian Conflict." *Journalism Practice* 10 (7):891–901. doi: 10.1080/17512786.2016.1163237.

Kheshti, Roshanak. 2015. *Modernity's Ear: Listening to Race and Gender in World Music*. New York: New York University Press.

Klid, Bohdan. 2007. "Rock, Pop and Politics in Ukraine's 2004 Presidential Campaign and Orange Revolution." *Journal of Communist Studies and Transition Politics* 23 (1):118–37.

Klymenko, Iryna. 2010. *Dyskohrafiya Ukrayinskoyi Etnomuzyky (Avtentychne Vykonannia) 1908–2010* [Discography of Ukrainian Ethno-music (Authentic Performance) 1908–2010]. Kyiv: Ministerstvo Kul'tury i Turyzmu Ukrajiny, Natsional'na Muzychna Akademia Ukraïny im. P. I. Chaikovskoho.

Kononenko, Natalie. 2004. "Karaoke Ivan Kupalo: Ritual in Post-Soviet Ukraine." *Slavic and East European Journal* 48 (2):177–202.

Kozelsky, Mara. 2008. "Casualties of Conflict: Crimean Tatars During the Crimean War." *Slavic Review* 67 (4):866–91.

Kulyk, Volodymyr. 2013. "Language Policy in the Ukrainian Media: Authorities, Producers and Consumers." *Europe-Asia Studies* 65 (7):1417–43.

Kunreuther, Laura. 2014. *Voicing Subjects: Public Intimacy and Mediation in Kathmandu*. Berkeley: University of California Press.

———. 2018. "Sounds of Democracy: Performance, Protest, and Political Subjectivity." *Cultural Anthropology* 27 (3):1–31. doi: 10.14506/ca33.1.01.

Kurshutov, Temur. 2005. "'Meydan'—Pervaya Krymskotatarskaya Radiostantsia ['Meydan'—The First Crimean Tatar Radio Station]." *Avdet*, February 15, 4.

Kuzio, Taras. 2011. "Soviet Conspiracy Theories and Political Culture in Ukraine: Understanding Viktor Yanukovych and the Party of Regions." *Communist and Post-Communist Studies* 44:221–32.

Kwan, Yin Yee. 2008. "The Transformation of the Accordion in Twentieth-Century China." *World of Music* 50 (3):81–99.

Lacey, Kate. 2013. *Listening Publics: The Politics and Experience of Listening in the Media Age*. Cambridge, UK: Polity Press.

Larkin, Brian. 2008. *Signal and Noise: Media, Infrastructure, and Urban Culture in Nigeria*. Durham, NC: Duke University Press.

Levin, Theodore Craig. 1980. "Music in Modern Uzbekistan: The Convergence of Marxist Aesthetics and Central Asian Tradition." *Asian Music* 12 (1):149–58.

———. 1996. "Dmitri Pokrovsky and the Russian Folk Music Revival Movement." In *Retuning Culture: Musical Changes in Central and Eastern Europe*, edited by Mark Slobin. Durham, NC: Duke University Press.

———. 2002. "Making Marxist-Leninist Music in Uzbekistan." In *Music and Marx: Ideas, Practice, Politics*, edited by Regula Burckhardt Qureshi, 190–203. New York: Routledge.

Levin, Theodore Craig, and Valentina Süzükei. 2006. *Where Rivers and Mountains Sing: Sound, Music, and Nomadism in Tuva and Beyond*. Bloomington: Indiana University Press.

Lovell, Stephen. 2015. *Russia in the Microphone Age: A History of Soviet Radio, 1919–1970*. Oxford: Oxford University Press.

Manabe, Noriko. 2015. *The Revolution Will Not Be Televised: Protest Music After Fukushima*. Oxford: Oxford University Press.

Marples, David. 2006. "Stepan Bandera: The Resurrection of a Ukrainian National Hero." *Europe-Asia Studies* 58 (4):555–66.

Martsenyuk, Tamara. 2014. "The State of the LGBT Community and Homophobia in Ukraine." *Problems of Post-Communism* 59 (2):51–62.

Mayerchyk, Maria, and Olha Plakhotnik. 2010. "The Radical FEMEN and the New Women's Activism." *Krytyka* 11 (11–12):7–10.

———. 2015. "Ukrainian Feminism at the Crossroad of National, Postcolonial, and (Post) Soviet: Theorizing the Maidan Events 2013-2014." Blog on www.krytyka.com, November 24, 2015.

Mbembe, Achilles. 2003. "Necropolitics." *Public Culture* 15 (1):11–40.

McCann, Brian. 2004. *Hello, Hello Brazil: Popular Music in the Making of Modern Brazil*. Durham, NC: Duke University Press.

McDonald, David A. 2013. *My Voice Is My Weapon: Music, Nationalism, and the Poetics of Palestinian Resistance*. Durham, NC: Duke University Press.

McGranahan, Carole. 2016. "Theorizing Refusal: An Introduction." *Cultural Anthropology* 31 (3):319–25. doi: 10.14506/ca31.3.01.

Medić, Ivana. 2014. "Arhai's *Balkan Folktronica*: Serbian *Ethno Music* Reimagined for British Market." Музикологија / *Musicology* 16:105–30.

Meintjes, Louise. 1990. "Paul Simon's *Graceland*, South Africa, and the Mediation of Musical Meaning." *Ethnomusicology* 34 (1):37–73.

———. 2003. *Sound of Africa: Making Music Zulu in a South African Studio*. Durham, NC: Duke University Press.

Meizel, Katherine. 2010. "Real-politics: Televised Talent Competitions and Democracy Promotion in the Middle East." In *Music and Media in the Arab World*, edited by Michael Frishkopf, 291–308. Cairo: American University in Cairo Press.

Miszczynski, Milosz, and Adriana Helbig, eds. 2017. *Hip Hop at Europe's Edge: Music, Agency, and Social Change*. Bloomington: Indiana University Press.

Mitchell, Tony. 2001. *Global Noise: Rap and Hip-Hop Outside the USA*. Music/Culture series. Middletown, CT: Wesleyan University Press.

Moore, Allan. 2002. "Authenticity as Authentication." *Popular Music* 21 (2):209–23.

Moore, David Chioni. 2001. "Is the Post- in Postcolonial the Post- in Post-Soviet? Toward a Global Postcolonial Critique." *PMLA* 116 (1):111–28.

Moorman, Marissa J. 2008. *Intonations: A Social History of Music and Nation in Luanda, Angola, from 1945 to Recent Times*. Athens: Ohio University Press.

Moreno, Jairo. 2016. "Imperial Aurality: Jazz, the Archive, and U.S. Empire." In *Audible Empire: Music, Global Politics, Critique*, edited by Ronald and Tejumola Olaniyan Radano, 135–60. Durham, NC: Duke University Press.

Morreale, Joanne. 1998. "Xena: Warrior Princess as Feminist Camp." *Journal of Popular Culture* 32 (2):79–86.

Mouffe, Chantal. "Agonistic Democracy and Radical Politics." *Pavilion*, accessed January 15, 2018. http://pavilionmagazine.org/chantal-mouffe-agonistic-democracy-and-radical-politics/.

Mrázek, Rudolf. 2002. *Engineers of Happy Land: Technology and Nationalism in a Colony*. Princeton, NJ: Princeton University Press.

Muñoz, José Esteban. 2009. *Cruising Utopia: The Then and There of Queer Futurity*. New York: New York University Press.

Murney, Maureen. 2007. "Our Women are Berehynia: (In)Authentic Femininity and Addiction in Western Ukraine." Toronto: Munk Centre for International Studies Briefings, 132–47.

Nelson, Amy. 2004. *Music for the Revolution: Musicians and Power in Early Soviet Russia*. University Park: Pennsylvania State University Press.

Nercessian, Andy. 2000. "A Look at the Emergence of the Concept of National Culture in Armenia: The Former Soviet Folk Ensemble." *International Review of the Aesthetics and Sociology of Music* 31 (1):79–94.

Nettl, Bruno. 2010. *Nettl's Elephant: On the History of Ethnomusicology.* Urbana: University of Illinois Press.

Niezen, Ronald. 2003. *The Origins of Indigenism: Human Rights and the Politics of Identity.* Berkeley: University of California Press.

Ninoshvili, Lauren. 2012. "'Wailing in the Cities': Media, Modernity, and the Metamorphosis of Georgian Women's Expressive Labor." *Music and Politics* 6 (2):1–15. doi: 10.3998/mp.9460447.0006.202.

Noll, William. 1991. "Music Institutions and National Consciousness among Polish and Ukrainian Peasants." In *Ethnomusicology and Modern Music History,* edited by Stephen Blum, Philip V. Bohlman, and Daniel M. Neuman. Urbana: University of Illinois Press.

Novak, David. 2011. "The Sublime Frequencies of New Old Media." *Public Culture* 23 (3):603–34.

———. 2013. *Japanoise: Music at the Edge of Circulation.* Durham, NC: Duke University Press.

———. 2017. "Project Fukushima! Performativity and the Politics of Festival in Post-3/11 Japan." *Anthropological Quarterly* 90 (1):225–54.

Ochoa Gautier, Ana María. 2006. "Sonic Transculturation, Epistemologies of Purification and the Aural Public Sphere in Latin America." *Social Identities* 12 (6):803–25.

———. 2014. *Aurality.* Durham, NC: Duke University Press.

———. 2016. "Acoustic Multinaturalism, the Value of Nature, and the Nature of Music in Ecomusicology." *boundary 2* 43 (1):107–41. doi: 10.1215/01903659-3340661.

O'Keeffe, Brigid. 2013. *New Soviet Gypsies: Nationality, Performance, and Selfhood in the Early Soviet Union.* Toronto: University of Toronto Press.

Olson, Laura J. 2004. *Performing Russia: Folk Revival and Russian Identity.* BASEES/RoutledgeCurzon Series on Russian and East European Studies. London: RoutledgeCurzon.

Ong, Aihwa. 1999. *Flexible Citizenship: The Cultural Logics of Transnationalism.* Durham, NC: Duke University Press.

———. 2006. *Neoliberalism as Exception: Mutations in Citizenship and Sovereignty.* Durham, NC: Duke University Press.

Ortmann, Stefanie, and John Heathershaw. 2012. "Conspiracy Theories in the Post-Soviet Space." *Russian Review* 71 (4):551–64. doi: 10.1111/j.1467-9434.2012.00668.x.

Ortner, Sherry B. 1974. "Is Female to Male as Nature Is to Culture?" In *Woman, Culture and Society,* edited by M. Z. Rosaldo and L. Lamphere. Stanford, CA: Stanford University Press.

———. 1995. "Resistence and the Problem of Ethnographic Refusal." *Comparative Studies in Society and History* 37 (1):173–93.

———. 2016. "Dark Anthropology and Its Others: Theory Since the Eighties." *HAU: Journal of Ethnographic Theory* 6 (1). doi: 10.14318/hau6.1.004.

Orwell, George. 2000 [1968]. "Notes on Nationalism." In *The Collected Essays, Journalism and Letters: As I Please, 1943–1946*, edited by Sonia Orwell and Ian Angus, 361–79. Boston: Nonpareil Books.

Oushakine, Serguei Alex. 2009. *The Patriotism of Despair: Nation, War, and Loss in Russia*. Culture and Society After Socialism series. Ithaca, NY: Cornell University Press.

Pareles, Jon. 2014. "Put Language Aside, Then Let the Music Take Time to Speak." *New York Times*, June 18, C2, Music Review. http://www.nytimes.com/2014/06/18/arts/music/dakhabrakha-plays-at-the-global-beat-festival.html.

Parker, James E. K. 2015. *Acoustic Jurisprudence: Listening to the Trial of Simon Bikindi*. Oxford: Oxford University Press.

Pavlychko, Solomea. 1996. "Feminism in Post-Communist Ukrainian Society." In *Women in Russia and Ukraine*, edited by Rosalind Marsh, 305–14. Cambridge, UK: Cambridge University Press.

Pavlyshyn, Marko. 2006. "Envisioning Europe: Ruslana's Rhetoric of Identity." *Slavic and East European Journal* 50 (3):469–85.

Petryna, Adriana. 2002. *Life Exposed: Biological Citizens After Chernobyl*. Princeton, NJ: Princeton Univeristy Press.

Phillips, Sarah D. 2014. "The Women's Squad in Ukraine's Protests: Feminism, Nationalism and Militarism on the Maidan." *American Ethnologist* 41 (3):414–26.

Pinkham, Sophie. 2014. "Are You Alive, Brother?" *n+1*, February 23. https://nplusonemag.com/online-only/online-only/are-you-alive-brother/.

Plokhii, Serhii. 2016. "Ukraine Sings to a Tune of New National Pride." Accessed May 18, 2016. https://next.ft.com/content/12fd7774-1c55-11e6-b286-cddde55ca122.

Porcello, Thomas, Louise Meintjes, Ana Maria Ochoa, and David W. Samuels. 2010. "The Reorganization of the Sensory World." *Annual Review of Anthropology* 39:51–66. doi: 10.1146/annurev.anthro.012809.105042.

Portnov, Andrii. 2013. "Memory Wars in Post-Soviet Ukraine (1991–2010)." In *Memory and Theory in Eastern Europe*, edited by Alexander Etkind, Uilleam Blacker, and Julie Fedor, 233–54. New York: Palgrave Macmillan.

Potoczniak, Anthony G. 2011. "Cultural Heritage in States of Transition: Authorities, Entrepreneurs, and Sound Archives in Ukraine." Ph.D. Dissertation, Anthropology Department, Rice University.

Quashie, Kevin. 2012. *The Sovereignty of Quiet: Beyond Resistence in Black Culture*. New Brunswick, NJ: Rutgers University Press.

Ranciere, Jacques. 2013. *The Politics of Aesthetics*. Translated by Gabriel Rockhill. New York: Bloomsbury Academic.

Raykoff, Ivan, and Robert Deam Tobin, eds. 2007. *A Song for Europe: Popular Music and Politics in the Eurovision Song Contest*. Burlington, VT: Ashgate.

Regev, Motti. 2007. "Ethno-National Pop-Rock Music: Aesthetic Cosmopolitanism Made from Within." *Cultural Sociology* 1 (3):317–41.

Reinelt, Janelle G. 2001. "Performing Europe: Identity Formation for a 'New' Europe." *Theatre Journal* 53 (3):365–87.

Risch, William Jay. 2015. "What the Far Right Does Not Tell Us About the Maidan." *Kritika: Explorations in Russian and Eurasian History* 16 (1):137–44.

Rollefson, J. Griffith. 2017. *Flip the Script: European Hip Hop and the Politics of Postcoloniality*. Chicago Studies in Ethnomusicology series. Chicago: University of Chicago Press.

Rosaldo, Renato. 1994. "Cultural Citizenship and Educational Democracy." *Cultural Anthropology* 9 (3):402–11.

Rubchak, M. J. 1996. "Christian Virgin or Pagan Goddess: Feminism versus the Eternally Feminine in Ukraine." In *Women in Russia and Ukraine*, edited by Rosalind Marsh, 315–30. Cambridge, UK: Cambridge University Press.

Said, Edward W. 1979. *Orientalism*. 1st Vintage Books ed. New York: Vintage Books.

Sakakeeny, Matt. 2010. "'Under the Bridge': An Orientation to Soundscapes in New Orleans." *Ethnomusicology* 54 (1):1–27.

———. 2015. "'Music.'" In *Keywords in Sound*, edited by David Novak and Matt Sakakeeny, 112–24. Durham, NC: Duke University Press.

Satie, Erik. 1996. *A Mammal's Notebook: Collected Writings of Erik Satie*. Edited by Ornella Volta. Translated by Antony Melville. Atlas Arkhive series, book 5. London: Atlas Press.

Schafer, R. Murray. 1994 [1977]. *The Soundscape: Our Sonic Environment and the Tuning of the World*. Rochester, VT: Destiny Books.

———. 1980. "Bricolage: There's Twang in Your Trash." *Music Educators Journal* 66 (7):32–37.

Schmelz, Peter J. 2009. "Introduction: Music in the Cold War." *Journal of Musicology* 26 (1):3–16. doi: 10.1525/jm.2009.26.1.3.

Schmitt, Carl. 1985 [1935]. *Political Theology: Four Chapters on the Concept of Sovereignty*. Translated by George Schwab. Chicago: University of Chicago Press.

Schönle, Andreas. 2001. "Garden of the Empire: Catherine's Appropriation of the Crimea." *Slavic Review* 60 (1):1–23.

Scott, James C. 1985. *Weapons of the Weak*. New Haven, CT: Yale University Press.

———. 2009. *The Art of Not Being Governed: An Anarchist History of Upland Southeast Asia*. New Haven, CT: Yale University Press.

Shakespeare, William. 2000 [1977]. *Shakespeare's Sonnets: Edited with Analytic Commentary by Stephen Booth*. New Haven, CT: Yale Nota Bene.

Shank, Barry. 2014. "The Anthem and the Condensation of Context." In *The Political Force of Musical Beauty*, 38–71. Durham, NC: Duke University Press.

Shay, Anthony. 1999. "State Folk Dance Ensembles and Folk Dance in 'The Field.'" *Dance Research Journal* 31 (1):29–56.

Shevchenko, Taras. 2013. *The Complete Kobzar: The Poems of Taras Shevchenko.* Translated by Peter Fedynsky. London: Glagoslav Publications.

Shohat, Ella, and Robert Stam. 2014. *Unthinking Eurocentrism: Multiculturalism and the Media.* 2nd ed. New York: Routledge.

"Signs of a Hipster Rebellion." 2013. *Economist, Prospero* (blog), accessed April 27, 2013. http://www.economist.com/blogs/prospero/2013/10/culture-ukraine.

Silverman, Carol. 2007. "Trafficking in the Exotic with 'Gypsy' Music: Balkan, Roma, Cosmopolitanism, and 'World Music' Festivals." In *Balkan Popular Culture and the Ottoman Ecumene: Music, Image, and Regional Political Discourse,* edited by Donna A. Buchanan. Lanham, MD: Scarecrow Press.

———. 2012. *Romani Routes: Cultural Politics and Balkan Music in Diaspora.* Oxford: Oxford University Press.

Simonett, Helena 2012. *The Accordion in the Americas: Klezmer, Polka, Tango, Zydeco, and More!* Urbana: University of Illinois Press.

Simpson, Audra. 2014. *Mohawk Interruptus: Political Life Across the Borders of Settler States.* Durham, NC: Duke University Press.

———. 2016. "Consent's Revenge." *Cultural Anthropology* 31 (3):326–33. doi: 10.14506/ca31.3.02.

Skinner, Frederick W. 2003. "Lenin and Beethoven: Beyond the 'Appassionata' Affair." *Beethoven Journal* 18 (2):62–65.

Slezkine, Yuri. 1992. "From Savages to Citizens: The Cultural Revolution in the Soviet Far North, 1928–1938." *Slavic Review* 51 (1):52–76.

Slobin, Mark, ed. 1996. *Retuning Culture: Musical Changes in Central and Eastern Europe.* Durham, NC: Duke University Press.

Snyder, Timothy. 2010a. *Bloodlands: Europe Between Hitler and Stalin.* London: Vintage Books.

———. 2010b. "A Fascist Hero in Democratic Kiev." Accessed November 21, 2010. http://www.nybooks.com/daily/2010/02/24/a-fascist-hero-in-democratic-kiev/.

———. 2015. "Integration and Disintegration: Europe, Ukraine, and the World." *Slavic Review* 74 (4):695–707.

Solomon, Thomas. 2005a. "'Every Way That I Can'?: Turkey and the Eurovision Song Contest." Society for Ethnomusicology Annual Meeting, Tucson, AZ.

———. 2005b. "'Listening to Istanbul': Imagining Place in Turkish Rap Music." *Studia Musicologica Norvegica* 31:46–67.

Sonevytsky, Maria. 2008. "The Accordion and Ethnic Whiteness: Toward a New Critical Organology." *World of Music* 50 (3):101–18.

———. 2012. "Wild Music: Ideologies of Exoticism in Two Ukrainian Borderlands." PhD Dissertation, Music Department, Columbia University.

———. 2019. "Overhearing Indigenous Silence: Crimean Tatars During the Crimean War." In *Hearing Crimea: Sound in Nineteenth-Century Wartime*, edited by Gavin Williams. Oxford: Oxford University Press.

Sonevytsky, Maria, and Adrian Ivakhiv. 2016. "Late Soviet Discourses of 'Nature' and the Natural: Musical Avtentyka, Native Faith and 'Cultural Ecology' After Chornobyl." In *Current Directions in Ecomusicology*, edited by Aaron S. Allen and Kevin Dawe, 135–46. New York: Routledge.

Spivak, Gayatri Chakravorty, Nancy Condee, Harsha Ram, and Vitaly Chernetsky. 2006. "Are We Postcolonial? Post-Soviet Space." *PMLA* 121 (3): 828–36.

Stahl, Matt. 2013. *Unfree Masters: Recording Artists and the Politics of Work*. Refiguring American Music series. Durham, NC: Duke University Press.

Stalin, J. V. 1913. "Marxism and the National Question." Marxists Internet Archive, accessed January 18, 2011. http://www.marxists.org/reference/archive/stalin/works/1913/03a.htm#s1.

Steingo, Gavin. 2016. *Kwaito's Promise: Music and the Aesthetics of Freedom in South Africa*. Chicago Studies in Ethnomusicology. Chicago: University of Chicago Press.

Steinholt, Yngvar B. 2013. "Kitten Heresy: Lost Contexts of Pussy Riot's Punk Prayer." *Popular Music and Society* 36 (1):120–24.

Sterne, Jonathan. 2003. *The Audible Past: Cultural Origins of Sound Reproduction*. Durham, NC: Duke University Press.

———. 2012. "Quebec's #Casseroles: On Participation, Percussion and Protest." Sound studiesblog.com, June 4. https://soundstudiesblog.com/2012/06/04/casseroles/.

Stokes, Martin. 2004. "Music and the Global Order." *Annual Review of Anthropology* 33:47–72.

———. 2010. *The Republic of Love: Cultural Intimacy in Turkish Popular Music*. Chicago Studies in Ethnomusicology series. Chicago: University of Chicago Press.

———. 2017. "The Musical Citizen." IMR Distinguished Lecture Series. Institute of Musical Research. http://www.the-imr.uk/media/.

Stoler, Ann Laura. 2008. "Imperial Debris: Reflections on Ruins and Ruination." *Cultural Anthropology* 23 (2):191–219.

Struve, Kai. 2014. "The Soviet Image of the Banderovtsy: Conflicting Memories and Propaganda from the Cold War to the Maidan." Danyliw Research Seminar on Contemporary Ukraine, last modified November 1. http://www.danyliwseminar.com/#!kai-struve/c195r.

Sugarman, Jane C. 1999. "Imagining the Homeland: Poetry, Songs, and the Discourses of Albanian Nationalism." *Ethnomusicology* 43 (3):419–58. doi: 10.2307/852556.

Sunderland, Willard. 2004. *Taming the Wild Field: Colonization and Empire on the Russian Steppe*. Ithaca, NY: Cornell University Press.

Taruskin, Richard. 1984. "The Authenticity Movement Can Become a Positivistic Purgatory, Literalistic and Dehumanizing." *Early Music* 12 (1):3–12.

———. 2001. "Nationalism." In *Grove Music Online*. http://www.oxfordmusiconline.com.

———. 2009. *The Danger of Music and Other Anti-Utopian Essays*. Berkeley: University of California Press.

Taussig, Michael. 1987. *Shamanism, Colonialism, and the Wild Man: A Study in Terror and Healing*. Chicago: University of Chicago Press.

Taylor, Charles. 2004. *Modern Social Imaginaries*. Public Planet Books. Durham, NC: Duke University Press.

Taylor, Timothy D. 1997. *Global Pop: World Music, World Markets*. New York: Routledge.

———. 2007. *Beyond Exoticism: Western Music and the World*. Durham, NC: Duke University Press.

———. 2014. "Fields, Genres, Brands." *Culture, Theory and Critique* 55 (2):159–74. doi: 10.1080/14735784.2014.897242.

———. 2016. *Music and Capitalism: A History of the Present*. Big Issues in Music series. Edited by Philip V. Bohlman and Ronald M. Radano. Chicago: University of Chicago Press.

Teitelbaum, Benjamin. 2017. *Lions of the North: Sounds of the New Nordic Radical Nationalism*. Oxford: Oxford University Press.

Tlostanova, Madina V., and Walter D. Mignolo. 2012. *Learning to Unlearn: Decolonial Reflections from Eurasia and the Americas*. Transoceanic Studies series. Columbus: The Ohio State University Press.

Tochka, Nicholas. 2013. "Pussy Riot, Freedom of Expression, and Popular Music Studies After the Cold War." *Popular Music* 32 (2):303–11.

———. 2016. *Audible States: Socialist Politics and Popular Music in Albania*. Oxford: Oxford University Press.

Tragaki, Dafni, ed. 2013. *Empire of Song: Europe and Nation in the Eurovision Song Contest*. Europea: Ethnomusicologies and Modernities no. 15. Lanham, UK: Scarecrow Press.

Trebunia, Vlad. 2010. "*Sharovarshchyna*." Web interview. http://www.gk-press.if.ua/node/2166.

Trnka, Susanna, Christine Dureau, and Julie Park. 2013. "Senses and Citizenships." In *Senses and Citizenships: Embodying Political Life*, edited by Susanna Trnka, Christine Dureau, and Julie Park, 1–30. New York: Routledge.

Trumpener, Katie. 2000. "Béla Bartók and the Rise of Comparative Ethnomusicology: Nationalism, Race Purity, and the Legacy of the Austro-Hungarian Empire." In *Music and the Racial Imagination*, edited by Ronald Radano and Philip V. Bohlman. Chicago: University of Chicago Press.

Tucker, Joshua. 2013. *Gentleman Troubadours and Andean Pop Stars: Huayno Music, Media Work, and Ethnic Imaginaries in Urban Peru.* Chicago Studies in Ethnomusicology series. Chicago: University of Chicago Press.

Turino, Thomas. 2000. *Nationalists, Cosmopolitans, and Popular Music in Zimbabwe.* Chicago: University of Chicago Press.

———. 2008. *Music as Social Life: The Politics of Participation.* Chicago: University of Chicago Press.

Uehling, Greta Lynn. 2004. *Beyond Memory: The Crimean Tatars' Deportation and Return.* New York: Palgrave Macmillan.

———. 2016. "Jamala, Eurovision, and Human Rights." *Savage Minds: Notes and Queries in Anthropology,* accessed June 16, 2016. http://savageminds.org/2016/06/16/jamala -eurovision-and-human-rights/.

Unger, Susanne. 2017. "More Thoughts on Resistence and Refusal: A Conversation with Sherry Ortner." *In Dialogue* (blog), "Comparative Studes in Society and History," April 16. http://cssh.lsa.umich.edu/2017/04/16/more-thoughts-on-resistance-and-refusal-a -conversation-with-sherry-ortner/.

Urban, Greg. 2008. "Citizenship as a Mode of Belonging by Choice." In *The Future of Citizenship,* edited by Jose V. Ciprut, 311–33. Cambridge, MA: MIT Press.

Verdery, Katherine. 1996. *What Was Socialism, and What Comes Next?* Princeton, NJ: Princeton University Press.

Visser, Oane, and Max Spoor. 2011. "Land Grabbing in Post-Soviet Eurasia: The World's Largest Agricultural Land Reserves at Stake." *Journal of Peasant Studies* 38 (2): 299–323.

Von Hagen, Mark. 1995. "Does Ukraine Have a History?" *Slavic Review* 54 (3):658–73.

Waksman, Steve. 2001. *Instruments of Desire: The Electric Guitar and the Shaping of Musical Experience.* Cambridge, MA: Harvard University Press.

Wanner, Catherine. 1996. "Nationalism on Stage: Music and Change in Soviet Ukraine." In *Retuning Culture: Musical Changes in Central and Eastern Europe,* edited by Mark Slobin, 136–55. Durham, NC: Duke University Press.

———. 2014. " 'Fraternal' Nations and Challenges to Sovereignty in Ukraine: The Politics of Linguistic and Religious Ties." *American Ethnologist* 41 (3):427–39.

Warner, Michael. 2002. "Publics and Counterpublics." *Public Culture* 14 (1):49–90.

Weidman, Amanda J. 2006. *Singing the Classical, Voicing the Modern: The Postcolonial Politics of Music in South India.* Durham, NC: Duke University Press.

———. 2007. "Stage Goddesses and Studio Divas in South India: On Agency and the Politics of Voice." In *Words, Worlds, and Material Girls: Language, Gender, Globalization,* edited by Bonnie S. McElhinny, 131–56. Berlin: Mouton de Gruyter.

———. 2015. " 'Voice.' " In *Keywords in Sound,* edited by David Novak and Matt Sakakeeny, 232–45. Durham, NC: Duke University Press.

Weiner, Isaac. 2014. *Religion Out Loud: Religious Sound, Public Space, and American Pluralism*. New York: New York University Press.

Werth, Alexander. 1949. *Musical Uproar in Moscow*. London: Turnstile Press. Reprint, Greenwood Press, 1973.

Whiteley, Sheila. 2006. "Popular Music and the Dynamics of Desire." In *Queering the Popular Pitch*, edited by Jennifer Rycenga and Sheila Whiteley, 249–62. New York: Routledge.

Williams, Brian Glyn. 2001. "The Ethnogenesis of the Crimean Tatars: An Historical Reinterpretation." *Journal of the Royal Asiatic Society* 11 (3):329–48.

Williams, Raymond. 1983. *Keywords: A Vocabulary of Culture and Society*. Oxford: Oxford University Press.

Witwicki, S. 1873. *O Huculach: Rys historyczny*. L'viv, Ukraine.

Wolff, Larry. 1994. *Inventing Eastern Europe: The Map of Civilization on the Mind of the Enlightenment*. Stanford, CA: Stanford University Press.

Wong, Deborah. 2004. *Speak It Louder: Asian Americans Making Music*. New York: Routledge.

Yakovlev, Yaroslav, and Vlad Rohlev. 2007. *Mudrist' Karpats'koho Mol'fara* [The Wisdom of the Carpathian *Mol'far*]. Film. Ukraine: Same Tak!

Yano, Christine Reiko. 2002. *Tears of Longing: Nostalgia and Nation in Japanese Popular Song*. Cambridge, MA: Harvard University Press.

Yefremov, Yevhen. 1985. "Doslidzhennia narodnopisennoho vykonavstva cherez modeli-uvannia invarianta pisni [Investigation of folksong performance through the simulation of song invariants]." *Ukrainske muzykoznavstvo* 20: 79–98.

——— 1997. "Rhythmic-Structural Types of Calendar Tunes in Kyivan Polissya." In *Polissya of Ukraine: Materials to Historical Ethnographical Research*, 245–59. L'viv, Ukraine: Institute for Folk Study of the National Academy of Sciences of Ukraine.

———. 2004. "Rytualy zaklykannia doshchu [Rituals of rain calling]." *Problemy etno-muzykolohii: Zbirnyk naukovykh prats* 2:192–209.

Yuksel', Gayana. 2004. "'DJ Bebek': Proyekt Budushchego ['DJ Bebek': Project of the Future]." *Golos Kryma* 28 (555), July 9.

Yurchak, Alexei. 1999. "Gagarin and the Rave Kids: Transforming Power, Identity, and Aesthetics in Post-Soviet Nightlife." In *Consuming Russia: Popular Culture, Sex, and Society Since Gorbachev*, edited by Adele M. Baker, 76–109. Durham, NC: Duke University Press.

———. 2005. *Everything Was Forever, Until It Was No More: The Last Soviet Generation*. Princeton, NJ: Princeton University Press.

———. 2014a. "Little Green Men: Russia, Ukraine and Post-Soviet Sovereignty." Last modified March 31, accessed April 2, 2014. http://anthropoliteia.net/2014/03/31/little-green-men-russia-ukraine-and-post-soviet-sovereignty/.

———. 2014b. "Revolutions and Their Translators: Maidan, the Conflict in Ukraine, and the Russian New Left." Last modified October 28. http://www.culanth.org /fieldsights/619-revolutions-and-their-translators-maidan-the-conflict-in-ukraine-and-the-russian-new-left.

———. 2015. "Bodies of Lenin: The Hidden Science of Communist Sovereignty." *Representations* 129 (1):116–57.

Zemtsovsky, Izaly. 2002. "Musicological Memoirs on Marxism." In *Music and Marx: Ideas, Practice, Politics*, edited by Regula Burckhardt Qureshi, 167–89. New York: Routledge.

Zhurzhenko, Tatiana. 2014. "Yulia Tymoshenko's Two Bodies." In *Women in Politics and Media: Perspective from Nations in Transition*, edited by Maria Raicheva-Stover and Elza Ibroscheva, 265–83. New York: Bloomsbury Academic.

Zychowicz, Jessica. 2011. "Two Bad Words: FEMEN and Feminism in Independent Ukraine." *Anthropology of East Europe Review* 29 (2):215–27.

INDEX

art object/artworks, 10, 77–80, 198n28
ArtPóle (АртПоле) festival, 11–17, *15*, 174, 186n17
Автентична Програма ("Authentic Program"), 12
АртПоле. *See* ArtPóle
ascriptive citizenship, 174
ASSR (Autonomous Soviet Socialist Republic), 121
AtlantSV (telecompany), 124
ATR television, 134–35
attachment to state, 7, 172–75
audible entanglements, 7, 172
audible exertion, 92, 97–98
audism, 173
auditions. *See* blind auditions
Aurality (Ochoa Gautier), 111–12, 190n39
aural practices, 116, 138
authentication. *See* stories of authentication
authenticity: *avtentyka*, 86–91, 97–99, 100–106, 151; gendered representations, 98–99; hip-hop, 133, 154; Hutsuls, 33, 83, 148; movement, 200n5; national, 109–10; performance, 12–13, 96–98; rituals, 36; rurality, 97
Authentic Program (Автентична Програма), 12
authoritarianism, 24, 171
auto-exoticism, 2, 5, 32, 38–44, 54, 57
Autonomous Soviet Socialist Republic (ASSR), 121
Avdiyevsky, Anatolij, 93
avtentyka: authenticity, 86–91, 97–99, 100–106, 151; defining, 88–91; disruptive timbres, 106–9; learning, 91–100; post-Soviet revivals, 151; voice, 87, 90–91, 95–99, 101, 106–7, 109–13

Baba Hannusya, 67–70, 73, 76
Baba Maria, 150
backwardness, 7, 94, 103, 162
Baibakov, Anton, 66
Bandera, Stepan, 72–73, 194n14
"Banderite group Dakh Daughters"

(Бендеровская группа Dakh Daughters), 71, 83
Banderivets (masculine), 75
Banderivka (feminine), 71–76, 83
Banderivtsi (Banderites, plural), 72–76
barbarism, 41, 66–67
bartka (ceremonial ax), 35
bass drum (*bubon*), 13
becoming Ukrainian, 170, 174–75
bel canto voice, 95–96
belonging: acoustic citizenship, 7, 173–74; *avtentyka*, 109–11; Eastern music, 116, 137; ethno-national, 32, 57, 70; networks of, 8; soundmarks, 156
Benjamin, Walter, 162–64
Berehynia (protector of the hearth), 42–43, 76, 83
Berlant, Lauren, 36
Bernstein, Anya, 44, 193n8
Bessire, Lucas, 115
Бендеровская группа Dakh Daughters ("Banderite group Dakh Daughters"), 71, 83
Беркут/Berkut (special police), 65
Бої (fight) (round of *Holos Kraïny*), 100
бурдон (drone), 97–98
Bhabha, Homi K., 82
Bilalov, Fevzi, 160
Bilaniuk, Laada, 195n3, 202n23, 209n7
binary politics, 3, 65–66, 81–83, 166
bingo cards, 179–80, *180*
biological citizenship, 173, 208–9n6
"Blackthorn Blossom" (Цвіте Терен), 92–93
blind auditions, 100–109
Bloch, Ernst, 8
body, 33, 42–44, 90–94, 97–98, 109, 111, 193n8
bond. *See* attachment to state
border epistemology, 4, 177
Boym, Svetlana, 162
Bozhychi (musical group), 101–2
branding, 43–44, 116, 177
bricolage, 142, 146, 153–59, 162, 206n9
Brown, Kate, 152
bubon (bass drum), 13

cultural capital, 134

cultural difference, 127

cultural expressions, 89–90, 94

cultural genocide, 136

cultural intimacy, 33, 36, 49

cultural memory, 161

cultural practices, 90, 93–94

cultural rights, 122–23

cultural sovereignty, 95, 116, 118, 122–26, 138, 150, 155–56, 161

DakhaBrakha: accordion, 152–55; activism, 206n5; ambassadors, 205nn2–3; "Carpathian Rap," 145–56; overview, 139–45; photo, *140*; provincialized sounds, 206n7; "Salgir Boyu," 156–61; steppe blues (степовій блюз), 207n14; world music, 164–66

DAKH Center of Contemporary Art, 145

Dakh Daughters, 58–73, *62*, 76–78, 80–84, 139, 194–95n2

"Dakh Daughters Band Euromaidan 2013" video, *59*

dance in 7/8 time (*qaytarma*), 13, 128, 204n13

"Dances" (Танці) (song by V.V.), 170

daré (Turkic frame drum), 130, 134, 157, 160

Daughtry, Martin, 163

davul (traditional Crimean Tatar drum), 130, 134

Day (magazine), 64

девушка (girl), 120

Державний заслужений Український народний хор ім. Григорія Верьовки (State Honored Ukrainian Folk Choir), 92

дикі ("wild"), 29, 192

дикість ("wildness"), 44–48

Дикі Танці (*Dyki Tantsi*), 29–33, 37–41, 47, 57

дикое поле (wild field), 4

дримба (jaw harp), 146

defiance, 42, 68, 71–72, 82, 89, 148

"delicate voice" (ніжний голос), 106

democracy. *See* liberal democracy

democratainment, 113, 177

demographic attrition, 172

demystification, 80

Deportacia (Deportation) (DJ Bebek), 130–34, *131*

deportation. *See* exile

desire: political, 18, 44, 56, 115, 125; postcolonial, 40, 57, 165; sovereignty, 16, 18, 56, 124, 175–76

de-territorialized popular musics, 129

Diachenko, Sergiy and Maryna, 52

dialect, 37, 50, 67–68, 76, 96

digital artifacts, 21–22, 77

dignity, 10, 33, 79, 81–82

Disappointment ("Відрада") (V.V.), 106

disavowal. *See* political ambivalence

disciplined vocality, 88, 91–98, 105, 111

discipline of vocal abandon, 90, 92–93, 98

discursive cleansing, 117, 125, 203n3

discursive Wildness, 2, 4–5, 11, 30, 55, 82, 91, 177

disembodied sonic markers, 144–45

disinformation, Russian, 135, 178–79, 210n13

disruptive timbres, 87, 99–100, 106–9

dissonance, 106

DJ Bebek, 130–34

Dolar, Mladen, 111

Donbas (region), 20, 63–64, 75

Donbas region, 12

Donetsk, 63–64, 75

doubled reality, 20, 80

doubled voice in rap, 147

doumbelek (goblet drum), 14

Dreamland (Kraina Mrij/Країна Мрій), 168–72, *169*, 175, 208n1

dress. *See* costumes

Drevo (singing group), 95, *96*, 101, 105

drone (бурдон) pitch, 97–98

drymba (jaw harp), 148–50, *149*

duet-as-duel format, 100, 106

Dyki Tantsi (Дикі Танці), 29–33, 37–41, 47, 56

earthy voice. *See avtentyka* voice

eastern borderlands, 12, 19, 24, 40, 77, 170, 172

information war, 23–24

infrastructural activism, 32–33, 51–56

infrastructure development, 57

institutionalized Soviet folklore, 89, 130, 147, 151, 200n7

instruments, 13–14, 61, 67–68, 152–56, 158, 160

internal folk, 68–69

internally displaced persons (IDPs), 134–35, 204n5

internet: accessibility, 126–27, 198n26; publics, 22, 58–59, 63–64, 69, 71, 76, 77, 80–81, 83–84; streaming, 134–35, 164–65

intimacy, 32–33, 35–40, 49, 52, 54, 57, 76

intimate belonging, 173

intimate public, 16

iron baba. See Rodina Mat'

Izdryk, Yurko, 50–51

Jamala, 135–37, *136*, 178–81, 204–5n14, 209n7

jaw harp (*drymba*) (дримба), 146, 148–50, *149*

Jemilev, Mustafa, 125

Junka, Laura, 82

juridico-political sovereignties, 118, 122, 150

"Kalyna moja, malyna moja" (Калина моя, малина моя), 150–51

Kant, Immanuel, 174

Карпатський Реп ("Carpathian Rap"), 146

Karpenko, Suzanna, 101–2, 106–8, 112

k'aval (end-blown flute), 132

kerpichi (yellow brick raw building materials), 119–20

Khalilov, Ridvan, 127–29

Khytsenko, Valentyna, 93

kitsch, 40, 49

Коли як не зараз, і хто як не ми ("If not now, when? If not us, who?") (protest chant), 70

коренной народ (Indigenous people, Russian), 17

корінний народ (Indigenous people, Ukrainian), 17

knowing and sounding, 5–6, 172–73

knowledge, 5, 25, 36, 52, 91

kolkhoz (collective farm), 11

kolomyika (Hutsul song form), 37

Kompanichenko, Taras, 176

korenizatsia (Soviet indigenization policy), 121–22

Kosmach (Hutsul village), 28–29, 34, 44, 73–74

Kosmats'ka Pysanka (Kosmach Easter Egg) (wedding band), 29

Kovalenko, Iryna, 145

kozhukh (traditional decorated vest), 44

Kraina Mrij/Країна Мрій (Dreamland), 168–72, 175

криївки (WWII underground bunkers)

Kryvorivnia (village), 46, 73

kwaito, 80–81

Kyiv, Ukraine, 191n45. *See also* Maidan Revolution; Radio Meydan

Kyivan Polissia region, 91–97

Kyiv Post (newspaper), 65

Kyiv Weekly (newspaper), 75

lament, 67–68, 76, 161, 198n25

"land art" summer festival. *See* ArtPóle

landmarks, 143–44

language hybrid (*surzhyk*), 17

language usage, 17, 116–17, 123–24, 175

late and post-Soviet eras, 19, 78, 92, 94–95, 99, 110

legitimacy, 18, 40, 88, 116, 172

Lenin, Vladimir, 9–10, 65–66

Leninist policy, 121–22

Leninopad (felling of Lenin statues), 65–66, 196n12

"Leninopad" (video), 70–71

"Let's go to the mountain valley!" (Гайда на полоннину), 67

Levin, Theodor, 94

liberal democracies, 16–17, 44, 171

Light (DakhaBrakha), 145–46

liminality, 3–4, 49, 77, 115, 121–25, 130, 133–38, 142

listening, 4, 9, 98, 120–21, 123, 171–76

little (мала), 4

Marié Abe
*Resonances of Chindon-ya:
Sounding Space and Sociality in
Contemporary Japan*

Frances Aparicio
*Listening to Salsa: Gender, Latin Popular
Music, and Puerto Rican Cultures*

Paul Austerlitz
*Jazz Consciousness: Music, Race,
and Humanity*

Harris M. Berger
*Metal, Rock, and Jazz: Perception and the
Phenomenology of Musical Experience*

Harris M. Berger
*Stance: Ideas about Emotion, Style,
and Meaning for the Study
of Expressive Culture*

Harris M. Berger and
Giovanna P. Del Negro
*Identity and Everyday Life: Essays
in the Study of Folklore, Music,
and Popular Culture*

Franya J. Berkman
*Monument Eternal: The Music
of Alice Coltrane*

Dick Blau, Angeliki Vellou Keil,
and Charles Keil
*Bright Balkan Morning: Romani Lives and
the Power of Music in Greek Macedonia*

Susan Boynton and Roe-Min Kok, editors
*Musical Childhoods and the
Cultures of Youth*

James Buhler, Caryl Flinn,
and David Neumeyer, editors
Music and Cinema

Patrick Burkart
Music and Cyberliberties

Thomas Burkhalter, Kay Dickinson,
and Benjamin J. Harbert, editors
*The Arab Avant-Garde: Music,
Politics, Modernity*

Julia Byl
*Antiphonal Histories: Resonant Pasts
in the Toba Batak Musical Present*

Daniel Cavicchi
Listening and Longing: Music Lovers in the Age of Barnum

Susan D. Crafts, Daniel Cavicchi, Charles Keil, and the Music in Daily Life Projec
My Music: Explorations of Music in Daily Life

Jim Cullen
Born in the USA: Bruce Springsteen and the American Tradition

Anne Danielsen
Presence and Pleasure: The Funk Grooves of James Brown and Parliament

Peter Doyle
Echo and Reverb: Fabricating Space in Popular Music Recording, 1900–1960

Ron Emoff
Recollecting from the Past: Musical Practice and Spirit Possession on the East Coast of Madagascar

Yayoi Uno Everett and Frederick Lau, editors
Locating East Asia in Western Art Music

Susan Fast and Kip Pegley, editors
Music, Politics, and Violence

Heidi Feldman
Black Rhythms of Peru: Reviving African Musical Heritage in the Black Pacific

Kai Fikentscher
"You Better Work!" Underground Dance Music in New York City

Ruth Finnegan
The Hidden Musicians: Music-Making in an English Town

Daniel Fischlin and Ajay Heble, editors
The Other Side of Nowhere: Jazz, Improvisation, and Communities in Dialogue

Wendy Fonarow
Empire of Dirt: The Aesthetics and Rituals of British "Indie" Music

Murray Forman
The 'Hood Comes First: Race, Space, and Place in Rap and Hip-Hop

Lisa Gilman
My Music, My War: The Listening Habits of U.S. Troops in Iraq and Afghanistan

Paul D. Greene and Thomas Porcello, editors
Wired for Sound: Engineering and Technologies in Sonic Cultures

Tomie Hahn
Sensational Knowledge: Embodying Culture through Japanese Dance

Edward Herbst
Voices in Bali: Energies and Perceptions in Vocal Music and Dance Theater

Deborah Kapchan
Traveling Spirit Masters: Moroccan Gnawa Trance and Music in the Global Marketplace

Deborah Kapchan, editor
Theorizing Sound Writing

Max Katz
Lineage of Loss: Counternarratives of North Indian Music

Raymond Knapp
Symphonic Metamorphoses:
Subjectivity and Alienation in Mahler's
Re-Cycled Songs

Victoria Lindsay Levine and
Dylan Robinson, editors
Music and Modernity among
First Peoples of North America

Laura Lohman
Umm Kulthūm: Artistic Agency and the
Shaping of an Arab Legend, 1967–2007

Preston Love
A Thousand Honey Creeks Later:
My Life in Music from Basie to Motown—
and Beyond

René T. A. Lysloff and
Leslie C. Gay Jr., editors
Music and Technoculture

Ian MacMillen
Playing It Dangerously: Tambura Bands,
Race, and Affective Block in Croatia
and Its Intimates

Allan Marett
Songs, Dreamings, and Ghosts:
The Wangga of North Australia

Ian Maxwell
Phat Beats, Dope Rhymes:
Hip Hop Down Under Comin' Upper

Kristin A. McGee
Some Liked It Hot: Jazz Women in Film
and Television, 1928–1959

Tracy McMullen
Haunthenticity: Musical Replay
and the Fear of the Real

Rebecca S. Miller
Carriacou String Band Serenade:
Performing Identity in the
Eastern Caribbean

Tony Mitchell, editor
Global Noise: Rap and Hip-Hop
Outside the USA

Christopher Moore and
Philip Purvis, editors
Music & Camp

Rachel Mundy
Animal Musicalities: Birds, Beasts,
and Evolutionary Listening

Keith Negus
Popular Music in Theory: An Introduction

Johnny Otis
Upside Your Head: Rhythm and Blues
on Central Avenue

Kip Pegley
Coming to You Wherever You Are:
MuchMusic, MTV, and Youth Identities

Jonathan Pieslak
Radicalism and Music: An Introduction
to the Music Cultures of al-Qa'ida, Racist
Skinheads, Christian-Affiliated Radicals,
and Eco-Animal Rights Militants

Lorraine Plourde
Tokyo Listening: Sound and Sense
in a Contemporary City

Matthew Rahaim
Musicking Bodies: Gesture and
Voice in Hindustani Music

John Richardson
Singing Archaeology:
Philip Glass's Akhnaten

Tricia Rose
Black Noise: Rap Music and Black Culture
in Contemporary America

David Rothenberg and
Marta Ulvaeus, editors
The Book of Music and Nature:
An Anthology of Sounds, Words, Thoughts

Nichole Rustin-Paschal
The Kind of Man I Am: Jazzmasculinity
and the World of Charles Mingus Jr.

Marta Elena Savigliano
Angora Matta: Fatal Acts of
North-South Translation

Joseph G. Schloss
Making Beats: The Art of
Sample-Based Hip-Hop

Barry Shank
Dissonant Identities: The Rock 'n' Roll
Scene in Austin, Texas

Jonathan Holt Shannon
Among the Jasmine Trees: Music and
Modernity in Contemporary Syria

Daniel B. Sharp
Between Nostalgia and Apocalypse:
Popular Music and the Staging of Brazil

Helena Simonett
Banda: Mexican Musical Life
across Borders

Mark Slobin
Subcultural Sounds: Micromusics
of the West

Mark Slobin, editor
Global Soundtracks: Worlds
of Film Music

Christopher Small
The Christopher Small Reader

Christopher Small
Music of the Common Tongue:
Survival and Celebration
in African American Music

Christopher Small
Music, Society, Education

Christopher Small
Musicking: The Meanings of
Performing and Listening

Maria Sonevytsky
Wild Music: Sound and Sovereignty
in Ukraine

Regina M. Sweeney
Singing Our Way to Victory:
French Cultural Politics and Music
during the Great War

Colin Symes
Setting the Record Straight: A Material
History of Classical Recording

Steven Taylor
False Prophet: Field Notes from
the Punk Underground

Paul Théberge
Any Sound You Can Imagine: Making
Music/Consuming Technology

Sarah Thornton
Club Cultures: Music, Media,
and Subcultural Capital

Michael E. Veal
Dub: Songscape and Shattered Songs
in Jamaican Reggae

ABOUT THE AUTHOR

Maria Sonevytsky is assistant professor of music (ethnomusicology) at the University of California, Berkeley. In 2015 Sonevytsky produced an album called *The Chornobyl Songs Project* on Smithsonian Folkways with Ensemble Hilka. She has performed with several bands, including Anti-Social Music, The Debutante Hour, and Zozulka.